Promoting and Marketing Your Crafts

by Edwin M. Field and Selma G. Field

An Audel® Book

Macmillan Publishing Company
New York

Maxwell Macmillan Canada
Toronto

Maxwell Macmillan International
New York   Oxford   Singapore   Sydney

Macmillan Publishing Company   Maxwell Macmillan Canada, Inc.
866 Third Avenue   1200 Eglinton Avenue East, Suite 200
New York, NY 10022   Don Mills, Ontario M3C 3N1

Macmillan Publishing Company is part of the Maxwell Communication Group of Companies.

Library of Congress Cataloging-in-Publication Data

Field, Edwin M.
    Promoting and marketing your crafts / by Edwin and Selma Field.
        p.   cm.
    Includes index.
    ISBN 0–02–537742–6
    1. Handicraft—Marketing.   I. Field, Selma G., 1925–
II. Title.
HD2341.F52   1993
745.5′068′8′—dc20   92–8205
                            CIP

Macmillan books are available at special discounts for bulk purchases for sales promotions, premiums, fund-raising, or educational use. For details, contact:

                    Special Sales Director
                    Macmillan Publishing Company
                    866 Third Avenue
                    New York, NY 10022

10 9 8 7 6 5 4 3 2 1
Printed in the United States of America

Dedication

This book is dedicated to our daughters Deborah, Jessica, and Shelly in appreciation of their gifts of education, inspiration, and stimulation.

Contents

Section Two—The P's at Work

Preface

Promoting and Marketing Your Crafts was written for those involved in the business of producing crafts who desire to sell the results of their creative efforts. The handcrafted pieces involved can be large or small, complex or simple, inexpensive or costly.

If you have already had experience selling the crafts you produce, the pages in this book can serve as a refresher and also offer helpful marketing suggestions.

If marketing the crafts you produce is a completely new experience, this book has the potential of "walking" you through all of the processes necessary to do a professional job with the assignment. While there can be a great deal of satisfaction gained from marketing and promoting your craft yourself, a sound method of guidance can also make the task easier and less stressful as you proceed step by step. The pages and chapters in this book have been arranged to provide you with this information.

How to Use This Book

Everyone has a different approach to reading a how-to book. Some will study it from cover to cover. For others a brief run-through will give an overview of the subject and enough familiarity with the various topics discussed to zero in on particular areas of interest.

Readers reactions to how-to books vary. In most instances, a book offering guidance and assistance within a specific target or interest area often takes on an instructional life of its own. A large number of readers may already be familiar with the subject matter, but feel more comfortable with the support received from reviewing a specific subject.

No matter how you use this book, recognize that the information it contains is the result of a great deal of experience, experimentation, and expertise. Use this book in any way it can be most effective for you. If, for example, you are most comfortable with the promotional aspects of business, but calculations cause you concern, concentrate on promoting your craft product and seek some assistance putting together a business plan.

Recognize, too, that not every technique or plan will work in every circumstance. Some programs require modifications while others may require a different approach. Always try to remain flexible in your handling of any project. In most instances, your personal lifetime experiences will provide you with the necessary background and judgment to handle any program changes or additions that may be necessary.

Many readers find it worthwhile to make notes in the margins or slip in markers for places or topics of special interest. However you read and use this book, you'll find yourself coming back to it time and time again to help you promote and market your craft.

About This Book's Contents

The chapters in this book have been developed with a specific sequence or flow in mind. The first chapter in this book offers a brief explanation and overview of marketing and promotional concepts as they relate to your craft business. The second chapter discusses the development of a business plan. It is written to help you establish costs, profit and loss—the so-called bottom line. Once the business aspects are clarified, the next step, outlined in Chapter Three, will assist you in working up a marketing plan. This plan is designed to position and sell your craft product effectively. Chapter Four provides guidance in obtaining television coverage for your product, while Chapter Five covers the same area for radio talk show exposure. Direct mail offers an excellent potential for sales—Chapter Six talks about using this method to promote your craft product.

Many other promotional tools and techniques available to the craftsperson are discussed in Chapter Seven. Just as there are promotional tools to assist with craft sales, there is also a wide variety of places where craft products can be sold effectively and profitably. Chapter Eight will highlight these shows, fairs, competitions, and exhibition spots for you. There are many low cost publicity vehicles to help promote your craft products, and Chapter Nine details these possibilities. Chapter Ten talks about the potential of wholesaling your craft, while Chapter Eleven gets down to the nitty-gritty of pricing, packaging, and positioning your craft items.

Fine craftspeople with unusual or unique products should be interested in protecting their craft product. It may take a copyright or a trademark. All craftspeople should know how to protect themselves against any possible liability caused by their products, displays, vehicles, or any other part of their business. Chapter Twelve talks about these important business areas and will help you make sound judgements about these specialties. Chapter Thirteen contains vital financial and business information for any craftsperson. No matter how outstanding and beautifully-created your craft product, you must know if you are making a profit. The government will want to know, too. This chapter shows you how to maintain records of sales and inventories, income and expenses, assets and liabilities, and other necessary financial information.

The handy appendix of this book will provide you with media outlets, major craft show lists, and other craft promotional and marketing information sources where applicable, charts and photographs have been included with the text to clarify some of the information. Finally, if you are seeking information about a specific area of craft marketing, the index is an easy guide to any of the informative data contained in the book.

Acknowledgments

The authors are grateful to the following individuals, organizations and companies for their assistance with this book.

American Images Company
34 Lawrence Road
Windsor Locks, CT 06096
Slate signs.

American Pie Company
Steve Falco
RD #1, Box 1431
Lake George, NY 12845
Fancy bird feeders.

Shirley Charron
3 Craigmoor Road, South
Ridgefield, CT 06877
Modern pewter.

Heartwood Furniture
P.O. Box 9
Worcester, NY 12197
Furniture.

Hinge Head Designs
301 10th Avenue - Suite 4A
New York, NY 10001
Creative artwork.

Peter P. Prince
104 Ludlow Street
Saratoga Springs, NY 12866
Creative stamp art.

Radio WVOS
P.O. Box 150
Liberty, NY 12754
A regional AM/FM radio station.

State of New Jersey
Dept. of the Treasury
Division of Taxation
CN 269
Trenton, NJ 08646

Sullivan County Democrat
Callicoon, NY 12723
A twice-weekly newspaper.

The Commonwealth of Massachusetts
Department of Revenue
100 Cambridge Street
Boston, MA 02204

Times Herald Record
40 Mulberry Street
Middletown, NY 10940
A regional daily newspaper.

Unique Things (Faith and Evelyn)
391 Main Street
Nashua, NH 03060
Handcrafted clothing.

WTZA-TV Channel 62
An independent TV station
P.O. Box 1609
721 Broadway
Kingston, NY 12401

Sanford Werfel
302 Old Georges Road
North Brunswick, NJ 08902
Artist.

CHAPTER I

What This Book Can Do for You

What This Book Can Do for You

It takes talent, time, and effort to be a craftsperson. It takes knowledge, organization, persistence, and determination to be a successful business-craftsperson. If you have the talent and are taking the time and making the effort to be a craftsperson, this book will give you the knowledge necessary to build a successful business with your craft products. It will help you get organized, inspire perseverance, and motivate determination.

This book, however, is not just for beginners in crafts or in the crafts business. Even those who have achieved a degree of success will find valuable tips for increasing profits because this book is based on the experience of countless professionals in the marketing field.

Learning how to market your crafts the way successful professionals do can make the difference between earning modest profits and reaping the rich rewards your talent deserves.

Most people believe that marketing is selling, but they are only partially right. Selling is really the end of the marketing process. When professional marketers use the term, *marketing* is the whole process from product development through customer purchase. That's why applying the principles of marketing will lead you on your way to developing a successful business.

A Marketing Capsule

The principles of marketing are often expressed as four P's: *Product, Price, Promotion* and *Place,* or a system of product distribution. To these four we add four: *Purpose, Projecting, Packaging* and *Positioning.* This book will teach you how to apply these eight principles to your business plan.

Indeed, it will begin by showing you how to customize a simple working business plan to follow in marketing your crafts. Then it will explain how to develop your own marketing plan to fulfill the objectives of your business plan. It will show you how to protect your product and your earnings, how to keep the records that let you know exactly what those earnings are, and how to make those earnings grow.

The book will help you take a businessperson's view of your product, and then package, price, position, place, and promote your work for maximum profits. It will assist you in analyzing the real purpose of your marketing efforts, so that you can make sound business projections and do effective planning for success.

Making the Eight P's Work for You

The first step in a marketing campaign is to determine your real purpose. Is your goal:

- to increase volume for existing products?
- to increase the price you get for the product you have crafted?
- to introduce your newest craft product?
- to establish yourself in a specific market or markets?
- to increase your bottom line, enhance your reputation?
- to attract capital, investors, or a buyout?
- to develop franchise opportunities?
- to meet competition?

Whether you are undertaking a marketing campaign independently, or with the help of a marketing professional, a clear-cut understanding of your purpose will help keep your campaign on target.

In developing a campaign for your craft product, it helps to project in advance who your potential customers are, where they are located, their economic range, their needs, and their attitudes or perceptions. Such projection of product demand is the essence of market research.

It is important to determine whether your potential customers are the ultimate consumers, or wholesalers, distributors, or retailers and to project a profile of that potential. Among the avenues of market research, specific projections are based on demographic and/or psychographic factors. Demographic research tells us who the customers are by age, education, sex, geographic area, and income. Psychographic research tells us who the customers are by how they think, what they think, and how they behave.

Demographic information can be secured from census reports, newspaper, radio, and television advertising department statistics, information from chambers of commerce, public information offices, and other similar sources. Psychographic research is based on interpretations of the potential customer's beliefs, attitudes, value systems, preferences, likes and dislikes, awareness, habits, cultural orientations, expectations, similarities, and differences. While many psychographic studies are the result of questionnaires and surveys, others are based on the kinds of cars people drive, where they shop, how they vacation, and other lifestyle indicators.

Research is also concerned with the buying process, satisfaction, and brand loyalty. The buying process consists of five distinct stages. They are:

- realization of a need or want to achieve a benefit;
- pre-purchase activity;
- purchase decision;
- purchase action;
- post-purchase feeling.

Satisfaction is usually an immediate response to the ownership or use of a particular product. Loyalty is demonstrated by a level of commitment to reuse or to purchase in the future from a particular craftsperson or manufacturer, or to recommend the work to others. Both satisfaction and product loyalty can be measured through research procedures. Both can be built into your marketing plan.

The important thing to know is that a great deal of general research material is readily available in public libraries from the government and from other agencies. It is also important to build up a database of information using your own experience and that of colleagues who will share information with you.

After you have made your purpose and projection decisions, you will want to begin asking yourself questions about your product or products. Does it meet an existing market demand or need? Are there people out there, potential purchasers, who want or need your product? Can the product be modified in any way to increase the current market or to meet the needs of other markets? Do you have to create a whole new market? Will your product be competing in a buyer's or seller's market?

You should be aware that products, like people, have life cycles. With this thought in mind, is your product in the: *Introductory Stage, Maturity Stage, Growth Stage,* or the *Declining Stage?* How will you market in each of these business phases? Will you diversify, intensify sales activities, aggressively promote, initiate innovative programs, or continue your marketing program as you have been? If you are introducing a new product, you might want to ask yourself: Does this product enhance or detract from current products? Is it a replacement? A totally new concept? A variation?

Your craft product may attract more attention and sell better with *packaging.* The importance of packaging in marketing is that it can help a potential customer make a decision. Packaging can identify and differentiate your craft product from those of others. Product packaging may protect, simplify handling and storage, serve as an advertisement, attract impulse buyers, and offer consumer information. Packaging can also attract attention for specific markets. Just as a similar detergent, for example, can be packaged for laundry, kitchen, or bath, or useful for crafts, sports, or repairs, craft products can be packaged for home, office, institutions of various types, gifts for special seasons, holidays or occasions, to name a few.

Color and design in packaging and in the product and product size can target products to specific markets. A product may be specifically packaged for and targeted to elite markets or to the masses, to the young or seniors, to the affluent or the budget conscious, to the corporate community or professionals, and tradespeople.

Pricing also plays an important role in the success of your craft product. The right price for a product can be essential to your marketing strategy. How much is too much and how much is too little? Your pricing plan must consider both the competition and the market segments you target, your costs, and the effects of volume on price and profits. What are your tactical approaches to price in the various stages of growth of your craft product? A craft product positioned for upscale markets may be priced substantially higher than a similar product positioned for the mass market. But in any market, charging too much can limit the numbers of buyers and send them to the competition.

Charging too little in some markets may prove equally disastrous. A low-priced product may be perceived as an inferior product rather than a good buy. There are a great many imported products that may have the handcrafted look. Many, in fact, are handcrafted and mass produced in third world countries where labor is cheap. Buyers are cautious and wary. Test marketing, marketing analysis and research can help to maximize your profits and to make sense of the pricing tightrope.

In contrast to place which refers to your craft items physical accessibility, *positioning* has to do with the most profitable competitive position for your product. Remember that the competition can be any other craft product that might conceivably wean away sales. While positioning has a great deal to do with perception and image, you can position by price, by product qualities or specific market segments. Among the related but distinct strategies involved are:

- achieving a distinct image for your craft product by emphasizing a feature or features its competitors may lack. As an example, lower calories from a dessert, faster relief from a over-the-counter pain killer, quicker response from a plumber, or housecalls by a physician. These features have the potential of positioning a product. In addition to its inherent beauty or artistic qualities, you can position a craft product for usefulness, for specific decorator application, for gift giving, for price, for uniqueness, or many other applications.
- achieving a distinct image for your craft product if it happens to be virtually identical to a product created by the competition. Money-saving generic brands are positioned by price. Other products may be targeted to specific markets. Maternity clothes for the professional woman, legal services for union members, and fitness services for office workers are just a few examples of products and services positioned for lifestyle markets. You might target your product to

grandparents, to gardeners, to homemakers, to computer buffs, to career men or women, to teenagers.

• creating a separate and distinct identity image to position your craft product in new market segments. Frozen dinners, for example, are positioned first for the primary market then for the hard hats, Swanson frozen dinners for men with big appetites, and again for gourmet appeal, the Le Menu line for such markets as the diet conscious, the adventurous, the ethnic, etc. Some simple applications of the identity-positioning principle are ceramic mugs sold to be used for hot beverages, as pen and pencil holders, for floral arrangements, for cappucino or expresso, for grandma's false teeth. Or, quilts as bed coverings, wall hangings, crib covers, seat covers, hot mats, pot holders, cozies, etc.

While your decisions on positioning may depend in great measure on the projecting you have done, these decisions will influence pricing, packaging, and promotion, and may even suggest changes in your product itself.

The ideal way to market your craft is to make it as easy as possible for customers to buy it. Simplifying this process is the basic *place* objective of marketing. Place, today, refers not only to the actual location where your craft product is available, but also to catalog sales, direct mail, telemarketing, and television accessibility, and even to sales through mobile vehicles.

Place decisions depend on who and where your customers are. Do you go to them or must they come to you? Have neighborhoods changed as they relate to interest in your craft product? What people and product transportation links exist? Does your current distribution system meet your buyer's needs? Do mall shows reach your market? Can regional shows improve your profits? Do you need or can you benefit from middlemen, wholesalers, agents, and/or consignment shops? Are you seeking mass markets or a target market? What market strategies have you developed? Convenience and accessibility are vital keys to a successful campaign.

The goal of effective *promotion* is to create an immediate positive interest in your craft product as well as to develop future sales. Positive responses can be generated in a number of ways. Public relations techniques are used to disseminate information that makes a positive case for your product. Public relations techniques differ from advertising in the public perception. Advertising is regarded as something the advertiser pays for. While advertising is a valuable sales tool, discerning consumers view it with less credibility than what they read, hear, or see in the media.

Public relations efforts frequently appear in the various media as editorial comment—what papers, magazines, radio or TV commentators or filmed programs say. These comments are gratuitous and in context. People tend to believe them, and to be influenced by them.

Depending on time and budget considerations, the PR/marketing specialist might exercise a variety of options, including, but not limited to, news releases, personal interviews, phone telemarketing, feature stories, sales letters, postcards, target media advertising, in-person visitations, billboards, institutional advertising, special events, audiovisual productions, television advertising, newspaper advertising, or cable advertising.

Promoting effectively can best be accomplished by using a variety of techniques, including developing media relations. Consider news releases, editorials, feature stories, TV, and radio appearances. Think about developing special events, or linking to events that tie in with your product line. Contests, giveaways, trade shows, charity events, or various special performances may be effective promotional tools.

Use publications effectively. The trade press, regional magazines, specialty press, and general news media should all be considered.

Develop and reinforce a personal selling program. Create a continuing and well-thought-out, professional direct-mail campaign. Develop a cost-effective advertising program. Develop a method to measure campaign results.

No matter how you plan to promote your product, there are certain sensible ground rules to follow:

A plan: set a specific promotional objective.
A budget: focus your resources whether limited or unlimited.
Timing/Schedule: plan your promotion. Be concerned. Be concerned for details.
Organization: Insure that your planned promotion is well implemented for success.

Through the pages of this book, you will have the opportunity to learn how to use the media—television, radio, newspapers and magazines—to publicize and promote your craft productions. You will understand how to retail your crafts yourself by direct mail, at mall shows, at local and regional fairs or in your own shop, and how to wholesale your products to boutiques and museum shops, buying chains, catalog outlets, and specialty stores. And you will learn how to decide whether it's more profitable to retail, wholesale, or do both.

Along the way, you will find advice from fellow business-craftspeople and successful marketers as well as many references to additional information sources.

The Craft of Crafting

The ability, skill, and talent to take a raw piece of metal, wood, paper, glass, ceramics, stone, leather, fabric, plastic, gem, crystal, or any combination of these materials and develop it into a creative, useful, attractive product is the benchmark of a craftsperson. Some craftpeople pursue their creativity on a full-time basis, seeking to earn their living from their craft. Other individuals do their creative work only part-time while holding down a full-time job. In many instances, their goal is to develop enough income from their creations to turn the part-time project into full-time work.

The creation of craft items for personal use, or for trade or sale, is ageless yet as modern as the twenty-first century. People have always valued and purchased craft articles for both their utilitarian value and their beauty. The origin of crafts can probably be traced to the beginning of history when wood or stone man and animal figures were created by cave dwellers to tell a story or to serve as playthings.

Throughout relatively recent time, every society and area has had its craftspeople and its craft specialties. Travel to the north and you will find Eskimo stone carvings; a trip up the St. Lawrence beyond Quebec, and wood carvers abound. In Belgium, lacemakers offer their craft items for sale. In the southwestern portion of the United States, craft collectors will find a wide range of handmade Indian jewelry. In the northeast and many other portions of the nation, country crafts of every type abound. Small wooden Kachinka dolls, each progressively smaller than the next, come from Russian craftspeople. Each culture of the world contributes its particular style of ceramic pottery. Different clays, glazes, and shapes differentiate one craft area from another. Certain areas of America are famous for their stylized quilts. Stained glass craftspeople have a long history dating back to the decoration of church windows worldwide. Today, their craft has proliferated and decorates not only religious buildings but business establishments and homes. Name the country or a particular section of a nation and a craft specialty will usually come to mind.

Today, crafts are prized particularly for their uniqueness, limited edition production, and for their decorative value. Because of the time it takes to visualize and handcraft a product, the supply is limited. Generally, because of the work, time, and skill involved, the cost of such handcrafted articles may be high compared to mass-produced items. This limited production, however, has the potential of increasing the value of handcrafted articles to the buyer.

On the other hand, manufactured craft articles are available and often flood the marketplace at low prices. It is not unusual for original, creative pieces to be used as models and mass-produced where labor and raw materials are inexpensive. These pieces are often referred to as *knockoffs*. The original artist will receive no remuneration for his or her work and will probably not even be credited with the creation. Some possible solutions may include trademarking, or copyrighting the craft work, signing or numbering original pieces to enhance the value, or where possible, seeking legal recourse.

Some General Notes on Craftmarkets

Cashing In on Collectables

Handcrafting, we know, goes back before recorded history. Archaeological digs and ancient tombs show us that collecting has also been an age-old characteristic of many cultures. The Faberge eggs are among the best known examples. Today, there are magazines, journals, papers, and books for serious collectors of everything from eggs to eggplants, from apples to zebras, from apricot seed carvings to Zulu masks.

There are some people who collect anything that has to do with their astrological sign—the Pisces fish, the Leo lion, the Aquarian waterbearer. There are others who collect turtles in every material, size, shape, or fanciful interpretation. Rainbows have their devotees, as do hearts. There are teapot collectors, salt cellar collectors, and collectors of caps, collars, buttons, and bottles. Dolls and doll clothes, teddy bears, rocking horses, carousel horses and memorabilia, monkeys, donkeys, elephants, cats, dogs, and a host of sports-related articles all claim fans who will travel great distances to add to their collections. Collectors tend to buy more and spend more than impulse buyers. And, almost any craft item can be adapted to attract collectors. This phenomenon should be considered in positioning a product, in changing a line, or in opening a market. Because there are known outlets for most collectables, costs for initial test marketing, promotion, and continuing advertising are less than for random products.

It is important to research collectable buyers as potentials for your product. Some of the questions you should ask are:

- Is the market interested in country crafts, folk art, traditional, continental, or contemporary products?
- Is the market interested in representational, photographic, or artistic interpretational products?
- In what stage of the market cycle is collecting this product?

How do you answer these questions? First, check the publications in the field. Check with mailing list companies to find out if they sell lists of periodical subscribers, and if so, how many, where they are, and if they are categorized by age, income, sex, or any other characteristic.

Check the competition. What are other craftspeople selling? In what price brackets? Where are they promoting? How are they doing? If they are successful, how can you differentiate your own product from theirs?

Think about the market. What products can you design in your own media that a collector might not yet have? Think about desk accessories, card cases, cuff links, ties, flatware, book covers, bibs or vests, pillows, planters, toys and games, picture frames, furnishings, etc., until you are inspired to develop a product or products for the collectable market.

The conservative approach is to produce a limited quantity to test in your potential market. This approach has the advantage of cutting your losses if the product does not sell. If, however, the product catches on and develops a life of its own, it will also attract imitators and competitors. On the highest price levels, a product of artistic merit and workmanlike quality properly showcased holds its own. Attention should be given, however, to some unique facet of the work to distinguish it—and you—from others. A flourish of a signature, or a distinctive identifying symbol adds value to your first-rate products, collectables or otherwise, and a piece of literature, a card or small leaflet describing the craft, the craftsperson, and/or a quotation, a story, or a brief history of the collectable can also make a higher price acceptable.

Fads and Fashions

Just as you can cash in on collectables, you can find that being attuned to fads and fashions can help fund your future. While many fads are based on films, television programs, books, and personalities whose products are protected by trademarking, registrations, and licensing agreements, other fads simply seem to spring up spontaneously or are cyclical. The yo-yo, for example, has come and gone a number of times in the twentieth century. Executive decision-making devices are popular during bull markets. Centennials, bi-centennials, and other commemorative events create a strong demand for special products. Birthdays of famous people in every field—music, art, science—boost the market for products inspired by their achievements. A popular play set in the Far East will create a market for oriental designs, just as a Twenties revival will call for flappers, fringes, and shades of Art Deco.

Your products can complement the fads, just as the fanny packs in leather, vinyl, and fabric have become popular products for joggers, travelers, and those who are fearful of purse-snatchers. Or, you can with ingenuity and promotional skill, create a fad with your product.

The secret in developing a fad is to find a widespread need, and to fill it, originally, dramatically, and highly visibly. That means that in addition to being creative in your craft, you have to find the right person or persons to wear it, use it, or flaunt it in a place or places where the rest of the world can see it.

If you'd like to try your hand at starting a fad with one of your designs, it makes great sense to cultivate columnists and commentators, talk show hosts and fashion writers as well as celebrities who are known pacesetters. Learning how to promote yourself and your product will be discussed later in this volume, and will stand you in good stead.

Whether you are looking to create a fad or not, it also makes sense to follow the trends projected in fashion, home decorating, and fine arts. People purchase crafts to complement wardrobes as well as decor. It is important for craftspeople to know which colors, styles, and textures are going to be popular each season; whether there's going to be a market for denims or silks, loomed wools or linens, laces or leather, chunky chains or delicate neckpieces. When short hair is in fashion, there is a change in the type of earrings people wear.

It helps sales to meet the market for whatever eclectic, period, or modern accessories are most in demand, or for the cobalt blue, black and white, or rainbow colors highlighted in homemaker magazines for the kitchens, bathrooms, or bedrooms of America. When pastels are popular, there is a market for soft accessories. When bold is beautiful, the bright colored accessories are most marketable.

Being attuned to fads and fashions makes good sense. Check out the leading magazines in each field applicable to your product. Visit the boutiques that spark fashion trends. Make it a point to review foreign trends and trends in other parts of the country. Read the columns that describe "what's hot and what's not." Adapting your products to popular demand puts money in your pocket.

Chapter Highlights

- The information in this book will help you take a business person's view of your product.
- This book is not just for beginners in the craft field. It can even provide valuable tips for increasing profits for those who have a great deal of experience in the business.
- Marketing is the whole process from product development through customer purchase. Learning how to market your craft product can often mean the difference between profit and loss.
- The four principles of marketing are expressed as product, price, promotion, and place. Each performs a role in marketing your craft product.
- Some additional principles that can be valuable when developing a craft marketing program are purpose, projecting, packaging, and positioning. These extra principles will provide further assistance when marketing your craft product.
- In marketing, it helps to project who your customers are, their locations, economic ranges, needs, attitudes, and perceptions.
- Research in marketing is concerned with many areas. Some of the more important include the buying process, satisfaction, and brand loyalty.
- The craft profession has a history that dates back to antiquity.

Today, there are magazines, journals, papers, books, and organizations devoted to the industry. Many of these sources are extremely useful when creating ideas for your craft products.

- Some craftspeople pursue their creativity on a full-time basis while others work only part-time at the business. A great deal depends on the individual's economic situation and business goals.
- No matter how a product is promoted, there are certain items that will assist you in making the process more successful. These include developing a plan, laying out a budget, setting a timeframe or schedule and making sure that the process is organized.
- Collectables have become an important part of the craft business. You can cash in on this market by developing or selling items that can become or complement collectables.
- It makes good sense to look closely at fads and fashions for new ideas when developing craft products. It is also possible that one of your craft products will create or develop into a fad or fashion.

Marketing Checklist

Test your present marketing quotient! The following checklist can be used to monitor the current marketing level of your craft business. If there is already a marketing program in place, score 10 points. If the procedure is partially in place, add 6 to 8 points to your final tally. Base your exact point score on actual program participation. If a marketing system is in the planning stages, but not actually in place, give yourself 5 points. A total of 75 to 100 points is an indication that your marketing program is safely on target. A lower score means that your marketing program requires attention.

Points

{ }   1–An active *long-range marketing plan* for your craft business, consisting of goals and objectives, has been developed and is in place.

{ }   2–An integrated *short-term marketing plan,* complete with business goals, runs parallel with your long-term plan. The objectives are designed to work with your long term goals.

{ }   3–Several *market research programs* have been undertaken to determine target markets and consumer demands for your line of craft products. The research is part of an ongoing program.

{ }   4–Based on market research and customer contacts, there has been a continuing emphasis on developing packages of satisfaction to enhance the sales of your craft product.

{ }   5–An integrated *advertising, promotion and/or publicity program* for your craft product is actively in place.

{ }   6–The many areas that impact on the *pricing* of your craft product have been evaluated. An attractive pricing formula has been developed.

{ }   7–A decision on the *positioning* of your line of craft products in the marketplace has been made. Based on sales and profits, the results are most satisfactory.

{ }   8–A number of different *sales techniques* have been experimented with to move your craft product into the market. Some of the most lucrative methods have been retained.

{ }   9–A three-year and a five-year business plan have been developed for your craft operation. It will assure that the economic stability of your business is constantly monitored.

{ }   10–Your craft business always operates with a budget so that you are aware at all times of your financial viability, expenses, profits, etc.

{ }   TOTAL

CHAPTER 2

Developing the Marketing for Your Product

Sculptor, weaver, paper maker, jeweler, glass blower, ceramicist, potter, metal crafter, leather worker, or whatever craft your talents take you into, there are serious decisions you must make about the product or products you want to develop for marketing.

A sculptor may make miniatures or massive marbles, chess men for collectors, or statues of beloved pets, one of a kind pieces, or models for molding or casting multiples. Weavers can create all manner of apparel for men, women, and children, wall hangings and other decorative objects, table napery, pillows, spreads, throws and other fabric furnishings. Papermakers' products may include bookmarks and book liners, greeting cards and stationery, jewelry, collages and other framable works, portfolio covers, desk sets, and more. The jeweler can work in a multitude of media, utilizing beach pebbles or semi-precious and precious stones, man-made materials or a variety of metals, fibers, clays, or shells.

These examples are sufficient to make the point that a talented craftsperson can craft products large and small. These products can be designed for markets ranging from infants and children—and their parents and grandparents, uncles and aunts—to sophisticated adults with a taste for the beautiful, the unusual, and the unique, through collectors of all ages and interests and corporate buyers for boardrooms, lobbies, offices, and grounds (Figs. 2–1, 2–2 and 2–3).

Fig. 2–1. There are a variety of product markets open to the craftsperson. Sculptures in metal, wood, ceramic, or stone, for example, may be created for business entities such as banks to decorate and call attention to the establishment. The purchase of an artistic item by a business also indicates an interest in the arts.

Fig. 2–2. Businesses of all types represent a prime market for creative works. The crafted item may be used to advertise a product line or simply as a decorative asset in a shop.

Fig. 2–3. Parks, public buildings, tourism sites, and recreation areas present marketing opportunities for craftspeople.

How do you decide what product to start out with? Should you concentrate on making multiples or singular creations? Should you develop small pieces or large? Should you tailor your product for tykes or teenagers, career women or homemakers, for country, colonial, or contemporary collectors, for the affluent or the middle income market, for the consumer or the gift buyer? Should your form encompass functionality or simply art for art's sake?

These questions are relevant even for the many craftspeople who have gone into business because they have developed one or more products. The questions—and answers—are a key to successful business growth.

A Product Is an Item To Be Sold

When products are produced or manufactured, they generally have separate identities for the producer or seller and the purchaser or consumer. This holds true whether the products are your handcrafted rings, briar pipes, glass bowls, leather belts, musical instruments, grandma-quilts, woven wear, manufactured auto parts, or ceramic plumbing fixtures.

For the manufacturer or producer, a product is *an item to be sold.* The craftsperson who creates a product that is not designed for the marketplace may have developed a work-of-art for his or her personal collection or a marvelous show piece, but certainly not a viable, consumer's product. It is basic to this discussion, therefore, that your product must be designed for a market.

A buyer, on the other hand, in order to receive full value and use from a product must *go into the marketplace and purchase the item.* To do otherwise will leave the buyer devoid of ownership, and lacking attendant personal product use and potential enjoyment.

Packages of Satisfaction

When someone buys any product, especially a craft product, the purchase is not merely a tangible one. The individual is purchasing *a package of satisfaction.* The components of this package might include, but not be limited to, feelings of physical or psychological satisfaction.

Pride of ownership, convenience of use, comfort in wearing, appreciation of the recipient if the product is purchased as a gift, snob appeal, nostalgia, avant-garde leadership, adaptability to a projected self-image, connoisseurship identification—these are only some of the intangibles a buyer may be seeking.

What we must realize, then, is what motivates buyers to buy a product is a complete, albeit varied, package, and not simply the product itself, the physically-produced wood carving, handcrafted jewelry, weaving, or ceramic piece. In developing an article for sale, therefore, consider how many intangible appeals can be incorporated in the product itself, in its presentation, and in its marketing.

In order to translate this concept into practical use, suppose you are marketing handcrafted briar pipes. The work and skill that goes into the design of your product, perfection itself, is obvious to everyone. If, however, you put yourself in the place of the potential purchaser, you may recognize that he or she may have some health concerns or sensitivity about using or giving a pipe. Will the buyer be concerned about personal appearance? Will the individual be intrigued with the lore of pipes and pipe smoking and want to know more? Is there an identification with distinguished or famous pipe smokers?

As you think about the varied packages of satisfaction which may attract the buyer, you may recognize that there are product features that you can build into the pipe to add intangible value. An exclusively-designed trap, for example, to catch tar residue might mitigate health concerns. The pipe might be designed in a variety of styles that complement a personality or facial structure or to identify with celebrities, past or present. For those seeking to purchase a gift for a pipe-smoking loved one, your case or tag may give them the information to speak knowledgeably or anecdotally about the product, process, or the producer.

Always remember that in addition to being the creator of the line of handcrafted briar pipes, you are also the salesperson responsible for marketing the product you have developed. Try to build as much marketing appeal, tangible and intangible, into the product itself. An extension of this product development is the preparation to give people advice and to discuss the best way to care for the briar pipe, the types of tobacco available, and a whole range of other subjects that might interest a pipe fancier or gift buyer. *You may be in the business of marketing your handcrafted product, but you are actually in the business of marketing a package of satisfaction.*

Consider yet another example. Suppose you want to market hand-crafted children's toys. Once again, your skill is obvious and the products you can make are most attractive. What features might you build into your product to appeal to the grandma and grandpa, ready to spoil the child; to the mother looking for something that will hold the youngster's attention or last from youngster to youngster; to the divorced dad who needs to demonstrate caring; and, oh yes, to the children themselves who see a toy simply as a plaything? Can you build in product safety? Can you build in perceived educational value? Can you build in gamesmanship? Can you build in heirloom characteristics or qualities? Can you make the product adaptable to both boys and girls?

As you develop the tangible product, build in as much of the package of satisfaction as your toy might possibly offer. You might, for example, add to the safety with smooth edges, rounded corners, lead-free paints, etc. You might add learning opportunities with alphabet trims or maps or spatial designs, primary and complimentary color wheels, nursery rhymes, number charts, or simply initials. Indeed if you are making toys, it would be a worthwhile investment of your time to study grade level curricula as well as parental guides and Saturday morning children's programs. One of the best books on children's toys is *Buy Me! Buy Me!* by Joanne Oppenheim. The author also publishes a periodical on children's toys which is must reading for the toycrafter.

When it comes to marketing your toys, you might be prepared with testimonials from parent groups or individuals whose children have enjoyed your work. Finally, you can offer gift boxing and/or shipping containers that are attractive enough to be used for storage. *Your handcrafted toy is not merely a tangible gift but a gift of a package of satisfaction. You are in the business of marketing your handcrafted product.*

Building Marketability into Your Product

Generally, most handcrafted items fall into the broad category of *consumer products* or *goods,* as products are sometimes referred to in the marketing field. Consumer goods are designed to meet a variety of needs or wants. Some products are designed for use or *convenience* such as handcrafted covers for toasters, bun baskets, teapots, articles of clothing, tableware, etc. Others are *specialty products*—jewelry and decorative items for house and garden fall into this category. There are also products that have consumer appeal such as handcrafted wooden name sign for door, porch, or lawn; name tag necklaces or an over-the-mantel woodcarving design.

While some people are impulse buyers, many consumers shop carefully before they buy. They may compare design and structure, price and value. Your handcrafted product is not immune from this comparison. Commercially-manufactured quilts or foreign imports, for example, can be purchased at outlets and shopping centers. Your own or your cottage-industry quilt has to stand up to and out from this inspection or *product-shopping* process. Your product has to be developed to compete on various levels if it is to succeed in the marketplace. This does not mean that it has to be less costly, but rather that it has to offer superior value.

Crafted quilts, for example, can offer better design, better workmanship, more interesting fabrics, custom-made sizes, lighter or heavier batting, pockets for pajamas or reading glasses, detachable trim, or many other distinctive features. They might be appliqued, embroidered, stamped, or bordered with laces, soutache, leather or ultrasuede; and they can be made to meet customer special orders.

It is important to recognize the importance of consumer shopping habits as they apply to your product or products. This will enable you to develop your product to meet the competition of the marketplace more successfully. It will also help you develop effective marketing strategies.

Incidentally, although we refer to the consumer, it should be noted that the individual buyer may be not be the target purchaser of your craft product line. In some instances, the purchaser may be a wholesale buyer making multiple purchases for a shop, gallery, museum, department store or even a chain. In other instances, the purchaser might be an architect or decorator selecting products such as handcrafted statuary, tapestries, or other decor for a bank, apartment, school, or office building.

The principles of product development remain the same, however. In developing to sell, you have to get a strong reading of your target market and design to meet its needs.

It is important to remember that the market for your craft product can be found virtually anywhere, and that there is a broad spectrum of consumers to draw upon. Your task is to seek these markets continually, determine their needs and wants, and then design your product or products to meet these needs and desires.

Looking at Product Markets

There are a number of steps you can take to help make these decision about your product. One is to spend as much time as you can at mall shows, craft shows, museum shops, boutiques, and galleries. It is important to note what sells quickly and what moves slowly or not at all. It helps to learn as much as possible about the people who buy the products and in what price range they are more likely to purchase. It is equally important to discover whether you would be comfortable selling in any of these settings.

Check as many gift catalogs as you can, looking to see what kinds of products appear issue after issue, what items go on sale from one issue to the next, what items appear to be in the beginning of their life cycle (a subject we'll discuss more later) and what products seem to be waning in consumer interest.

Profit is the bottom line of marketing. The object in bringing a product to market is to make a profit. The objective is to determine how you can utilize your time to make the most of your talents.

Read the trade papers in the retail field that covers the commercial products in your area of expertise. Look to established, successful business ventures, department stores, specialty stores, and other retail establishments. Learn to estimate their markups, not only to help you later in pricing your product, but to help you determine what product to make. Many specialty stores, for example, will mark up a product 300 percent for initial selling, cut back to 150 percent, 100 percent and 50 percent markups for sales; but certain goods will have higher percentage markups than others.

The markup or profit per item is a major factor to consider. Can you get a higher markup on a framed wall hanging than a portfolio though each take the same time to make? Can you charge more for a pair of booties than for a pair of handknit socks? Can a lace curtain panel bring more than a lace apron; a wooden toy or an equally detailed box? Will a woven rug garner a higher price tag than an article of clothing, a quilted casserole holder more than a tea cozy or a ceramic teapot more than a covered casserole? Will a leather desk set sell for more than a pocketbook or an attache case?

Of equal importance as markup is how many items can be sold. At the risk of mentioning the obvious, two items sold at a profit of $200 each can bring as much as 200 sold at a profit of $2 each. The question, then, is how large are the potential markets for the $2 item or the $200 item?

It was mentioned in passing that you should determine the milieu in which you feel comfortable selling because this, too, will help you decide how to tailor your product. Mall shows, for example, generally feature lower-priced products than juried craft shows. Retail prices at juried shows are frequently lower than at galleries, museum shops, and boutiques, but in the latter cases you will be receiving wholesale prices. How and where you plan to sell your wares may also determine whether you want to produce small, light pieces, or larger, heavier ones.

Customers may have or develop a general idea about the selling price of many items, but many products are "blind", that is their price is based more on abstract values than actual costs and percentage markups. In other words, their price is set at what the market is willing to pay. This is best seen in the fine arts. However, many craftspeople have developed products which are works of art and command fine art prices.

Making Your Product Distinctive

Once you have determined what and where you might sell, there are some considerations that can help to give your product an advantage in the marketplace.

Product Personalization

Personalization or individualization of products frequently adds to their sales potential as well as their selling price. Products may be personalized by the addition of initials, names, or professional or career symbols. They may also be individualized with collector interest items. Someone looking for a gift for a cat lover might find a belt buckle shaped like a sleeping kitten an ideal gift, when otherwise a belt buckle would have no appeal at all.

People are also willing to pay more for one-of-a-kind items. Limited editions command higher prices than mass multiples. The addition of the craftsperson's signature or identifying logo adds value to a product for many consumers and also encourages buyers to become collectors of favorite craftspeople's products. In cases where craft becomes art, signed pieces have a higher intrinsic value than unsigned.

Product Uniqueness

Many buyers look to "make a statement" with the jewelry, clothing, or accessories they wear, the furnishings they display, and the presents they give. For these people, even those who are price-conscious, the product must be something that is a conversation piece, the kind of thing that makes perfect strangers stop them on the street or in a shop and say: "How interesting. How unusual. Where did you get that?" These products are not necessarily a function of price but of design, material, color, or size. The design must be good artform but often incorporating the unexpected, the whimsical, or the exaggerated, the miniature or the oversized adds value to the product. The material is always of quality, but once again is utilized in an atypical way. Colors are bold and striking or combined with excitement. Beyond this, these products demonstrate an undefinable sense of style. Even when they are not signed, they are frequently identifiable and customers form a kinship with others who acquire them and follow the crafter from show to show, shop to shop. They are the pieces that wind up in the "What's Hot?" columns or in high fashion model photos, decorating magazines, and slick ad shots.

This quality is frequently developed by creating a product that can be used in more ways than one, especially in some unexpected way. The ceramic belt buckle or Christmas tree ornament that can be used as an oversized pendant is one example of this. The baby quilt that becomes a wall hanging or the gold-plated yo-yo that becomes a desk accessory are others. A square of handpainted silk or handwoven fabric might be a scarf, but also a pillow cover; or with the addition of a ribbon or a braided cord, an apron. Two squares might become a blouse; a single length glamorous table runner, a sash, a turban, or a sarong.

In a home we visited recently, we admired what we thought was a wonderful wood sculpture of a child's tricycle posed on a room dividing ledge. "Where did you find it," we asked and were told it was the work of an area toy crafter and actually was a tyke-sized working model trike. "We also bought a wooden wagon we use as a picnic-table centerpiece and a train set for the mantel," our hosts said. "We like his toys for girls and boys, but his creative displays appeal to the kids in all of us."

One of the exercises educators use to develop innate creativity is to have youngsters list as many uses as possible for any mundane article. You can take a page from these educators and try to think of the variety of ways and settings in which your product can be used. The object, of course, is to find those ways and settings which will enable you to expand your markets, your prices, and your sales. One talented craftsperson incorporated special issue postage stamps and first day of issue covers into one-of-a-kind watercolor paintings. Another used stamps to cover jewelry boxes, mirror frames, and desk sets.

The wonderful beauty of craftsmanship is that there is an opportunity to develop basic product models and in the process build in a unique quality, so that literally no two items are precisely the same. This is an important consideration in product development. Whether it is the difference in brush strokes, the blend of color, the variety in trim or fabric design, the finish of the wood, the flow of the glaze, or the bubbles in the glass, crafted products are expected to be different, if only minutely so. It is this difference that gives buyers not only an exciting opportunity to make choices but also the special satisfaction of ownership or giftsmanship.

Product Life Cycle

Like man, and every other creature and product on earth, your handcrafted product will have a life cycle. The life cycle for a product starts from the point at which the product is launched into the marketplace. It spans the period when sales grow to a peak through the time when they decline to a point where it is not financially viable to continue production. In the final stages of the life cycle, it becomes a losing proposition to expend the time, energy, or dollars to market the item.

While some products have longer life cycles than others, every

Fig. 2–4. Hospitals and a large assortment of other not-for-profit organizations can be prime markets for the work of many craftspeople. In the examples shown, unique handcarved wooden Trees of Life are prepared and used by community organizations in their fund-raising efforts. While the woodcarving is the focal point of the craft piece, contributors to the particular cause have their names placed on the wood or metal leaves of the Tree of Life. This picture shows the trunk detail of a sculpture entitled "A Tradition of Caring," commissioned for CGH Medical Center, Sterling, IL. *(Courtesy Sanford Werfel, artist).*

Fig. 2–5. Another example of a Tree of Life showing the "leaves" for the addition of donors' names. This one is entitled "Whispering Leaves," and is an exclusive design for Chapel of Hope, Hobbs, NM. *(Courtesy Sanford Werfel, artist)*

Fig. 2–6.   This wall sculpture with hand-carved portrait, building, and logo was designed and built for Eger Nursing Home, Staten Island, NY. *(Courtesy Sanford Werfel, artist)*

craft item that you produce will experience the product life cycle. Most often, it will move through four distinct stages. These stages are clearly defined and if you pay close attention, you can watch the cycle forming, rising, and finally deflating even as yeast dough might. The analogy is apt. You begin by mixing the ingredients to *create the product*. The mixture of dough is then kneaded into a round bread-like shape. The mixture is covered, placed in a warm place, and gradually it *begins to rise*. At some point, the mixture, risen as far as possible, *matures*. At this point, if the risen dough is not baked, gradually the dough ball will *decline* in size and finally become useless as a product.

If you are introducing a completely new product line, there are several steps that usually precede the *market introduction stage*. Initially, your new craft product will be in the *developmental stage*. You will be designing and developing the product and seeking out the raw materials necessary for production. You will also be considering product packaging and any supplementary or complementary marketing tools that might enhance the product. These might include descriptive brochures, order blanks, and even protective liability insurance.

When you have gone through the developmental stage, you will probably be ready to launch your newest handcrafted item into the marketplace. Now, the product life cycle clock begins to tick.

The first stage your craft product will encounter is the *market introduction* or *pioneering stage*. Any product weakness or problem can be identified and corrected during the early part of this stage. The marketing introduction stage, experience has shown, is when your greatest energy should be expended in promotion. The heaviest portion of the advertising and promotional budget allocated to the new product will be needed here to develop exposure and basic demand for your product.

After your craft product has gone through the introductory stage, with the proper application of business guidance, marketing skills, promotion, and a modicum of luck, it next enters the *growth stage* of its life cycle. At this point, if the product is a good one, sales begin an upward spiral that requires special attention. First, of course, as sales increase, you may have to adjust the product to meet production and distribution demand.

As the product becomes more successful, competitors in the marketplace may recognize its sales potential, and you may find others bringing similar products to market. To keep your advantage, you may maximize product quality, develop variations to differentiate your product from the competition, or expand the areas of product distribution. The reasoning for the latter strategy is to make it easier for buyers to find and purchase your product.

In many instances, however, an increase in competition from similar products may also trigger a general increase in sales. This is especially true when certain items, for whatever reason, come into vogue. There was a time, for example, when nearly every jewelry maker featured at least one stickpin design, and nearly every woman bought at least one stickpin. Popular films, best sellers, or historic events will trigger a spate of similar products, sometimes ethnic in character, sometimes nostalgic, sometimes futuristic. These products may have shorter life cycles than old standards, but in many cases they peak at higher levels.

In the third level of the life cycle, a product reaches its *maturity stage*. From a practical standpoint, this means that your product and all of the products similar to yours in the entire marketplace begin to saturate the market and the demand is not as strong as it was during the growth stage. The maturity stage varies with different products so that you will have to keep a close watch on consumer demand for and sales of your product. You also have to watch the market share your competitors may be developing as this can force the price of your product down and lower your profits.

At some point, if your product does not change, it will enter the *market decline stage*. This is the stage at which a new product begins to take its place in the marketplace. It may be that the market has been saturated, or that changes in demographics or lifestyle limit the need for or appeal of the product, or simply that something else has come into vogue. Sales begin to fall, and buyers look to other products. Examples of products in the market decline stage are those connected with the Desert Storm interlude. T-shirts, jackets, and other memorabilia emblazoned with Desert Storm photographs, insignia, and slogans, the ubiquitous yellow ribbons and the patriotic stars and stripes, highly popular and salable during the war, no longer find a ready market except for collectors.

Visually, a product life cycle chart is similar to the bell curve usually used to graft the range of intelligence. The bell with its short introductory lip, its rising and falling cap, and its declining lip can be plotted on a graph. The vertical axis charts the sales income in dollars on the graph. The horizontal axis shows the timeframe of the sales. Plotting the line reveals the different stages of the product life cycle (Fig. 2–7). As dollars are charted over given time periods, the curve develops and the stages of the life cycle become apparent. In the introductory stage, the line begins to move up the dollar axis. If the introductory stage of the new product spans a short period of time, the line slopes upward quite rapidly; if long, the slope is more gradual. The dollars continue to be charted by time period as the product moves through the various stages of the product life cycle. When the chart is completed, it clearly pictures the dollar flow over time.

Plotting the chart, however, is more than an exercise. The picture is an excellent study of the marketability of your current product. It also serves as a useful tool for making decisions about other items that you may wish to market. As you see the sales curve falling, you begin to work on product changes that might slow the decline, or on new products that might start a new upward curve.

A product life cycle, however, does not always positively and absolutely end with its market decline stage. Witness the yo-yo, the hula-hoop, the thermometer with a weather forecasting, color-changing strip and many other items that have returned after a hiatus of years, each to successfully begin its product life cycle anew. In addition, there are usually consumers in the marketplace who maintain a warm spot in their heart for a particular product. It matters little that the mass market has decided that it no longer cares for or wants to purchase the item. The result is that a market, albeit a smaller one, remains for certain products long after the product life cycle chart may have pronounced its death knell.

Product Choices and Planning

Among the most important lessons that the craftsperson can glean from the marketing departments of manufacturers of all sizes, nationwide, is the necessity for _product adaptation and/or improvement_. If a product no longer sells well, either it should be modified to meet current needs and wants, or it should be set aside for a new product that may have greater marketing potential. If there is a change in the society and the marketplace that may affect your product, you should be prepared to meet the challenge.

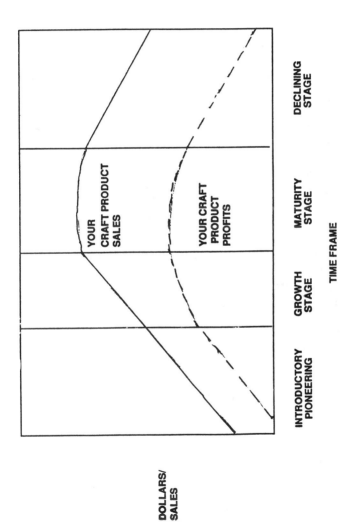

Fig. 2-7.   The Product Life Cycle.

A number of steps are required to put new craft product on the market. In a large business, these steps may involve planning, meetings, consultants, and delegation of responsibilities. In a small operation, each of these steps usually falls directly to you, and you generally handle them routinely. It's important, however, to set definite timeframes for working on and completing each step.

Making a wise product choice is the first step. Major manufacturers and marketers know that to be successful, products should always be geared to existing consumer needs or to needs which can be developed in the marketplace. Major marketers spend a great deal to study buyers' attitudes, behavioral patterns, selective purchasing processes, and shifts from one type of product to another. It is generally costly to conduct this type of research, but it can and should be done if there is to be a major investment in production. In another chapter of this book we will discuss how the process works.

It may also be worthwhile to test market the appeal of your new product. While major marketers test market in specific areas with typical or special demographics, you can test market in less costly and less complex ways. You can, for example, make several samples and take them to a small craft show to test buyer response, or you can simply show a sample, or a mock-up, to groups of people and elicit their comments. Show it to individuals other than family and friends so that the reaction is not prejudiced by kindness. Try to get a reasonably large sampling of people who might be typical of your market. If there are any problems with the product design or value, you want to find the weak spots before you go into full scale production.

Product Marketing Strategies

Test marketing may also help you establish the niche that best accommodates you product. Even in a niche market, however, it is good marketing strategy to differentiate your product from others in the market or that might be attracted to it by your success. In a sense, *product differentiation* is keeping ahead of or at least apart from the competition.

This requires product development concentration on such areas as value, relevance, and perceived or developed needs of the potential consumer. Even the best of products benefits from attention to the complete range of maketing strategies. These include a promotional

Fig. 2–8. *Courtesy Sanford Werfel, artist*

Fig. 2–9. *Courtesy Sanford Werfel, artist*

Fig. 2–10. *Courtesy Sanford Werfel, artist*

strategy for letting consumers know about your product and for creating an interest in it; a pricing strategy both for profitability and for positioning in the competitive, price-conscious marketplace; a distribution strategy for getting your product to the consumer; and an overall strategy for meshing your efforts.

These strategies will be useful whether the market for your craft product or the product itself is a completely new one or if you have made a product change and you are re-introducing a modified product. Marketing strategy factors may also encourage upgrading of both product and price. For example, perhaps someone bought one of your small woven wall hangings a number of years ago for $25. Currently more affluent, the consumer might now be able to purchase a special-order hanging from you for $1000. Have you kept in touch with that consumer over the years? Was your initial product labeled or marked in any way so that the buyer could get in touch with you? Can you upgrade your product? What strategies can you develop to prosper with your customers?

If your product has been on the market for some time, you may also be considering a slight change or a marketing reorientation strategy. The ordinary glass marble continues to respond to marketing reorientation strategies. For years, marbles were marketed as popular playthings. As the population shifted to the cities, marbles were replaced by stickballs and other competitive sports. In their current market reorientation, marbles are sold by the pound, for flower arranging, for fish tanks, for light catchers, and for kaleidoscopes.

The application of marketing strategies can play an important role in the successful sale of products. The investment of your time in reviewing the various strategy segments and in implementing those which are applicable can add an assurance factor to the business of marketing your crafts.

Chapter Highlights

- The manufacturer of a craft product must remember that the item has been developed to be sold.
- The consumer not only purchases a product, but buys a package of satisfaction.
- Some products are developed for convenience or utility while others

are designed for decoration or other selective purposes. It is important to understand the shopping habits of the consumer.

- It is important to investigate as many sources as possible to determine which craft products are selling best in the marketplace.
- Profit is the bottom line in marketing. The objective is to determine how you can utilize your time to make the most of your talents.
- While the markup or profit per item is a major factor to consider, the potential volume of sales is equally important.
- Customers may have a general idea about the cost of a product but many items are "blind" and prices are based more on abstract values or "what the market can bear" than on actual costs.
- Product personalization or product individualization adds to sales potential. Always try to differentiate your handcrafted product from others.
- Building in a unique quality enhances product value.
- Every product goes through a life cycle which includes a series of four clearly defined stages.
- As a manufacturer of a craft item, it is vital to recognize the importance of product adaptation and improvement.

CHAPTER 3

Protecting Your Craft Product

An important area to consider and understand, before your craft product has been widely distributed, is that of protecting your craft product. The government of the United States provides three distinct options to protect the work of craftspeople. These include federal copyrights, trademarks, and patents.

Copyrights and trademarks are best suited to helping craftspeople protect against potential infringement of their product name, promotional concepts, symbols, designs, and the like. Patent regulations, on the other hand, are useful for the craftsperson who has invented a completely new product or product adaptation and wishes to protect the invention.

The Patent

Patent regulations, as they relate to product design and originality, are complex. If you want to protect your unique product or adaptation legally, you should consult a patent attorney who specializes in product patents.

Patents are granted only to the original inventor. A patent cannot be obtained on a mere idea or suggestion. If you do obtain a patent on your invention, the Patent Office will, at your request, publish in the department's weekly Official Gazette a notice that your patent is available for licensing or sale. There is a small fee for this service, but it can produce investors or purchasers for your invention.

In addition to patent attorneys and agents, there are patent promotion organizations who represent that they can handle all details concerned with your invention. It is strongly suggested that you contact your personal attorney or the Better Business Bureau in your area or theirs to check on the reputation of these organizations before giving them any information or making any commitment to use their services.

Sometimes securing a patent can serve two purposes. It provides product protection, and also allows you to launch a related business venture. An example is the wood chair business of the Heartwood Furniture Company in Worcester, NY (Fig. 3–1). Each handcrafted chair has a built-in, patented hardware assembly device that makes the line unique. The completed chairs are sold at craft shows. The company also sells do-it-yourself plans at shows and by direct mail. The plans allow others to duplicate the chairs for their own use. In order to produce the furniture, however, do-it-yourselfers have to purchase the patented Flexibolt hardware from the Heartwood Company.

The Copyright

What It Is and How It Works

A *copyright* is a form of legal protection provided by the United States government for an individual, firm, or organization which has created a new work of any type of writing, art, or music. This protection means that anyone who wishes to use the work for any purpose must receive prior consent from the copyright holder.

The copyright law can protect certain of your original artistic endeavors against potential infringement. Included in the visual arts category are pictorial, graphic, or sculptured works, including two-dimensional and three-dimensional works of fine, graphic, and applied art; photographs, prints and art reproductions, maps, globes, charts, technical drawings, diagrams, architectural works, and models.

The acquisition of a copyright does not protect an idea, system, method, device, or trademark material. However, it does protect the

Fig. 3–1. Here is an example of a craft product design that has been patented by its inventor. This company not only markets the completed chairs at craft shows and in other venues, but also sells the patented hardware and plans so that do-it-yourselfers can build their own furniture. (*Courtesy Heartwood Furniture*)

originator's, author's, or copyright holder's specific expression in artistic form, as well as literary or musical pieces. Single words, or short phrases are not sufficient for those seeking copyright protection, nor are such things as slogans. What is required are full arrangements if copyright protection for music is being considered; completed bodies of text if written material is to be copyrighted, and a definitive artistic piece.

Today, your copyrighted work is automatically protected for 50 to 100 years depending on several factors. Protection for creative work produced prior to January 1, 1978 lasted 28 years with renewal rights of from 28 to 47 years. In order to determine the exact length of your copyright protection, check the information circulars issued by the Copyright Office.

The copyright department makes it clear that "works of artistic craftsmanship" are registerable. You would use form VA to make application for copyright registration. The statute makes it clear that the protection offered by a copyright extends to *their form,* and not, like a patent, to *the items' mechanical or utilitarian aspects.* The *design of a useful article* is considered copyrightable only if, and only to the extent that such design incorporates pictorial, graphic, or sculptural features that can be identified separately from, and are capable of existing independently of, the utilitarian aspects of the article.

An interesting application of a copyright to an artistic piece was recently displayed at a regional craft show. Copyrighted *Hinge Heads,* the original, creative art work, use blocks of wood that are turned into oversized heads. Huge rows of teeth dominate the character. A mechanism allows the jaws of these square, individually-hinged heads to open and close. Included in the line are sweatshirts and other items using the copyrighted Hinge Head figures.

How Long Does Copyright Registration Take?

The Copyright Office, Library of Congress, Washington, DC will send you, on request, informational booklets and data sheets describing each step of the copyright process. One information sheet details the length of time it will take you to register your copyright.

A copyright registration is effective on the date of receipt in the Copyright Office of all the required elements in acceptable form, regardless of the length of time it takes to process the application and mail the certificate of registration. The length of time required by the Copyright Office to process an application varies depending on the amount of material received and the personnel available to handle it. It must also be kept in mind that it may take a number of days for mailed material to reach the Copyright Office and for the certificate of registration to reach the recipient after being mailed by the Copyright Office.

You will receive an acknowledgement that your application for copyright registration has been received (the offices receive more than 500,000 applications annually), but you may expect:

- A letter or telephone call from a copyright examiner if further information is needed; and
- A certificate of registration to indicate the work has been registered, or if the application cannot be accepted, a letter explaining why it has been rejected.

You might not receive either of these until at least 120 days have passed. If you want to know when the Copyright Office receives your material, you should send it via registered or certified mail and request a return receipt.

For further information, write:

Information Section, LM-401
Copyright Office - Library of Congress
Washington, DC 20559

You may photocopy blank copyright application forms; but photocopied forms submitted to the Copyright Office must be clear, legible, and on a good grade of 8 ½ × 11 white paper suitable for automatic feeding through a photocopier. The forms should be printed, preferably in black ink, head-to-head (so that when you turn the sheet over, the top of page 2 is directly behind the top of page 1). Forms not meeting these requirements will be returned to the originator.

How to Register Your Work

In order to register your work for a copyright, three elements are required. All of the elements must all be enclosed in the same mailing envelope.

1—You will have to fill out copyright application form VA. Fig. 3–2 shows the VA application form and the copyright department's instructions necessary for completing the application. Form VA and instructions are available from the Register of Copyrights.

2—Include in the packet a non-refundable filing fee of $20.00.

3—Send a non-returnable deposit of the material you intend to register for a copyright. The deposit requirements will vary depending on whether the work has been seen or published at the time of registration.

- If the visual is *published,* send two complete copies with the copyright application. If the visual art is *unpublished,* one complete copy must be sent with the copyright application. The copy you use should represent the entire copyrightable content of the work that you wish to register.

- Identifying material deposited to represent visual art shall consist of photographs, photostats, slides, drawings or other two-dimensional representations of the work. The identifying material shall include as many pieces as necessary to show the entire copyrightable content of the work, including the copyright notice if it appears on the work. All pieces of identifying material other than transparencies must be no less than 3 × 3 inches in size, and no more than 9 × 12 inches, but preferably 8 × 10 inches. At least one piece of identifying material must, on its front, back, or mount, indicate the title of the work and an exact measurement of one or more dimensions of the work.

Your copyrightable material should be mailed to:

Register of Copyrights
Copyright Office
Library of Congress
Washington, DC 20559

When and How to Use Your Copyright

You can use the copyright that you have obtained for your work on all publicly-distributed copies that will be visually perceived. It is your responsibility, as copyright owner, to post or make this notice visible. The symbol or wording should appear in the form specified by the Copyright Department.

The required form of the notice for copies consists of three elements. (1) the symbol ©, the word *Copyright*, or the abbreviation

FORM VA

UNITED STATES COPYRIGHT OFFICE

REGISTRATION NUMBER

VA   VAU

EFFECTIVE DATE OF REGISTRATION

Month   Day   Year

DO NOT WRITE ABOVE THIS LINE. IF YOU NEED MORE SPACE, USE A SEPARATE CONTINUATION SHEET.

1

TITLE OF THIS WORK ▼   NATURE OF THIS WORK ▼ See instructions

PREVIOUS OR ALTERNATIVE TITLES ▼

PUBLICATION AS A CONTRIBUTION If this work was published as a contribution to a periodical, serial, or collection, give information about the collective work in which the contribution appeared.   Title of Collective Work ▼

If published in a periodical or serial give: Volume ▼   Number ▼   Issue Date ▼   On Pages ▼

2 a

NAME OF AUTHOR ▼   DATES OF BIRTH AND DEATH
                                    Year Born ▼ Year Died ▼

Was this contribution to the work a "work made for hire"?   AUTHOR'S NATIONALITY OR DOMICILE
Name of Country
☐ Yes   OR { Citizen of ▶
☐ No   { Domiciled in▶

WAS THIS AUTHOR'S CONTRIBUTION TO THE WORK
Anonymous?   ☐ Yes ☐ No
Pseudonymous? ☐ Yes ☐ No
If the answer to either of these questions is "Yes," see detailed instructions.

NOTE

Under the law, the "author" of a "work made for hire" is generally the employer, not the employee (see instructions). For any part of this work that was "made for hire" check "Yes" in the space provided, give the employer (or other person for whom the work was prepared) as "Author" of that part, and leave the space for dates of birth and death blank.

NATURE OF AUTHORSHIP Check appropriate box(es). **See Instructions**
☐ 3-Dimensional sculpture   ☐ Map   ☐ Technical drawing
☐ 2-Dimensional artwork   ☐ Photograph   ☐ Text
☐ Reproduction of work of art ☐ Jewelry design ☐ Architectural work
☐ Design on sheetlike material

b

NAME OF AUTHOR ▼   DATES OF BIRTH AND DEATH
                                    Year Born ▼ Year Died ▼

Was this contribution to the work a "work made for hire"?   AUTHOR'S NATIONALITY OR DOMICILE
Name of Country
☐ Yes   OR { Citizen of ▶
☐ No   { Domiciled in▶

WAS THIS AUTHOR'S CONTRIBUTION TO THE WORK
Anonymous?   ☐ Yes ☐ No
Pseudonymous? ☐ Yes ☐ No
If the answer to either of these questions is "Yes," see detailed instructions.

NATURE OF AUTHORSHIP Check appropriate box(es). See instructions
☐ 3-Dimensional sculpture   ☐ Map   ☐ Technical drawing
☐ 2-Dimensional artwork   ☐ Photograph   ☐ Text
☐ Reproduction of work of art ☐ Jewelry design ☐ Architectural work
☐ Design on sheetlike material

3 a

YEAR IN WHICH CREATION OF THIS WORK WAS COMPLETED
◀Year This information must be given in all cases.

b DATE AND NATION OF FIRST PUBLICATION OF THIS PARTICULAR WORK
Complete this information ONLY if this work has been published.
Month▶   Day▶   Year▶
◀ Nation

4

See instructions before completing this space.

COPYRIGHT CLAIMANT(S) Name and address must be given even if the claimant is the same as the author given in space 2. ▼

TRANSFER If the claimant(s) named here in space 4 are different from the author(s) named in space 2, give a brief statement of how the claimant(s) obtained ownership of the copyright. ▼

APPLICATION RECEIVED

ONE DEPOSIT RECEIVED

TWO DEPOSITS RECEIVED

REMITTANCE NUMBER AND DATE

DO NOT WRITE HERE OFFICE USE ONLY

MORE ON BACK ▶ • Complete all applicable spaces (numbers 5-9) on the reverse side of this page.
• See detailed instructions.   • Sign the form at line 8.

DO NOT WRITE HERE
Page 1 of _____ pages

Fig. 3–2. These copyright forms are used when applying for a copyright. The forms are supplied, on request, by the Register of Copyrights.

EXAMINED BY	FORM VA
CHECKED BY	
CORRESPONDENCE ☐ Yes	FOR COPYRIGHT OFFICE USE ONLY

DO NOT WRITE ABOVE THIS LINE. IF YOU NEED MORE SPACE, USE A SEPARATE CONTINUATION SHEET.

PREVIOUS REGISTRATION Has registration for this work, or for an earlier version of this work, already been made in the Copyright Office?
☐ Yes ☐ No If your answer is "Yes," why is another registration being sought? (Check appropriate box) ▼
a. ☐ This is the first published edition of a work previously registered in unpublished form.
b. ☐ This is the first application submitted by this author as copyright claimant.
c. ☐ This is a changed version of the work, as shown by space 6 on this application.
If your answer is "Yes," give: **Previous Registration Number** ▼   **Year of Registration** ▼

5

DERIVATIVE WORK OR COMPILATION Complete both space 6a & 6b for a derivative work; complete only 6b for a compilation.
a. Preexisting Material Identify any preexisting work or works that this work is based on or incorporates. ▼

b. Material Added to This Work Give a brief, general statement of the material that has been added to this work and in which copyright is claimed. ▼

6

See instructions before completing this space.

DEPOSIT ACCOUNT If the registration fee is to be charged to a Deposit Account established in the Copyright Office, give name and number of Account.
Name ▼   **Account Number** ▼

7

CORRESPONDENCE Give name and address to which correspondence about this application should be sent.   Name/Address/Apt/City/State/Zip ▼

Area Code & Telephone Number ▶

Be sure to give your daytime phone number ◀

CERTIFICATION* I, the undersigned, hereby certify that I am the
Check only one ▼
☐ author
☐ other copyright claimant
☐ owner of exclusive right(s)
☐ authorized agent of _____
              Name of author or other copyright claimant, or owner of exclusive right(s) ▲

of the work identified in this application and that the statements made
by me in this application are correct to the best of my knowledge.

Typed or printed name and date ▼ If this application gives a date of publication in space 3, do not sign and submit it before that date.
                                                                                            date ▶

Handwritten signature (X) ▼

8

MAIL CERTIFI-CATE TO	Name ▼	• Complete all necessary spaces • Sign your application in space 8
Certificate will be mailed in window envelope	Number/Street/Apartment Number ▼	1. Application form 2. Nonrefundable $20 filing fee in check or money order payable to Register of Copyrights 3. Deposit material
	City/State/ZIP ▼	Register of Copyrights Library of Congress Washington, D.C. 20559

9

*17 U.S.C. § 506(e): Any person who knowingly makes a false representation of a material fact in the application for copyright registration provided for by section 409, or in any written statement filed in connection with the application, shall be fined not more than $2,500.

May 1991—150,000   ☆U.S. GOVERNMENT PRINTING OFFICE: 1991-282-170/20,018

Fig. 3–2, cont.

■Filling Out Application Form VA

Detach and read these instructions before completing this form.
Make sure all applicable spaces have been filled in before you return this form.

BASIC INFORMATION

When to Use This Form: Use Form VA for copyright registration of published or unpublished works of the visual arts. This category consists of "pictorial, graphic, or sculptural works," including two-dimensional and three-dimensional works of fine, graphic, and applied art, photographs, prints and art reproductions, maps, globes, charts, technical drawings, diagrams, and models.

What Does Copyright Protect? Copyright in a work of the visual arts protects those pictorial, graphic, or sculptural elements that, either alone or in combination, represent an "original work of authorship." The statute declares: "In no case does copyright protection for an original work of authorship extend to any idea, procedure, process, system, method of operation, concept, principle, or discovery, regardless of the form in which it is described, explained, illustrated, or embodied in such work."

Works of Artistic Craftsmanship and Designs: "Works of artistic craftsmanship" are registrable on Form VA, but the statute makes clear that protection extends to "their form" and not to "their mechanical or utilitarian aspects." The "design of a useful article" is considered copyrightable "only if, and only to the extent that, such design incorporates pictorial, graphic, or sculptural features that can be identified separately from, and are capable of existing independently of, the utilitarian aspects of the article."

Labels and Advertisements: Works prepared for use in connection with the sale or advertisement of goods and services are registrable if they contain "original work of authorship." Use Form VA if the copyrightable material in the work you are registering is mainly pictorial or graphic; use Form TX if it consists mainly of text. NOTE: Words and short phrases such as names, titles, and slogans cannot be protected by copyright, and the same is true of standard symbols, emblems, and other commonly used graphic designs that are in the public domain. When used commercially, material of that sort can sometimes be protected under state laws of unfair competition or under the Federal trademark laws. For information about trademark registration, write to the Commissioner of Patents and Trademarks, Washington, D.C. 20231.

Architectural Works: Copyright protection extends to the design of buildings created for the use of human beings. Architectural works created on or after December 1, 1990, or that on December 1, 1990, were unconstructed and embodied only in unpublished plans or drawings are eligible. Request Circular 41 for more information.

Deposit to Accompany Application: An application for copyright registration must be accompanied by a deposit consisting of copies representing the entire work for which registration is to be made.

Unpublished Work: Deposit one complete copy.

Published Work: Deposit two complete copies of the best edition.

Work First Published Outside the United States: Deposit one complete copy of the first foreign edition.

Contribution to a Collective Work: Deposit one complete copy of the best edition of the collective work.

The Copyright Notice: For works first published on or after March 1, 1989, the law provides that a copyright notice in a specified form "may be placed on all publicly distributed copies from which the work can be visually perceived." Use of the copyright notice is the responsibility of the copyright owner and does not require advance permission from the Copyright Office. The required form of the notice for copies generally consists of three elements: (1) the symbol "©", or the word "Copyright," or the abbreviation "Copr."; (2) the year of first publication; and (3) the name of the owner of copyright. For example: "© 1991 Jane Cole." The notice is to be affixed to the copies "in such manner and location as to give reasonable notice of the claim of copyright." Works first published prior to March 1, 1989, must carry the notice or risk loss of copyright protection.

For information about notice requirements for works published before March 1, 1989, or other copyright information, write: Information Section, LM-401, Copyright Office, Library of Congress, Washington, D.C. 20559.

LINE-BY-LINE INSTRUCTIONS

Please type or print using dark ink.

1 SPACE 1: Title

Title of This Work: Every work submitted for copyright registration must be given a title to identify that particular work. If the copies of the work bear a title (or an identifying phrase that could serve as a title), transcribe that wording *completely* and *exactly* on the application. Indexing of the registration and future identification of the work will depend on the information you give here. For an architectural work that has been constructed, add the date of construction after the title; if unconstructed at this time, add "not yet constructed."

Previous or Alternative Titles: Complete this space if there are any additional titles for the work under which someone searching for the registration might be likely to look, or under which a document pertaining to the work might be recorded.

Publication as a Contribution: If the work being registered is a contribution to a periodical, serial, or collection, give the title of the contribution in the "Title of This Work" space. Then, in the line headed "Publication as a Contribution," give information about the collective work in which the contribution appeared.

Nature of This Work: Briefly describe the general nature or character of the pictorial, graphic, or sculptural work being registered for copyright. Examples: "Oil Painting"; "Charcoal Drawing"; "Etching"; "Sculpture"; "Map"; "Photograph"; "Scale Model"; "Lithographic Print"; "Jewelry Design"; "Fabric Design."

2 SPACE 2: Author(s)

General Instruction: After reading these instructions, decide who are the "authors" of this work for copyright purposes. Then, unless the work is a "collective work," give the requested information about every "author" who contributed any appreciable amount of copyrightable matter to this version of the work. If you need further space, request Continuation Sheets. In the case of a collective work, such as a catalog of paintings or collection of cartoons by various authors, give information about the author of the collective work as a whole.

Name of Author: The fullest form of the author's name should be given. Unless the work was "made for hire," the individual who actually created the work is its "author." In the case of a work made for hire, the statute provides that "the employer or other person for whom the work was prepared is considered the author."

What is a "Work Made for Hire"? A "work made for hire" is defined as: (1) "a work prepared by an employee within the scope of his or her employment"; or (2) "a work specially ordered or commissioned for use as a contribution to a collective work, as a part of a motion picture or other audiovisual work, as a translation, as a supplementary work, as a compilation, as an instructional text, as a test, as answer material for a test, or as an atlas, if the parties expressly agree in a written instrument signed by them that the work shall be considered a work made for hire." If you have checked "Yes" to indicate that the work was "made for hire," you must give the full legal name of the employer (or other person for whom the work was prepared). You may also include the name of the employee along with the name of the employer (for example: "Elster Publishing Co., employer for hire of John Ferguson").

"Anonymous" or "Pseudonymous" Work: An author's contribution to a work is "anonymous" if that author is not identified on the copies or phonorecords of the work. An author's contribution to a work is "pseudonymous" if that author is identified on the copies or phonorecords under a fictitious name. If the work is "anonymous" you may: (1) leave the line blank; or (2) state "anonymous" on the line; or (3) reveal the author's identity. If the work is "pseudonymous" you may: (1) leave the line blank; or (2) give the pseudonym and identify it as such (for example: "Huntley Haverstock, pseudonym"); or (3) reveal the author's name, making clear which is the real name and which is the pseudonym (for example: "Henry Leek, whose pseudonym is Priam Farrel"). However, the citizenship or domicile of the author must be given in all cases.

Dates of Birth and Death: If the author is dead, the statute requires that the year of death be included in the application unless the work is anonymous or pseudonymous. The author's birth date is optional, but is useful as a form of identification. Leave this space blank if the author's contribution was a "work made for hire."

Author's Nationality or Domicile: Give the country of which the author is a citizen or the country in which the author is domiciled. Nationality or domicile must be given in all cases.

Fig. 3–2, cont.

Nature of Authorship: Catagories of pictorial, graphic and sculptural authorship are listed below. Check the box(es) that best describe(s) each author's contribution to the work.

3-Dimensional sculptures: fine art sculptures, toys, dolls, scale models, and sculptural designs applied to useful articles.

2-Dimensional artwork: watercolor and oil paintings; pen and ink drawings; logo illustrations; greeting cards; collages; stencils; patterns; computer graphics; graphics appearing in screen displays; artwork appearing on posters, calendars, games, commercial prints and labels and packaging, as well as 2-dimensional artwork applied to useful articles.

Reproductions of works of art: reproductions of preexisting artwork made by, for example, lithography, photoengraving, or etching.

Maps: cartographic representations of an area such as state and county maps, atlases, marine charts, relief maps and globes.

Photographs: pictorial photographic prints and slides and holograms.

Jewelry designs: 3-dimensional designs applied to rings, pendants, earrings, necklaces and the like.

Designs on sheetlike materials: designs reproduced on textiles, lace and other fabrics; wallpaper; carpeting; floor tile; wrapping paper and clothing.

Technical drawings: diagrams illustrating scientific or technical information in linear form such as architectural blueprints or mechanical drawings.

Text: textual material that accompanies pictorial, graphic or sculptural works such as comic strips, greeting cards, games rules, commercial prints or labels, and maps.

Architectural works: designs of buildings, including the overall form as well as the arrangement and composition of spaces and elements of the design. NOTE: Any registration for the underlying architectural plans must be applied for on a separate Form VA, checking the box "Technical drawing."

3 SPACE 3: Creation and Publication

General Instructions: Do not confuse "creation" with "publication." Every application for copyright registration must state "the year in which creation of the work was completed." Give the date and nation of first publication only if the work has been published.

Creation: Under the statute, a work is "created" when it is fixed in a copy or phonorecord for the first time. Where a work has been prepared over a period of time, the part of the work existing in fixed form on a particular date constitutes the created work on that date. The date you give here should be the year in which the author completed the particular version for which registration is now being sought, even if other versions exist or if further changes or additions are planned.

Publication: The statute defines "publication" as "the distribution of copies or phonorecords of a work to the public by sale or other transfer of ownership, or by rental, lease, or lending"; a work is also "published" if there has been an "offering to distribute copies or phonorecords to a group of persons for purposes of further distribution, public performance, or public display." Give the full date (month, day, year) when, and the country where, publication first occurred. If first publication took place simultaneously in the United States and other countries, it is sufficient to state "U.S.A."

4 SPACE 4: Claimant(s)

Names(s) and Address(es) of Copyright Claimant(s): Give the name(s) and address(es) of the copyright claimant(s) in this work even if the claimant is the same as the author. Copyright in a work belongs initially to the author of the work (including, in the case of a work made for hire, the employer or other person for whom the work was prepared). The copyright claimant is either the author of the work or a person or organization to whom the copyright initially belonging to the author has been transferred.

Transfer: The statute provides that, if the copyright claimant is not the author, the application for registration must contain "a brief statement of how the claimant obtained ownership of the copyright." If any copyright claimant named in space 4 is not an author named in space 2, give a brief statement explaining how the claimant(s) obtained ownership of the copyright. Examples: "By written contract"; "Transfer of all rights by author"; "Assignment"; "By will." Do not attach transfer documents or other attachments or riders.

5 SPACE 5: Previous Registration

General Instructions: The questions in space 5 are intended to find out whether an earlier registration has been made for this work and, if so, whether

Fig. 3–2, cont.

there is any basis for a new registration. As a rule, only one basic copyright registration can be made for the same version of a particular work.

Same Version: If this version is substantially the same as the work covered by a previous registration, a second registration is not generally possible unless: (1) the work has been registered in unpublished form and a second registration is now being sought to cover this first published edition; or (2) someone other than the author is identified as a copyright claimant in the earlier registration, and the author is now seeking registration in his or her own name. If either of these two exceptions apply, check the appropriate box and give the earlier registration number and date. Otherwise, do not submit Form VA; instead, write the Copyright Office for information about supplementary registration or recordation of transfers of copyright ownership.

Changed Version: If the work has been changed, and you are now seeking registration to cover the additions or revisions, check the last box in space 5, give the earlier registration number and date, and complete both parts of space 6 in accordance with the instruction below.

Previous Registration Number and Date: If more than one previous registration has been made for the work, give the number and date of the latest registration.

6 SPACE 6: Derivative Work or Compilation

General Instructions: Complete space 6 if this work is a "changed version," "compilation," or "derivative work," and if it incorporates one or more earlier works that have already been published or registered for copyright, or that have fallen into the public domain. A "compilation" is defined as "a work formed by the collection and assembling of preexisting materials or of data that are selected, coordinated, or arranged in such a way that the resulting work as a whole constitutes an original work of authorship." A "derivative work" is "a work based on one or more preexisting works." Examples of derivative works include reproductions of works of art, sculptures based on drawings, lithographs based on paintings, maps based on previously published sources, or "any other form in which a work may be recast, transformed, or adapted." Derivative works also include works "consisting of editorial revisions, annotations, or other modifications" if these changes, as a whole, represent an original work of authorship.

Preexisting Material (space 6a): Complete this space **and** space 6b for derivative works. In this space identify the preexisting work that has been recast, transformed, or adapted. Examples of preexisting material might be "Grunewald Altarpiece" or "19th century quilt design." Do not complete this space for compilations.

Material Added to This Work (space 6b): Give a brief, general statement of the **additional** new material covered by the copyright claim for which registration is sought. In the case of a derivative work, identify this new material. Examples: "Adaptation of design and additional artistic work"; "Reproduction of painting by photolithography"; "Additional cartographic material"; "Compilation of photographs." If the work is a compilation, give a brief, general statement describing both the material that has been compiled **and** the compilation itself. Example: "Compilation of 19th century political cartoons."

7,8,9 SPACE 7,8,9: Fee, Correspondence, Certification, Return Address

Deposit Account: If you maintain a Deposit Account in the Copyright Office, identify it in space 7. Otherwise leave the space blank and send the fee of $20 with your application and deposit.

Correspondence (space 7): This space should contain the name, address, area code, and telephone number of the person to be consulted if correspondence about this application becomes necessary.

Certification (space 8): The application cannot be accepted unless it bears the date and the **handwritten signature** of the author or other copyright claimant, or of the owner of exclusive right(s), or of the duly authorized agent of the author, claimant, or owner of exclusive right(s).

Address for Return of Certificate (space 9): The address box must be completed legibly since the certificate will be returned in a window envelope.

Copr.; (2) the year of first publication; and (3) the name of the owner of the copyright. The notice should be affixed to all copies of your work in such a manner and location as to give reasonable notice of the claim of copyright.

The Trademark

The use of a *trademark* provides craftspeople with a legal form of government protection. Trademark protection is designed to shield identifying product symbols, devices, names, words, designs, logos, or even distinctive sounds that you may originate, against infringement. When in force, this protection gives you, as the trademark originator, the right to demand that your prior consent be given before any of your distinctive marks are used for any purpose. Some consider the trademark as the intellectual property of the person who originated the concept or the trademark holder.

In some instances people develop copyrightable, patentable, or trademarkable works when they are working for or under contract to publishers, agencies, or corporations. In these instances, there may be an agreement or an understanding that the copyright, patent, or trademark will belong to the organization rather than the originator.

A symbol such as the Quaker "portrait" on all Quaker Oats products, the Heinz symbol with the small green pickle on all Heinz products, the Nestle name with special distinctive graphic line over the last "e" in the product name, or the word Coca-Cola in script are typical trademark identifications. A trademark has value. Consider for a moment the value in dollars of any of the trademark examples listed at the beginning of this paragraph. The interesting thing about a trademark is that the older it gets and the more it is used, the higher its value.

In the instance of craft products, it is not unusual for a special name to be selected and trademarked by the craftsperson to identify and promote the product. For example, there is a company that produces a unique, colorful, handcrafted line of bird feeders. The firm, which headquarters in Lake George, NY, calls itself the *American Pie Company Inc.* They have trademarked this company name. In addition, the name has been woven into a red, white and blue logo containing stars and portion of the American flag (Fig. 3–3).

In addition to providing protection against infringement, a trade-

Fig. 3–3. This craft company, producers of specialty bird feeders, has a trademarkable name. They carry out the logo theme by printing the name and art work in red, white, and blue. *(Courtesy American Pie Company)*

mark has important promotional potential so that your choice of a trademark, symbol, or name requires a great deal of attention. When you use a trademark, you are, in effect, promoting your product, your company, and your reputation as a master craftsperson.

When you create a name to be trademarked, work for originality, word play, acronyms, word and letter combinations, or other choices that are unique. If somehow the name selected is a common noun, it may not receive trademark registration. If, for example, you select such words as hose, window, building, or grating for a trademark, you will find that these nouns cannot be registered. The best choices for trademarks are logos and letter combinations. Think about some of the famous trademarked names—IBM, EXXON, GM, CITIBANK. Try not to select a plural name or a name in its possessive form for your trademark.

Do not try to trademark generic words. These are words which define a general group or class. If, for example, you were the owner of a Christmas tree farm, and wanted to trademark the words "Christmas Tree" to identify the products of your farm, this would not be acceptable. To get around such naming dilemma, perhaps you try to trademark the word "Tannenbaum." This, too, would not be permitted because it is the German word for Christmas tree. On the other hand, you might trademark the words "Christmas Tree" if the name was for your company's newest product, a line of woodsmen's axes.

Graphically, there are many techniques that can make your selected trademark even more effective. When your trademark is a word, capital letters are suggested as being most effective. If this is not possible, capitalize the lead letters. Develop some special graphic treatment for the trademark to differentiate it from surrounding words. You may want to enclose the trademarked word in quotes, or use special typefaces, or text treatments. If possible, test market your trademark to get consumer reaction to the design and concept. If viewers respond by easily relating your trademark to your product, you have a winner. If not, you may have to send the graphics back to the drawing board.

Always remember that the prime purpose of using a trademark is to identify your product as separate and distinct from others. A good trademark can draw consumers whose perception of the name identification will encourage product purchase. Trademarks, e.g., Exxon, also have strong promotional applications, such as on gas pumps. Always identify your trademarks when they are used in these applications just as in any non-promotional situation, such as on trucks.

The Service Mark

A *service mark* can be protected under the trademark process. While a trademark is generally used to identify a product or product as a brand name, a service mark is usually used, particularly in advertising, to identify services or intangibles.

How Trademarking Works

Your trademark serves a dual purpose. It protects you as the creator of the mark or brand from the unlawful use of your created property. Trademarks and service marks also protect the public from being fooled into believing that they are using or purchasing anything but your original product. The best examples of this situation are knock-off watches purchased in outlets or on street corners. *Knock-offs* are cheap copies of an original with well-known names placed on a conspicuous part of the product. If the perpetrators of these frauds can be located, the legitimate trademark holder has a legal claim against them.

Your trademark rights arise from either (1) the use of your mark, or (2) a bona fide intention to use your mark, along with the filing of an application to actually register your mark. This intention goes along with the filing of an application to federally register that mark on the government's Principal Register.

Protecting against Infringements

Trademark infringement may take a number of forms. The major techniques used by unethical competitors are designed to cause consumer confusion. Your trademark can be duplicated by an infringer. The use of a design that is very, very similar to yours, may also be a tactic selected by some unscrupulous competitors.

You should be prepared to guard against situations where a drop in your market share might conceivably diminish the value and effectiveness of your trademark, and thus you will no longer be able to battle trademark-infringing competitors vigorously. Once you react in this fashion, the competition may become even more active and hostile, causing a dangerous downward spiral.

Before You Use a Trademark

As a trademark owner, before you can file an application for a federal registration, you must use the mark on products which are actually sold in commerce. This means that there should be real transactions or sales of your products in either interstate commerce, or commerce between the United States and a foreign country. Another option is for you to have the genuine intention to use your mark on your product in a commercial venture. This simply means that you are genuinely trying to sell your product in the consumer marketplace.

From a practical business standpoint, in the United States, *you are the trademark's owner when you use it.* Registering your trademark is a legal and official matter entitling you to certain advantages which will be enumerated later in this section.

The Life of a Trademark

Unlike copyright or patent rights, trademark rights can last indefinitely. Your mark, however, must continue to perform a so-called source-indicating function. This means that your product is alive, well, and active in the marketplace. The term of the federal trademark registration is ten years, with ten-year renewable terms. However, between the fifth and sixth year after the date of registration, as registrant, you must file an affidavit stating that the mark is currently in use in commerce. If no affidavit is filed, the registration will be cancelled. When you no longer find use for your trademark, it becomes free to return to the marketplace for general use.

Registration Benefits

While federal registration is not necessary for trademark protection of your product, registration on the Principal Register in the trademark office can provide you with certain advantages and protection. According to Patent and Trademark Office information, these include:

- The filing date of the application is the date that you first use the mark with your product or advertising in commerce.
- You have the right to sue in federal court for infringement of your trademark.
- You have the right to recover profits, damages, and costs in a federal

court infringement action. There is also the possibility of recovering triple damages and attorneys' fees.

- You have the right to constructive notice of a claim of ownership. Legally, this eliminates a good faith defense for a party adopting your trademark subsequent to the date of registration.
- You have the right to deposit your trademark registration with Customs. You would do this in order to stop the importation of products which bear an infringing mark.
- Legally, the fact that you have obtained such a registration provides you with prima facie evidence of the validity of your registration, ownership of the mark, and exclusive right to use the mark in commerce in connection with the products and/or services detailed in your certificate.
- Your registration has the possibility of incontestability. This means that your registration constitutes conclusive evidence of your exclusive right, with certain limited exceptions, to use your registered trademark in commerce.
- Your registration provides limited grounds for anyone who intends to attack your registration once it has been in place for five years.
- Your registration provides for criminal penalties and triple damages if anyone is caught counterfeiting your registered trademark.
- Your registration serves as a basis for filing trademark applications in those foreign countries where trademarks are recognized.

How to Display Your Trademark

Once your federal trademark registration is issued, you may give notice of the registration by using the small circled R symbol (®), or the phrase "Registered in U.S. Patent and Trademark Office," or "Reg. U.S. Pat. & Tm. Off."

Although registration symbols may not be used lawfully prior to registration, many trademark owners use a **TM** or **SM** (if the mark identifies a service) symbol to indicate a claim of ownership, even if no federal trademark application is pending.

The Trademark Registration Process

There is a system for shepherding the item you wish to trademark through the registration process. According to the Patent and Trademark Office, the PTO is responsible for the federal registration of trademarks. When an application is filed, it is reviewed to determine if it meets the requirements for receiving a filing date. If the filing requirements are not met, the entire mailing, including the fee, is returned to the applicant. If the application meets the filing requirements, it is assigned a serial number, and the applicant is sent a filing receipt.

The first part of the registration process is a determination by the Trademark Examining Attorney as to whether the mark may be registered. An initial determination of registerability, listing any statutory grounds for refusal as well as any procedural informalities in the application, is issued about three months after filing. The applicant must respond to any objections raised within six months, or the application will be considered abandoned. If, after reviewing the applicant's response, the Examining Attorney makes a final refusal of registration, the applicant must appeal to the Trademark Trial and Appeal Board, an administrative tribunal within the PTO.

Once the Examining Attorney approves the mark, the mark will be published in the Trademark Official Gazette, a weekly publication of the PTO. Any other party then has 30 days to oppose the registration of the mark, or request an extension of time to oppose. An opposition is similar to a proceeding in the federal district courts, but is held before the Trademark Trial and Appeal Board. If no opposition is filed, the application enters the next stage of the registration process.

If the mark is published based upon its actual use in commerce, a registration will be issued approximately 12 weeks from the date the mark was published.

If, instead, the mark is published based upon the applicant's statement of a bona fide intention to use the mark in commerce, *a notice of allowance* will be issued approximately 12 weeks from the date the mark was published. The applicant then has six months from the date of the notice of allowance to either (1) use the mark in commerce and *submit a statement of use,* or (2) request a six-month *extension of time* to file a statement of use (see forms and instructions). The applicant may request additional extensions of time only as noted in the instructions on the back of the application form.

Grounds for Refusing to Issue a Trademark

There are a number of reasons that the Examining Attorney will refuse registration of a trademark. The Patent and Trademark Office suggests that the following are statutory grounds for refusing your selected name, slogan, word, etc.

1—It does not function as a trademark to identify your product as coming from a particular source.

2—It is deemed to be immoral, deceptive, or scandalous.

3—It may disparage or falsely suggest a connection with persons, institutions, beliefs, or national symbols, or bring them into contempt or disrepute.

4—It consists of or simulates the flag or coat of arms or other insignia of the United States, or a State or municipality, or any foreign nation.

5—It is the name, portrait, or signature of a particular living individual, unless he/she has given written consent; or is the name, signature or portrait of a deceased President of the United States during the life of his widow, unless she has given consent.

6—It so resembles a mark already registered with the PTO as to be likely, when used on or in connection with the goods of the applicant, to cause confusion, or to cause mistake, or to deceive.

7—It is merely descriptive or deceptively misdescriptive of the goods or services.

8—It is primarily geographically descriptive or deceptively misdescriptive of the goods or services of the applicant.

9—It is primarily merely a surname.

A mark will not be refused registration on the grounds listed in 7, 8 and 9 if the applicant can show that, through use of the mark in commerce, the mark has become distinctive so that it now identifies to the public the applicant's goods or services. Marks which are refused registration on the grounds listed in numbers 1, 7, 8, and 9 may be registered on the Supplemental Register, which contains terms or designs considered capable of distinguishing the owner's goods or services, but that do not yet do so. A term or design cannot be considered for registration on the Supplemental Register unless it is in use in commerce in relation to all the goods and services identified in the application, and an acceptable allegation of use has been submitted. Additional information on this subject is available in a booklet provided by the Patent and Trademark Office.

Filing for a Trademark

A trademark application consists of a written application form, a drawing of the mark, the required filing fee, and, only if the application is filed based upon prior use of the mark in commerce, three specimens showing actual use of the mark on or in connection with the goods or services. Separate applications must be filed for each mark.

The trademark filing fee for each class of goods or services for which an application is made is $175. This fee must be submitted for an application to be given a filing date. Information on other fee designations are available in the Patent and Trademark booklet.

In order to obtain all of the necessary information you require to register your trademark, and the necessary forms which must be filled out, write to:

The Commissioner of Patents and Trademarks
Washington, DC 20231

Indicate in your correspondence exactly what information and forms you require.

Trademark application forms (Figs. 3–4, 3–5, 3–6, and 3–7) are available from the Commissioner of Patents and Trademarks.

Liability Insurance

Today's society is extremely litigious. When you produce a craft product and put it into the marketplace, you expose yourself to the possibility of legal action if anyone claims injury resulting from the product.

- Consider the possibilities. Though you have designed and guarded against it, a parent may claim that a child cut his finger on a toy you produced. The parents sue you for damages.
- The handle of a large ceramic craft pitcher that you have produced comes off and the pitcher falls and breaks the customer's toe. The individual takes liability action against you.
- You've developed some attractive, colorful plastic flowers. A child manages to eat one of your creations, and ends up in the hospital emergency room. The parents institute suit for the hospital costs plus many extras.

These are just some examples of your potential exposures.

The surest way to protect yourself against consumer liability charges is to *secure liability insurance for your craft product line.* This type of insurance is available through any business insurance broker, and will protect you against consumer claims. If a claim is made against you, the insurance company may provide legal defense, or may pay the claim against you outright.

TRADEMARK/SERVICE MARK APPLICATION, PRINCIPAL REGISTER, WITH DECLARATION	MARK (Identify the mark)
	CLASS NO. (If known)

TO THE ASSISTANT SECRETARY AND COMMISSIONER OF PATENTS AND TRADEMARKS:

APPLICANT NAME:

APPLICANT BUSINESS ADDRESS:

APPLICANT ENTITY: (Check one and supply requested information)

☐ Individual - Citizenship: (Country) _____

☐ Partnership - Partnership Domicile: (State and Country) _____
Names and Citizenship (Country) of General Partners: _____
_____

☐ Corporation - State (Country, if appropriate) of Incorporation: _____

☐ Other: (Specify Nature of Entity and Domicile) _____
_____

GOODS AND/OR SERVICES:

Applicant requests registration of the above-identified trademark/service mark shown in the accompanying drawing in the United States Patent and Trademark Office on the Principal Register established by the Act of July 5, 1946 (15 U.S.C. 1051 et. seq., as amended.) for the following goods/services: _____
_____
_____

BASIS FOR APPLICATION: (Check one or more, but NOT both the first AND second boxes, and supply requested information)

☐ Applicant is using the mark in commerce on or in connection with the above identified goods/services. (15 U.S.C. 1051(a), as amended.) Three specimens showing the mark as used in commerce are submitted with this application.
• Date of first use of the mark anywhere: _____
• Date of first use of the mark in commerce which the U.S. Congress may regulate: _____
• Specify the type of commerce: _____
(e.g., interstate, between the U.S. and a specified foreign country)

• Specify manner or mode of use of mark on or in connection with the goods/services: _____
(e.g., trademark is applied to labels, service mark is used in advertisements)

☐ Applicant has a bona fide intention to use the mark in commerce on or in connection with the above identified goods/services. (15 U.S.C. 1051(b), as amended.)
• Specify intended manner or mode of use of mark on or in connection with the goods/services: _____
(e.g., trademark will be applied to labels, service mark will be used in advertisements)

☐ Applicant has a bona fide intention to use the mark in commerce on or in connection with the above identified goods/services, and asserts a claim of priority based upon a foreign application in accordance with 15 U.S.C. 1126(d), as amended.
• Country of foreign filing: _____ • Date of foreign filing: _____

☐ Applicant has a bona fide intention to use the mark in commerce on or in connection with the above identified goods/services and, accompanying this application, submits a certification or certified copy of a foreign registration in accordance with 15 U.S.C. 1126(e), as amended.
• Country of registration: _____ • Registration number: _____

Note: Declaration, on Reverse Side, MUST be Signed

PTO Form 1478 (REV. 9/89)
OMB No. 06510009
Exp. 5-31-91

U.S. DEPARTMENT OF COMMERCE/Patent and Trademark Office

Fig. 3–4. These trademark forms are used when applying for a trademark. The forms are supplied, on request, by the Commissioner of Patents and Trademarks.

DECLARATION

The undersigned being hereby warned that willful false statements and the like so made are punishable by fine or imprisonment, or both, under 18 U.S.C. 1001, and that such willful false statements may jeopardize the validity of the application or any resulting registration, declares that he/she is properly authorized to execute this application on behalf of the applicant; he/she believes the applicant to be the owner of the trademark/service mark sought to be registered, or, if the application is being filed under 15 U.S.C. 1051(b), he/she believes applicant to be entitled to use such mark in commerce; to the best of his/her knowledge and belief no other person, firm, corporation, or association has the right to use the above identified mark in commerce, either in the identical form thereof or in such near resemblance thereto as to be likely, when used on or in connection with the goods/services of such other person, to cause confusion, or to cause mistake, or to deceive; and that all statements made of his/her own knowledge are true and all statements made on information and belief are believed to be true.

_____   _____
Date   Signature

_____   _____
Telephone Number   Print or Type Name and Position

INSTRUCTIONS AND INFORMATION FOR APPLICANT

To receive a filing date, the application must be completed and **signed by the applicant** and submitted along with:

1. The prescribed fee for each class of goods/services listed in the application;
2. A drawing of the mark in conformance with 37 CFR 2.52;
3. If the application is based on use of the mark in commerce, three (3) specimens (evidence) of the mark as used in commerce for each class of goods/services listed in the application. All three specimens may be the same and may be in the nature of: (a) labels showing the mark which are placed on the goods; (b) a photograph of the mark as it appears on the goods, (c) brochures or advertisements showing the mark as used in connection with the services.

Verification of the application - The application must be signed in order for the application to receive a filing date. Only the following person may sign the verification (Declaration) for the application, depending on the applicant's legal entity: (1) the individual applicant; (b) an officer of the corporate applicant; (c) one general partner of a partnership applicant; (d) all joint applicants.

Additional information concerning the requirements for filing an application are available in a booklet entitled **Basic Facts about Trademarks**, which may be obtained by writing:

U.S. DEPARTMENT OF COMMERCE
Patent and Trademark Office
Washington, D.C. 20231

Or by calling: (703) 557-INFO

This form is estimated to take 15 minutes to complete. Time will vary depending upon the needs of the individual case. Any comments on the amount of time you require to complete this form should be sent to the Office of Management and Organization, U.S. Patent and Trademark Office, U.S. Department of Commerce, Washington D.C., 20231, and to the Office of Information and Regulatory Affairs, Office of Management and Budget, Washington, D.C. 20503.

Fig. 3–4, cont.

AMENDMENT TO ALLEGE USE UNDER 37 CFR 2.76, WITH DECLARATION	MARK (Identify the mark)
	SERIAL NO.

TO THE ASSISTANT SECRETARY AND COMMISSIONER OF PATENTS AND TRADEMARKS:

APPLICANT NAME:

Applicant requests registration of the above-identified trademark/service mark in the United States Patent and Trademark Office on the Principal Register established by the Act of July 5, 1946 (15 U.S.C. 1051 et. seq., as amended). Three specimens showing the mark as used in commerce are submitted with this amendment.

☐ Check here if Request to Divide under 37 CFR 2.87 is being submitted with this amendment.

Applicant is using the mark in commerce on or in connection with the following goods/services:

_____

_____

(NOTE: Goods/services listed above may not be broader than the goods/services identified in the application as filed)

Date of first use of mark anywhere: _____

Date of first use of mark in commerce
which the U.S. Congress may regulate: _____

Specify type of commerce: (e.g., interstate, between the U.S. and a specified foreign country) _____

Specify manner or mode of use of mark on or in connection with the goods/services: (e.g., trademark is applied to labels, service mark is used in advertisements) _____

The undersigned being hereby warned that willful false statements and the like so made are punishable by fine or imprisonment, or both, under 18 U.S.C. 1001, and that such willful false statements may jeopardize the validity of the application or any resulting registration, declares that he/she is properly authorized to execute this Amendment to Allege Use on behalf of the applicant; he/she believes the applicant to be the owner of the trademark/service mark sought to be registered; the trademark/ service mark is now in use in commerce; and all statements made of his/her own knowledge are true and all statements made on information and belief are believed to be true.

Date	Signature
Telephone Number	Print or Type Name and Position

PTO Form 1579 (REV. 9/89)
OMB No. 06510023
Exp. 6-30-92

U.S. DEPARTMENT OF COMMERCE/Patent and Trademark Office

Fig. 3–5. Additional trademark forms.

INSTRUCTIONS AND INFORMATION FOR APPLICANT

In an application based upon a bona fide intention to use a mark in commerce, applicant must use its mark in commerce before a registration will be issued. After use begins, the applicant must submit, along with evidence of use (specimens) and the prescribed fee(s), either:

(1) an Amendment to Allege Use under 37 CFR 2.76, or
(2) a Statement of Use under 37 CFR 2.88.

The difference between these two filings is the timing of the filing. Applicant may file an Amendment to Allege Use before approval of the mark for publication for opposition in the **Official Gazette**, or, if a final refusal has been issued, prior to the expiration of the six month response period. Otherwise, applicant must file a Statement of Use after the Office issues a Notice of Allowance. The Notice of Allowance will issue after the opposition period is completed if no successful opposition is filed. Neither Amendment to Allege Use or Statement of Use papers will be accepted by the Office during the period of time between approval of the mark for publication for opposition in the **Official Gazette** and the issuance of the Notice of Allowance.

Applicant may call (703) 557-5249 to determine whether the mark has been approved for publication for opposition in the **Official Gazette**.

Before filing an Amendment to Allege Use or a Statement of Use, applicant must use the mark in commerce on or in connection with **all** of the goods/services for which applicant will seek registration, **unless** applicant submits with the papers, a request to divide out from the application the goods or services to which the Amendment to Allege Use or Statement of Use pertains. (See: 37 CFR 2.87, Dividing an application)

Applicant **must** submit with an Amendment to Allege Use or a Statement of Use:

(1) the appropriate fee of $100 per class of goods/services listed in the Amendment to Allege Use or the Statement of Use, and

(2) three (3) specimens or facsimiles of the mark as used in commerce for each class of goods/services asserted (e.g., photograph of mark as it appears on goods, label containing mark which is placed on goods, or brochure or advertisement showing mark as used in connection with services).

Cautions/Notes concerning completion of this Amendment to Allege Use form:

(1) The goods/services identified in the Amendment to Allege Use must be within the scope of the goods/services identified in the application as filed. Applicant may delete goods/services. Deleted goods/services may not be reinstated in the application at a later time.

(2) Applicant may list dates of use for only one item in each class of goods/services identified in the Amendment to Allege Use. However, applicant must have used the mark in commerce on all the goods/services in the class. Applicant must identify the particular item to which the dates apply.

(3) Only the following person may sign the verification of the Amendment to Allege Use, depending on the applicant's legal entity: (a) the individual applicant; (b) an officer of corporate applicant; (c) one general partner of partnership applicant; (d) all joint applicants.

This form is estimated to take 15 minutes to complete. Time will vary depending upon the needs of the individual case. Any comments on the amount of time you require to complete this form should be sent to the Office of Management and Organization, U.S. Patent and Trademark Office, U.S. Department of Commerce, Washington D.C., 20231, and to the Office of Information and Regulatory Affairs, Office of Management and Budget, Washington, D.C. 20503.

Fig. 3–5, cont.

STATEMENT OF USE UNDER 37 CFR 2.88, WITH DECLARATION	MARK (Identify the mark)
	SERIAL NO.

TO THE ASSISTANT SECRETARY AND COMMISSIONER OF PATENTS AND TRADEMARKS:

APPLICANT NAME:

NOTICE OF ALLOWANCE ISSUE DATE:

Applicant requests registration of the above-identified trademark/service mark in the United States Patent and Trademark Office on the Principal Register established by the Act of July 5, 1946 (15 U.S.C. 1051 et. seq., as amended). Three (3) specimens showing the mark as used in commerce are submitted with this statement.

☐ Check here only if a Request to Divide under 37 CFR 2.87 is being submitted with this Statement.

Applicant is using the mark in commerce on or in connection with the following goods/services: (Check One)

☐ Those goods/services identified in the Notice of Allowance in this application.

☐ Those goods/services identified in the Notice of Allowance in this application except: (Identify goods/services to be deleted from application)

Date of first use of mark anywhere: _____

Date of first use of mark in commerce which the U.S. Congress may regulate: _____

Specify type of commerce: (e.g., interstate, between the U.S. and a specified foreign country) _____

Specify manner or mode of use of mark on or in connection with the goods/services: (e.g., trademark is applied to labels, service mark is used in advertisements) _____

The undersigned being hereby warned that willful false statements and the like so made are punishable by fine or imprisonment, or both, under 18 U.S.C. 1001, and that such willful false statements may jeopardize the validity of the application or any resulting registration, declares that he/she is properly authorized to execute this Statement of Use on behalf of the applicant; he/she believes the applicant to be the owner of the trademark/service mark sought to be registered; the trademark/service mark is now in use in commerce; and all statements made of his/her own knowledge are true and all statements made on information and belief are believed to be true.

Date	Signature
Telephone Number	Print or Type Name and Position

PTO Form 1580 (REV. 9/89)
OMB No. 06510023
Exp. 6-30-92

U.S. DEPARTMENT OF COMMERCE/Patent and Trademark Office

Fig. 3–6. Additional trademark forms.

INSTRUCTIONS AND INFORMATION FOR APPLICANT

In an application based upon a bona fide intention to use a mark in commerce, applicant must use its mark in commerce before a registration will be issued. After use begins, the applicant must submit, along with evidence of use (specimens) and the prescribed fee(s), **either**:

(1) an Amendment to Allege Use under 37 CFR 2.76, or
(2) a Statement of Use under 37 CFR 2.88.

The difference between these two filings is the timing of the filing. Applicant may file an Amendment to Allege Use before approval of the mark for publication for opposition in the **Official Gazette**, or, if a final refusal has been issued, prior to the expiration of the six month response period. Otherwise, applicant must file a Statement of Use after the Office issues a Notice of Allowance. The Notice of Allowance will issue after the opposition period is completed if no successful opposition is filed. Neither Amendment to Allege Use or Statement of Use papers will be accepted by the Office during the period of time between approval of the mark for publication for opposition in the **Official Gazette** and the issuance of the Notice of Allowance.

Applicant may call (703) 557-5249 to determine whether the mark has been approved for publication for opposition in the **Official Gazette.**

Before filing an Amendment to Allege Use or a Statement of Use, applicant must use the mark in commerce on or in connection with **all** of the goods/services for which applicant will seek registration, **unless** applicant submits with the papers, a request to divide out from the application the goods or services to which the Amendment to Allege Use or Statement of Use pertains. (See: 37 CFR 2.87, Dividing an application)

Applicant **must** submit with an Amendment to Allege Use or a Statement of Use:

(1) the appropriate fee of $100 per class of goods/services listed in the Amendment to Allege Use or the Statement of Use, and

(2) three (3) specimens or facsimiles of the mark as used in commerce for each class of goods/services asserted (e.g., photograph of mark as it appears on goods, label containing mark which is placed on goods, or brochure or advertisement showing mark as used in connection with services).

Cautions/Notes concerning completion of this Statement of Use form:

(1) The goods/services identified in the Statement of Use must be identical to the goods/services identified in the Notice of Allowance. Applicant may delete goods/services. Deleted goods/services may not be reinstated in the application at a later time.

(2) Applicant may list dates of use for only one item in each class of goods/services identified in the Statement of Use. However, applicant must have used the mark in commerce on all the goods/services in the class. Applicant must identify the particular item to which the dates apply.

(3) Only the following person may sign the verification of the Statement of Use, depending on the applicant's legal entity: (a) the individual applicant; (b) an officer of corporate applicant; (c) one general partner of partnership applicant; (d) all joint applicants.

This form is estimated to take 15 minutes to complete. Time will vary depending upon the needs of the individual case. Any comments on the amount of time you require to complete this form should be sent to the Office of Management and Organization, U.S. Patent and Trademark Office, U.S. Department of Commerce, Washington D.C., 20231, and to the Office of Information and Regulatory Affairs, Office of Management and Budget, Washington, D.C. 20503.

Fig. 3–6, cont.

REQUEST FOR EXTENSION OF TIME UNDER 37 CFR 2.89 TO FILE A STATEMENT OF USE, WITH DECLARATION	MARK (Identify the mark)
	SERIAL NO.

TO THE ASSISTANT SECRETARY AND COMMISSIONER OF PATENTS AND TRADEMARKS:

APPLICANT NAME:

NOTICE OF ALLOWANCE MAILING DATE:

Applicant requests a six-month extension of time to file the Statement of Use under 37 CFR 2.88 in this application.

☐ Check here if a Request to Divide under 37 CFR 2.87 is being submitted with this request.

Applicant has a continued bona fide intention to use the mark in commerce in connection with the following goods/services: (Check one below)

☐ Those goods/services identified in the Notice of Allowance in this application.

☐ Those goods/services identified in the Notice of Allowance in this application except: (Identify goods/services to be **deleted** from application) _____

This is the _____ request for an Extension of Time following mailing of the Notice of Allowance.
        (Specify first - fifth)
If this is not the first request for an Extension of Time, check one box below. If the first box is checked, explain the circumstance(s) of the non-use in the space provided:

☐ Applicant has not used the mark in commerce yet on all goods/services specified in the Notice of Allowance; however, applicant has made the following ongoing efforts to use the mark in commerce on or in connection with each of the goods/services specified above:

_____

If additional space is needed, please attach a separate sheet to this form

☐ Applicant believes that it has made valid use of the mark in commerce, as evidenced by the Statement of Use submitted with this request; however, if the Statement of Use is found by the Patent and Trademark Office to be fatally defective, applicant will need additional time in which to file a new statement.

The undersigned being hereby warned that willful false statements and the like so made are punishable by fine or imprisonment, or both, under 18 U.S.C. 1001, and that such willful false statements may jeopardize the validity of the application or any resulting registration, declares that he/she is properly authorized to execute this Request for Extension of Time to File a Statement of Use on behalf of the applicant; he/she believes the applicant to be the owner of the trademark/service mark sought to be registered; and all statements made of his/her own knowledge are true and all statements made on information and belief are believed to be true.

Date _____   Signature _____

Telephone Number _____   Print or Type Name and Position _____

PTO Form 1581 (REV. 9/89)
OMB No. 06510023
Exp. 6-30-92   U.S. DEPARTMENT OF COMMERCE/Patent and Trademark Office

Fig. 3–7. Additional trademark forms.

INSTRUCTIONS AND INFORMATION FOR APPLICANT

Applicant must file a Statement of Use within six months after the mailing of the Notice of Allowance in an application based upon a bona fide intention to use a mark in commerce, UNLESS, within that same period, applicant submits a request for a six-month extension of time to file the Statement of Use. The request **must**:

    (1) be in writing,
    (2) include applicant's verified statement of continued bona fide intention to use the mark in commerce,
    (3) specify the goods/services to which the request pertains as they are identified in the Notice of Allowance, and
    (4) include a fee of $100 for each class of goods/services.

Applicant may request four further six-month extensions of time. No extension may extend beyond 36 months from the issue date of the Notice of Allowance. Each request must be filed within the previously granted six-month extension period and must include, in addition to the above requirements, a showing of **GOOD CAUSE**. This good cause showing must include:

    (1) applicant's statement that the mark has not been used in commerce yet on all the goods or services specified in the Notice of Allowance with which applicant has a continued bona fide intention to use the mark in commerce, **and**

    (2) applicant's statement of ongoing efforts to make such use, which may include the following: (a) product or service research or development, (b) market research, (c) promotional activities, (d) steps to acquire distributors, (e) steps to obtain required governmental approval, or (f) similar specified activity .

Applicant may submit one additional six-month extension request during the existing period in which applicant files the Statement of Use, unless the granting of this request would extend beyond 36 months from the issue date of the Notice of Allowance. As a showing of good cause, applicant should state its belief that applicant has made valid use of the mark in commerce, as evidenced by the submitted Statement of Use, but that if the Statement is found by the PTO to be defective, applicant will need additional time in which to file a new statement of use.

Only the following person may sign the verification of the Request for Extentsion of Time, depending on the applicant's legal entity: (a) the individual applicant; (b) an officer of corporate applicant; (c) one general partner of partnership applicant; (d) all joint applicants.

This form is estimated to take 15 minutes to complete. Time will vary depending upon the needs of the individual case. Any comments on the amount of time you require to complete this form should be sent to the Office of Management and Organization, U.S. Patent and Trademark Office, U.S. Department of Commerce, Washington D.C., 20231, and to the Office of Information and Regulatory Affairs, Office of Management and Budget, Washington, D.C. 20503.

Fig. 3–7, cont.

If the cost of a straight liability insurance policy is too high for your budget, consider a deductible. This means that if there is a liability claim against you, and the insurance company determines that the claim is justifiable, you would be liable to pay the initial $100 or $200 (or whatever the deductible amount is) of the claim. Your insurer would be obligated to pay the balance.

Chapter Highlights

- Craftspeople can take advantage of three different government protective registrations to guard their work against competitive infringement.
- A federal patent is useful to craftspeople who have invented new products or made a specific product adaptation, and wish protection from potential infringement of these works.
- A federal copyright is helpful to craftspeople who have developed original, artistic, literary, or musical creations and seek protection against potential infringement of their work.
- A federal trademark is useful to craftspeople who desire to shield identifying product symbols, names, words, designs, logos, or even distinctive sounds they have developed from potential infringement of the work.
- The procedures for patent, copyright, and trademark applications must be accurately followed to secure the proper registrations from the government agencies.
- Each of the specific protective agencies that craftspeople will use to guard their interest in their product require that applications be made and filled out completely.
- In addition to application forms, all three government protective agencies require that specified filing fees accompany all applications.
- If a craftsperson is seeking to patent a newly-developed product, there are patent attorneys who can assist in moving the process through the system.
- Liability insurance on your craft product can provide you with legal and monetary protection against damage claims that arise from the display, sale, and use of your craft product.

CHAPTER 4

Pricing Your Product

Selling Price = Cost + Profit. Sounds easy, doesn't it?

It's not that simple.

In thinking about how to price your product there are a number of concepts to keep in mind. Some of these are basics that bear repeating; others are more sophisticated aspects of the marketing mix because pricing realistically is an integral part of the overall mix, and it cannot be realistically separated from the whole program.

The objective of pricing is to assure a profit. It is important to be competitive in the marketplace but that's a secondary consideration. Unless your craft is a hobby that you are willing to continue to subsidize, you can't stay in business if your prices do not cover your costs plus a reasonable profit.

Defining Costs

What are your costs? Some are connected directly to your product easy to identify: the cost of raw materials, including any freight, shipping, or handling charges, and the cost of packaging, labeling, or tagging can generally be calculated on a per item basis. These costs of goods are basics, easiest to figure but frequently the smallest part of the total cost of production.

In some instances, the cost of materials can be substantially reduced by volume purchasing with quantity discounts. You can also frequently secure discounts for immediate payment or for payment within specified periods of time, usually 10, 20 or 30 days from invoice date or 10 days from end of month, or some other agreed upon terms.

In addition to the cost of materials, what other costs are involved? For starters, there are the items generally classified as *overhead* or *operating expenses*. These include rent or space ownership costs such as mortgage payments, utilities including gas and electric, heating, air-conditioning, water, cleaning, and repairs. Then there are such items as insurance, taxes, office supplies, postage, and telephone and fees for lawyers, accountants, and other professionals. There are also the expenses of advertising, printing, and travel related to production, delivery, and/or direct sales. Show registrations, food and lodging away from home, and business entertainment are other costs which must be considered.

Fixed Costs/Overhead/Non-Variable Expenses

Overhead or operating expenses are also called *fixed costs;* that is, they will remain approximately the same no matter how many units of how many items you produce. These costs are related to the actual operation of your business: rent, utilities, insurance, depreciation, and to some extent, salaries. They are sometimes called *non-variable expenses*. Another term for them is *indirect costs*. Once contracted, they are obligations whether you produce a lot or a little.

Variable Expenses

Other expenses, however, are variable, controllable to a greater degree, and more easily attributable on a per unit basis to production. These might include, as we mentioned previously, the cost of materials including packaging, mailing, shipping, or other delivery costs, and labor costs if paid on a piecework or contract basis. We will discuss later in this chapter some concerns about the attribution of fixed costs to per unit pricing, but for the moment in order to make clear the basic concepts, let us proceed with generalities.

All of these costs can ultimately be expressed in dollars and cents. In the beginning, you may have to estimate them, but after a period of time you will have hard figures to allocate on a per item basis.

Both fixed and variable costs are shown in Fig. 4–1, which illustrates the concept of *breakdown*—the point at which revenues from

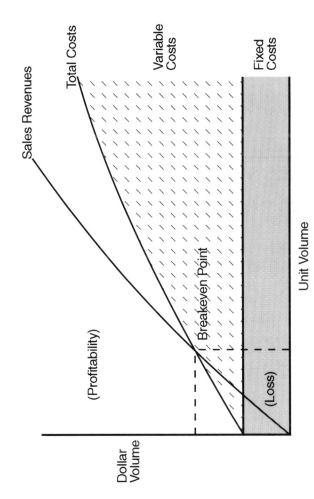

Fig. 4–1. Pricing Breakeven.

the sale of products are the same as total costs. Below this point, you are losing money; above it, your business is profitable.

The Role of Fixed Costs in Pricing

How you deal with fixed costs may lead you to misprice or over-price your products in terms of competition or in terms of what the market will bear. When you are starting up, for example, you may envision producing 1,000 units during the first year, 2,000 units in the second year, and 5,000 units at full capacity. While your variable expenses will change with each unit increased, your fixed costs will remain approximately the same. So, for example, fixed costs of $5,000 at full capacity translate to $1.00 a unit, but at startup they translate to $5.00 per unit. These numbers are important to know not only because they will affect the profitability of your business, but also because many accountants and business marketers advise clients to consider fixed costs on a long range basis rather than short range. That is, calculate your fixed costs based on full production for pricing purposes. On a long range basis, you might say, then, that you are subsidizing your fixed costs with your capital investment until you get up to full capacity production.

Depreciation, a Fixed Cost

One fixed cost which bears further discussion is depreciation. The cost of tools, equipment, furniture, and fixtures, and other articles with a lifespan that will cover the operation for any length of time should be apportioned to operating expense annually over the period of their lifespan. These items are often called *capital assets,* as are buildings and vehicles. Even if you pay cash for these items, the government will not allow you to deduct their costs in one year except under unusual tax regulations. The costs of capital assets, instead, are "written off" or depreciated over the life of the asset. For example, if you have a tool that you bought for $100 that you expect to last for 20 years, the cost or depreciation per year is only $5. If you use that tool to make 100 products, the cost of that tool per product is only five cents. If you use it to make 1000 products, the cost per product is a half cent. The objective of allowing for depreciation is to build up a reserve for the replacement of each asset. To accomplish this, you would "fund" or actually save your depreciation expense in a separate account annually. Few small businesses do this. However, even if you do not fund or save depreciation, it is important to keep a record of each of your business assets, its original costs, its anticipated lifespan, and the annual costs attributable to its depreciation. This record is important because your depreciation expense is a legitimate deduction from income on your tax returns. There are also tax regulations which affect the length of time for which capital goods can be depreciated.

It should be noted that many factors in addition to anticipated lifespan might affect this expense. Obsolescence resulting from new technology, for example, may make a tool or machine less efficient than a newly-developed device. Breakage, unavailability of replacement parts, loss of small tools, and other factors also affect usability. While these costs may not be easily estimated in advance, they will create expenses that are both tax deductible and attributable to the costs of doing business.

Labor Costs

Having calculated all of your fixed and variable expenses, you must then add the cost of labor, including your own. Unless you are working with precious metals, costly jewels, or other raw materials of great intrinsic value, labor is a substantial factor of the cost of production. The cost of labor includes actual salaries or wages plus benefits plus various taxes.

For example, if you pay an assistant $10 an hour for a 40-hour week, his or her wages will be $400 per week, or $20,800 for a year (52 × $400).

If, however, you give that employee a two-week vacation with pay and hire a replacement at the same rate, the cost to you goes up by $800 ($400 × 2) The same is true if you allow for sick days, personal days, and/or holidays. That is, if you replace the employees for those days, your costs also increase. In addition, if you provide health insurance or other benefits, the costs of these are also part of your labor costs.

Moreover, you will also owe the cost of taxes based on wages. These include the employer's share of social security and medicare costs; federal and state unemployment insurance costs; and disability and worker's compensation insurance. These costs are calculated as percentages of total salaries or wages paid and, in some instances, on employee benefits including meals, lodging, personal use of a vehicle, paid vacations, bonuses, etc.

Contract or Piecework Labor Costs

You can avoid employment taxes and fringe benefits if you use *contracted* or *piece work* labor rather than salaried labor. The contractor is paid an agreed-upon price for an agreed-upon number of production processes or units. Pieceworkers, as the name implies, are paid an agreed-upon price for each process they perform or piece they produce.

In many areas of the country, cottage industries have grown up, serving as part of the contract or piecework labor force. Quilt makers, for example, may have people cutting the pieces to match varying design specifications. Other workers may stitch the face of the quilts into the completed design pattern. Still others will assemble the completed quilt face, batting, and back. Finally, others will stitch through or tie the completed quilts.

The piecework process also lends itself to crafted furniture and wooden toys, to ceramic pouring, glazing and firing, and to a host of other crafts where distinct processes can be performed in varying stages.

While the cost of distributing and picking up the materials in from the various processors must also be calculated, the piecework or contract arrangement has several advantages. It can give you a fixed cost per unit. It avoids employment insurance and employment taxes. It can reduce the amount of your overhead costs for space and utilities, and it can increase your production capabilities.

Calculating the Value of Your Own Labor

All of the foregoing can be calculated on the basis of actual or projected expenses. There is another cost, however, that is more difficult to quantify, and many craftspeople make the sad mistake of not including it in their product costs. This is the cost of your own or your family's labor. There is a tendency to think that the cost of your labor is really profit. It is not. You can understand this more easily if you consider what might happen if you were to start another business while continuing this one, or if you were to become ill for a period of time, or if there were any other circumstances which would require you to hire and pay someone to do the work you or your family members do.

Even if you recognize that there is a cost that should be attached to your labor for the purpose of establishing how much your product actually costs you, there is a question about how to calculate the amount. There are several ways to answer this question. At the low end, you might calculate that your labor is at least worth minimum wage, the lowest hourly rate that another employer could legally pay you. At the high end, you might consider what your skills could actually bring on the open market, or alternatively, what you would have to pay someone for the same work.

Many craftspeople are willing to take a great deal less for their own services than they might earn in the professions, for example, or in the corporate world, or in teaching, or in other pursuits, because they like the lifestyle and the creative options of crafting. This is a decision that is personal, but is nevertheless a business decision. It should be made consciously and not left to chance. Whatever method you use, your resulting calculations should be included in the cost of your product.

Establishing Your Costs

Taking all of these factors into account, you will have an initial formula that looks something like this: Total cost of goods sold = Cost of materials + Cost of labor, including personal and family labor + All other expenses of the business.

If you are working with just one product, in order to find your costs per product, you take your total costs and divide them by the number of pieces produced. For example, if your total costs are $36,000 and you can produce 36,000 pieces, your cost per piece is $1. If you can produce only 3,600 pieces, your cost per piece is $10. If you are working with several products, costs other than materials should be allocated proportionately to the time it takes to produce each and the numbers of each produced.

Establishing Your Price

Having established your costs, the next step is to use this information as a base for establishing your selling price. The ordinary rule of thumb for setting the selling price of craft products is to double your costs. This gives you what is called a 100% *markup* on cost. Markups are also sometimes expressed as a percentage of selling price: a 100% markup on cost is the equivalent of a 50% markup on selling price. So that if an item costs you $10, you would add 100% and sell it for $20.

Sound easy? Once again, it's not that simple.

If you are selling directly to the consumer, the selling price or the retail price might then be $20. However, if you are selling the item wholesale, to a museum or a gallery, a boutique or a department store, to a mail order shop or a television home shopping network, or to some other middleman organization that will retail it to the consumer, that organization, too, will want to cover its costs of selling and to make a profit. Middleman markups generally run 50% to 100% of their costs. This means that if you sell to them for $20, their selling price for your product could run from $30 to $40.

This raises several additional questions. If a middleman organization can sell your product to the consumer for $40, should you sell it to the consumer for less? And, if a middleman is adding 50% to 100% to your product to cover selling expenses and a profit, are you entitled to add the same 50% to 100% if you are selling directly?

Alternatively, you can establish wholesale prices considerably lower than your own retail selling price if you consider that you are giving the middleman volume or quantity discounts. This takes into account your reduced sales expense as well as your ability to secure your own discounts for volume purchases.

Many organizations which retail craft products impose restrictive agreements on the craftspeople from whom they buy. Among these are agreements that the craftspeople will not sell their products within specified nearby geographic areas; that they will not sell identical products, and that craftspeople's consumer prices will not undercut the retailer.

All of these factors must be considered in pricing your product for both wholesale and retail sales.

Pricing in the Competitive Marketplace

Another factor which is of vital consideration is *competitive position*. If other people are selling products similar to yours, a competitive strategy would suggest that your prices compare favorably with those of the successful competitors.

You may find, however, that there may be sellers of similar products with a wide range of prices, some higher and some lower than yours. In this instance, you should look to other factors that may affect what people are willing to pay. These factors may be customer services and/or conveniences, credit card options, distinctive packaging, exclusive sales settings, etc. An out-of-the way-craft outlet warehouse without customer amenities, for example, can afford to sell the same product for less than a high-rental boutique in a fashionable shopping neighborhood or mall. The warehouse is trading convenience for price, and guessing that the customer will give up the convenience of the mall for a lower price.

In utilizing a competitive strategy to set prices, you can price above or below the competition. You can set prices over the competition's if you can offer non-price services which are meaningful in your market. The convenient, quality location we mentioned above is one type of non-price service. A lifetime guarantee might be another. Coordinating colors, costumes, or furnishings, or identifying gifts by age groups for children or interest groups for adults are also services on which some buyers place extra value. Other service considerations might include free gift wrapping and/or delivery; or a gift registry for brides, babies, or graduates. Free personalization or other exclusivity options also can permit you to price above the competition.

If you are in a price-sensitive market, you may find that you can increase your volume of sales by pricing below the competition, or by beating competitors' prices. This, of course, means that you may be reducing your margin of profit on each sale because you believe that your increased number of sales will add up to a greater total profit. On the other hand, you may be able to keep your margin of profit if you can reduce your own costs by limiting services, restricting your products to fast-turnover items, controlling your investment in inventory, and constantly monitoring every expense.

Reduced Prices, Sales, and Closeouts

Many craftspeople have been successful using a *reduced-price strategy* on some items. Since this reduces your profit margin on these items, you have to increase your volume and/or limit your costs; or compensate for these *loss leaders* with other items of higher price. Your emphasis in product advertising or promotion should rely heavily on pricing specials. If you have a number of products in your line, the reduced-price product should be an item that is generally a good seller, a fast mover in the marketplace. This means, of course, that you must closely control your product inventory.

A reduced price strategy must be constantly monitored from a number of different positions. Every component of product production and sales has to be evaluated as to its cost and effect on price. You must also be aware that a reduced-price strategy in the marketplace can lead to responses from your competition. In many instances, your competitors can match your pricing structure, and the resulting price war can only be costly to both parties.

Reduced pricing does not necessarily mean across the board cost-cutting. There are other techniques that can be used as effectively. An *announced sale* for a limited period of time can generate additional business. Many people tend to react positively when they see or hear the word "sale." A sale can be effective if you want to stimulate new business, or if you want to expose the marketing public to the product lines you have available.

A sale can be a reason for your established customers to return to your booth or store. Many craftspeople send out advance notices to shows where they will be exhibiting. The notices, often printed on postcards, offer special discounts when used at the show. Some craftspeople turn the sale process into a ritual. Once a year, twice a year, at certain seasons, year-in and year-out, they conduct their annual, bi-annual, pre-holiday, or inventory clearance sale. Customers come to expect the sales and look forward to buying at the events.

Couponing is big business in this country, and it can be applied effectively to craft products. Each day, hundreds of thousands of coupons, in effect discounts against prevailing product price, enter the marketplace. Consumers are used to the process and respond. A coupon can be as complex as a full color ad in a newspaper, or designed simply as a fast-print flyer to be distributed at shows and other events.

The coupon gives the consumer the opportunity to purchase your product at full price less the discount (10% - 20% - 50%, etc.) noted on the coupons you have distributed. Coupons can also entitle buyers to two products for the price of one, a free gift with each purchase, or other bonuses.

When using coupons for promotional purposes, it is important to clearly state on the printed material the specific rules for use. For example, discount coupons might not be accepted with any other product promotion or on specific sales items. It is also a good idea to limit the time period during which the coupon will be honored.

There are times when a product or a product line does not sell well. Your expectations may be at one level while actual product sales remain at another. At some point, you may make a decision that it is time to clear the line out of your inventory. You may require space or need the capital tied up in the products. At this point, you may decide to have a *closeout*. You can calculate your costs to determine reasonable prices for the closeout line of products. If advertising is part of your normal business process, the closeouts should be noted in your ads. If you plan on disposing of the closeouts at a show, a section of your booth, generally close to the front but off to the side, should be allocated for the sale merchandise. Signage should indicate the prices and reasons for the bargains.

The sale, discount, or closeout process can often work to your advantage, not only to clear inventory but also to serve as a magnet. Consumers arriving for the sale or closeouts should be given an opportunity to review your complete line of products in addition to the specials. Appropriate signage indicating "new", "designer", "limited edition", "signed pieces", and other distinguishing identification can enhance sales of fully-priced items.

Added-Value Pricing

There are times when you can charge a higher price than your competitors, and not suffer economic fallout. If the price of your product is secondary to other considerations for the consumer, this approach can work for you. Customers may be willing to pay a higher price to gain something of additional value to them, thus *added-value* pricing. These features are usually qualitative or related to the concept of the package of satisfaction.

As we discussed previously, your product may be available in an exclusive or a convenient location and thus in the consumer's mind a higher price may be justified. The consumer may be willing to pay a higher price for any service, or special knowledge you may be able to offer along with your product. Perhaps one of the most justifiable reasons for pricing above competition is exclusivity, originality, or uniqueness. If the consumer cannot purchase a similar product from any other source and wants that product immediately, the higher product price may be acceptable.

You may also find that you can charge more for the same item if you have established yourself through both promotion and talent as an artisan whose works are expected to go up in value, to be represented in museum or distinguished private collections, or to be otherwise singled out for recognition.

Price Lining

You may decide to sell one or more of your products to a select market. This strategy, known as *price lining*, targets a special portion of the consumer market with a product in a specific price range. For example, you might specialize in large white ceramic soup tureens with an established price of $150. Among the advantages of price lining is that it makes it easy for consumers to make a decision. People come to know that this is the product you have for sale and its price. Your inventory is simplified, as is your advertising and promotion. While your market is limited to those people seeking white soup tureens in the $150 price category, you can position the product in the market, as a quality wedding gift, for example, or for gourmet chefs, or for housewarming gifts, etc. Other products in your line may be positioned for other markets.

Creative Pricing

Another frequently effective pricing strategy is *multiple pricing*. This technique depends heavily on the size, type, and cost of the products in your line. Some items do not lend themselves to this process. Multiple pricing works this way. Suppose your product is a line of small, handcrafted wooden toys priced individually to sell for $3.98. You might try packaging or selling the toys in multiples of two for $7.00

or $7.50, or five for $15.00. The multiple pricing system is particularly useful for a special sale or clearance but also encourages greater volume purchases in any event.

Another pricing technique also depends on numbers. The figures five (5), eight (8), and nine (9) often play a significant role in pricing. Some marketers attach psychological value to the use of these numbers in setting a price structure for their products. Consumers, according to these marketing people, prefer to purchase items with prices that are rounded down rather than buying products with prices that are rounded up. Rounded down examples are $19.95, $29.98 and $39.99. Rounded up examples are $20.00, $30.00 and $40.00.

Experiential Pricing

Sometimes, formulas to the contrary, experience can help you set prices. Products which do not move at certain prices may sell if they are raised in certain markets or cut in others. Major concerns test market at various price levels before establishing selling prices. This is fine if you can afford to do it. If not, you can get the same insight with experience. It is important to remember that overall profit is a function of both the number of pieces sold and the profit per piece. Monitoring sales volume at various prices in similar circumstances is an effective experiential guide to pricing.

Pricing Questions

You can see that pricing has many aspects and that it may differ in various situations to which pricing techniques and applications can be applied. It is frequently difficult to decide exactly which process or method is more effective. It becomes obvious that the most businesslike approach is to continually monitor your product's price structure, the costs that go into the production of the items, and, of course, competitive positions. While many craft purchases are the result of impulse buying, knowledgeable consumers can be turned away by prices that are thought to be too low as well as those that are perceived as being too high.

You might want to consider the following questions as you develop your own price structure:

1—Have you priced your craft products at a level sufficiently high to insure a reasonable profit margin?

2—When you set the price structure for your products, are fixed and variable costs included?

3—Do you make product cost monitoring a continuous business process?

4—Are you flexible enough in your pricing structure to insure that the levels of profitability remain stable?

5—Have you developed a price structure that is consistent with the consumer image of your product?

6—If you decide to reduce the price of one of your products, do you calculate the possible reaction of competition?

7—Have you ever considered price lining, carrying a product line only in a specific price range?

8—Have you ever considered multiple pricing, selling a package of two or more of your products?

9—Do you try to find the price-volume combination that will maximize your profits?

10—Do you recognize that even if your ceramic kiln, woodworking lathe or other facility is not in use for periods of time, certain costs are active and remain in place?

11—Do your craft product markups always cover operations, sales expenses, profit, and any price reductions you may institute?

12—There are a number of factors that are vital to developing an effective pricing strategy. Do you include in your calculations the lifecycle of your product, the projected annual sales volume, the effectiveness of your distribution system, competition, and any regulatory forces that may impact on your product?

Fig. 4–2 shows some general questions and concerns in setting your pricing.

Sales Tax

It is important to understand and follow regulations regarding the sales tax which may be in effect in each state where you will be doing business. In most cases, the rule is that a sales tax must be collected for each retail product sold. The exact amount differs from state to state

YOUR COSTS

Have all of the costs of development, manufacture, and sales been considered and included in the pricing structure?

COMPETITION

Does your pricing take into consideration competitive products? Have you considered pricing above, below, or in line with competition? Or, do you plan to meet competition in ways other than price.

PRICING POSITION

What type of pricing position are you planning to take? Below, do you intend to become a price leader? Are you thinking about discounting, price lining, couponing, or using a variety of pricing techniques.

SALES METHODS

What effect will your product distribution or sales methods play in the pricing structure of your product? Will you sell directly at shows or from you own shop or workshop? Will you wholesale to galleries, boutiques, or other retail outlets? Or, will you sell to architects, decorators, building managers, etc.?

PROMOTIONAL TECHNIQUES

What type of strategies have you developed for product promotion? Will you advertise, publicize, develop catalogues, use special events, etc.?

PRODUCT LIFE CYCLE

In which stage of its product life cycle is your product? Are you prepared to move your pricing strategy to match changing product life cycles?

PRODUCT IMAGE

Have you considered the image you intend to develop and project for your product? Will the process add to the pricing of your product?

THE ECONOMY

The economic climate fluctuates. Are you prepared to meet the challenges of economic downturns (or upturns) with a pricing strategy?

Fig. 4–2. Pricing Factors.

Massachusetts Department of Revenue ST-1
Data Integration Bureau
100 Cambridge Street
Boston, MA 02204
5475506
CERTIFICATE NUMBER

SALES AND USE TAX REGISTRATION

The vendor herein named is registered to sell tangible personal property at retail or for resale, pursuant to the General Laws, Chapters 62C, 64H and 64I. This registration is effective **only** for the registrant at the location specified herein. Any change of name or address renders this registration null and void.

S A M P L E

IDENTIFICATION NUMBER

ISSUE DATE

250M-11-88-807251

This registration must be displayed for customers to see and is not assignable or transferable.

COMMISSIONER OF REVENUE

Fig. 4–3. A Sales Tax Registration Form issued by the State of Massachusetts, Department of Revenue. Most states with sales tax in effect, require that the registration form be displayed at your craft booth at a show. *Courtesy State of Massachusetts, Department of Revenue.*

and also in counties and cities within each state. Every state has its own regulations and forms which must be submitted to the State Tax Department or State Department of Revenue. When collected, all sales taxes must be turned into the proper department.

Figs. 4–3 through 4–6 show sample sales tax documentation from Massachusetts and New Jersey.

MASSACHUSETTS DEPARTMENT OF REVENUE
5% SALES TAX SCHEDULE
INCLUDING MEALS, PREPARED FOOD AND/OR
ALCOHOLIC BEVERAGES, EFFECTIVE JAN. 1, 1979

AMOUNT OF SALE	TAX	AMOUNT OF SALE	TAX
$.10 - $.29	$.01	$7.70 - $7.89	$.39
.30 - .49	.02	7.90 - 8.09	.40
.50 - .69	.03	8.10 - 8.29	.41
.70 - .89	.04	8.30 - 8.49	.42
.90 - 1.09	.05	8.50 - 8.69	.43
1.10 - 1.29	.06	8.70 - 8.89	.44
1.30 - 1.49	.07	8.90 - 9.09	.45
1.50 - 1.69	.08	9.10 - 9.29	.46
1.70 - 1.89	.09	9.30 - 9.49	.47
1.90 - 2.09	.10	9.50 - 9.69	.48
2.10 - 2.29	.11	9.70 - 9.89	.49
2.30 - 2.49	.12	9.90 - 10.09	.50
2.50 - 2.69	.13	10.10 - 10.29	.51
2.70 - 2.89	.14	10.30 - 10.49	.52
2.90 - 3.09	.15	10.50 - 10.69	.53
3.10 - 3.29	.16	10.70 - 10.89	.54
3.30 - 3.49	.17	10.90 - 11.09	.55
3.50 - 3.69	.18	11.10 - 11.29	.56
3.70 - 3.89	.19	11.30 - 11.49	.57
3.90 - 4.09	.20	11.50 - 11.69	.58
4.10 - 4.29	.21	11.70 - 11.89	.59
4.30 - 4.49	.22	11.90 - 12.09	.60
4.50 - 4.69	.23	12.10 - 12.29	.61
4.70 - 4.89	.24	12.30 - 12.49	.62
4.90 - 5.09	.25	12.50 - 12.69	.63
5.10 - 5.29	.26	12.70 - 12.89	.64
5.30 - 5.49	.27	12.90 - 13.09	.65
5.50 - 5.69	.28	13.10 - 13.29	.66
5.70 - 5.89	.29	13.30 - 13.49	.67
5.90 - 6.09	.30	13.50 - 13.69	.68
6.10 - 6.29	.31	13.70 - 13.89	.69
6.30 - 6.49	.32	13.90 - 14.09	.70
6.50 - 6.69	.33	14.10 - 14.29	.71
6.70 - 6.89	.34	14.30 - 14.49	.72
6.90 - 7.09	.35	14.50 - 14.69	.73
7.10 - 7.29	.36	14.70 - 14.89	.74
7.30 - 7.49	.37	14.90 - 15.09	.75
7.50 - 7.69	.38	15.10 - 15.29	.76

CONTINUED ON REVERSE ⟶

Fig. 4–4. A 5% Sales Tax Schedule indicating the sales tax to be charged for varying sale amounts. *Courtesy State of Massachusetts, Department of Revenue.*

MORLEY F-1115-OJ484

AMOUNT OF SALE	TAX	AMOUNT OF SALE	TAX
$15.30 - $15.49	$.77	$22.70 - $22.89	$1.14
15.50 - 15.69	.78	22.90 - 23.09	1.15
15.70 - 15.89	.79	23.10 - 23.29	1.16
15.90 - 16.09	.80	23.30 - 23.49	1.17
16.10 - 16.29	.81	23.50 - 23.69	1.18
16.30 - 16.49	.82	23.70 - 23.89	1.19
16.50 - 16.69	.83	23.90 - 24.09	1.20
16.70 - 16.89	.84	24.10 - 24.29	1.21
16.90 - 17.09	.85	24.30 - 24.49	1.22
17.10 - 17.29	.86	24.50 - 24.69	1.23
17.30 - 17.49	.87	24.70 - 24.89	1.24
17.50 - 17.69	.88	24.90 - 25.09	1.25
17.70 - 17.89	.89	25.10 - 25.29	1.26
17.90 - 18.09	.90	25.30 - 25.49	1.27
18.10 - 18.29	.91	25.50 - 25.69	1.28
18.30 - 18.49	.92	25.70 - 25.89	1.29
18.50 - 18.69	.93	25.90 - 26.09	1.30
18.70 - 18.89	.94	26.10 - 26.29	1.31
18.90 - 19.09	.95	26.30 - 26.49	1.32
19.10 - 19.29	.96	26.50 - 26.69	1.33
19.30 - 19.49	.97	26.70 - 26.89	1.34
19.50 - 19.69	.98	26.90 - 27.09	1.35
19.70 - 19.89	.99	27.10 - 27.29	1.36
19.90 - 20.09	1.00	27.30 - 27.49	1.37
20.10 - 20.29	1.01	27.50 - 27.69	1.38
20.30 - 20.49	1.02	27.70 - 27.89	1.39
20.50 - 20.69	1.03	27.90 - 28.09	1.40
20.70 - 20.89	1.04	28.10 - 28.29	1.41
20.90 - 21.09	1.05	28.30 - 28.49	1.42
21.10 - 21.29	1.06	28.50 - 28.69	1.43
21.30 - 21.49	1.07	28.70 - 28.89	1.44
21.50 - 21.69	1.08	28.90 - 29.09	1.45
21.70 - 21.89	1.09	29.10 - 29.29	1.46
21.90 - 22.09	1.10	29.30 - 29.49	1.47
22.10 - 22.29	1.11	29.50 - 29.69	1.48
22.30 - 22.49	1.12	29.70 - 29.89	1.49
22.50 - 22.69	1.13	29.90 - 30.09	1.50

ON ANY CHARGE OVER $30.09, ADAPT
ABOVE AMOUNTS OR MULTIPLY BY .05.
THE TAX MUST BE COMPUTED ON THE
TOTAL SALE AND NOT ON PRICES OF IN-
DIVIDUAL ITEMS INCLUDED IN THE SALE.

ST-3, 5% Rate   COMMISSIONER OF REVENUE

Fig. 4–4, cont.

THIS SECTION FOR DEPARTMENTAL USE ONLY				
Federal or Primary Ident. No.	Tax Type	Business Code	Date Received	Doc. Loc. No.
	TMWH ☐ TMMT ☐ TMSV ☐ TMST ☐ TMRO ☐			
Type of Registration		Mode Required		Screening Personnel
New Case Single	New Case Cons.	Addl. Tax Single	Addl. Tax Cons.	Addl. Loc. Single	Addl. Loc. Cons.	TMTP ☐ TMRE ☐ TXPR ☐	

DO NOT WRITE ABOVE THIS LINE

FORM TA-1 APPLICATION FOR ORIGINAL REGISTRATION AS

CHECK AS MANY AS APPLY

Mail to:
The Commonwealth of Massachusetts

MASS. DOR
(Department of Revenue)

Data Integration Bureau
P.O. Box 7022
Boston, Massachusetts 02204

Use Form TA-2 to Register Additional Locations or to Add a New Tax for a Previously Registered Location

1. A ☐ Employer under the Income Tax Withholding Law — No Fee
B 1. ☐ Sales and/or Use Tax on Goods Vendor
2. ☐ Sales and/or Use Tax on Services Vendor
3. ☐ Meals Tax on Food and/or Alcoholic Beverages — One $10 Fee
4. ☐ Purchasing in MA for Out-of-State Resale Only
C ☐ Operator under Room Occupancy Excise — $10 Fee
D ☐ Governmental or Charitable Exempt Purchaser — No Fee
E ☐ Chapter 180 Organization Selling Alcoholic Beverages — No Fee
F ☐ Use Tax Purchaser — No Fee

2. Federal Identification Number   3. Social Security Number   4. No. of Locations

PRINCIPAL PLACE OF BUSINESS

5. Name of Owner, Partnership or Legal Corporate Name

Name (cont.)

6. Number and Street (P. O. Box is NOT acceptable)

7. City or Town

8. State   9. Zip Code   10. (Area Code) Telephone Number

GENERAL INFORMATION

11. Indicate Type of Organization:
☐ Corporation ☐ Partnership
☐ Trust or Assoc. ☐ Other (Specify):
☐ Individual
☐ Fiduciary

12. Indicate Type of Business:
☐ Retail Trade ☐ Finance
☐ Wholesale Trade ☐ Real Estate
☐ Manufacturing ☐ Service
☐ Construction ☐ Other (Specify):
☐ Governmental

13. Describe Nature of Business

14. Business Code

15. CHECK applicable box
PROFIT ☐
NON-PROFIT ☐

If a Corporation, Trust, Association, Fiduciary, or Partnership — YOU MUST COMPLETE Schedule TA-3 with Name, Title, and Social Security Number of Executive Officers or General Partners

16. If a Subsidiary Corporation — Enter Name of Parent Corporation ➤ Name   Federal Identification No.

17. If Individual (Sole Owner) Enter Name of Parent Corporation ➤ Name   Social Security No.

18. Reasons for Applying:
☐ Started New Business
☐ Purchased Going Business—Enter Name, Address, and Federal Identification Number of Previous Owner
☐ Organizational Change—Previous Federal I.D. Number MUST be entered, or Application will be returned.
☐ Other (Specify and attach explanation)

BACKGROUND INFORMATION

19. Are any Massachusetts tax returns due or any Massachusetts taxes owed by your firm? If yes, please explain. ☐ Yes ☐ No

20. Has your Certificate of Registration issued to you ever been revoked? ☐ Yes ☐ No

EXEMPT ORGANIZATIONS

21. If you are applying for exempt purchaser status, be sure to include a copy of your IRS letter of exemption under Section 501 (c)(3) of the Internal Revenue Code. Subordinate organizations covered under an IRS group exemption letter should include a copy of the group exemption ruling and a copy of the organization's directory page listing the organization as an approved subordinate. Both of the questions below must be answered.
A. Are you exempt from paying U.S. income taxes? ☐ Yes ☐ No   B. Are you exempt from paying local property taxes? ☐ Yes ☐ No

Fig. 4–5. A Sales Tax Application Registration Form. Front side.
Courtesy State of Massachusetts, Department of Revenue.

MODE REQUIRED: TXPR ☐ TXEL ☐ LOCN ☐ FLEN ☐ LCTX ☐	ADMINISTRATIVE CODES
TMLC ☐ TMFE ☐ TMWH ☐ TMST ☐ TMMT ☐ TMRO ☐ TMSV ☐	ADTX_____ ADFE_____
CERT. CODE MAIL CODE LOC. NUM. EFF. DTE. 1st LOC. FILING ENTITY CODES	ADTE_____ ADLT_____
WH____SL ___ MT____RO___SV___	ADLC_____

DO NOT WRITE ABOVE THIS LINE

LOCATION OF BUSINESS

22. Trade Name

Trade Name (cont.)

23. Number and Street (P. O. Box is NOT acceptable)

24. City or Town

25. State   26. Zip Code   27. (Area Code) Telephone Number   28. Loc. Code

29. Send Certificates to: ☐ Principal Place of Business   ☐ Location of Business

30. Send Tax Forms to: ☐ Principal Place of Business   ☐ Location of Business   ☐ Other   IF OTHER, COMPLETE SCHEDULE TA-4

31. Indicate if this location is Seasonal. (See instructions) ☐ Yes ☐ No   32. Indicate 12 month ESTIMATE of tax to be withheld, collected or paid for EACH
If "yes," check month(s) or partial month(s) business operates.   applicable tax. Check the appropriate box(es).

Check Month(s)	Jan	Feb	Mar	Apr	May	Jun	Jul	Aug	Sep	Oct	Nov	Dec	Check Appropriate Box(es)	$0 - $100	$101 - $1,200	$1,201 - $25,000	Over $25,000
Withholding													Withholding				
Sales and/or Use													Sales and/or Use				
Sales and/or Use on Services													Sales and/or Use on Services				
Meals													Meals				
Room Occupancy													Room Occupancy				
													Use Tax Purchaser				

TAX TYPE INFORMATION			Fee Entry
WITHHOLDING	33. Date you were first required to withhold taxes at this location. Mo. Day Yr.	34. Number of Employees at this location. NO FEE	
SALES AND/OR USE TAX	35. Date you were first required to collect sales/use taxes at this location. Mo. Day Yr.	36. Enter fee of $10.00. No fee is required if you are now registered at this location to collect meals or sales on services tax. ➤	$
SALES AND/OR USE TAX ON SERVICES	37. Date you were first required to collect sales/use tax on services at this location. Mo. Day Yr.	38. Enter fee of $10.00. No fee is required if you are currently registered at this location as a vendor collecting sales/use tax on goods or meals. ➤	$
MEALS TAX ON FOOD AND/OR ALCOHOLIC BEVERAGES	39. Check if you serve ☐ Food ☐ Beer ☐ Wine ☐ Alc. Bev.	40. Check if food/beverage vending machine ☐ 41. Date you were first required to collect meals tax. Mo. Day Yr. 43. Seating Capacity	
	42. Name and Address on Liquor License at this location		
	44. Enter fee of $10.00 unless you have applied for registration as a sales and/or use tax on goods vendor in Item 36, a sales on services vendor in Item 38 or are already licensed as a sales and/or use tax on goods or a sales/use tax on services vendor at this location. ➤		$
ROOM OCCUPANCY	45. Date you were first required to collect room occupancy tax. Mo. Day Yr.	46. Number of Rooms 47. Enter $10.00 Fee if you are a hotel, motel or lodging house operator. ➤	$
USE TAX PURCHASER	48. Date you were first required to pay use tax. Mo. Day Yr.	NO FEE	
49. TOTAL FEE(S) this location. Add Items 36 or 38, and 47; or Items 44 and 47, whichever is more.		➤	$
50. TOTAL FEE(S) from attached Form(s) TA-2 (additional locations)		➤	$
51. TOTAL FEE(S) all locations. Add Item 49 and Item 50. Pay this Amount. Make check payable to Commonwealth of Massachusetts		➤	$

SIGN HERE

I HEREBY CERTIFY THAT THE STATEMENTS MADE HEREIN HAVE BEEN EXAMINED BY ME AND ARE, TO THE BEST OF MY KNOWLEDGE AND BELIEF, TRUE AND CORRECT. Signed under the pains and penalties of perjury.

Sign
Here ➤ _____
Date   Must be signed by Owner, Partner or Officer   Title

Please note that the signing of this application is evidence that you may be the person individually and personally responsible for any sums required to be paid to the Commonwealth, under Massachusetts General Laws, Chapter 62B, Sec. 5; Chapter 64G, Sec. 7B; Chapter 64H, Sec. 16 and Chapter 64I, Sec. 17.
MAIL TO: The Commonwealth of Massachusetts, MASS. DOR (Department of Revenue) P.O. Box 7022, Boston, MA 02204.

Fig. 4–5. A Sales Tax Application Registration Form. Reverse side.
Courtesy State of Massachusetts, Department of Revenue.

CIS-1
(6-90)

STATE OF NEW JERSEY
DIVISION OF TAXATION
APPLICATION FOR REGISTRATION
Read instructions before completing this form
ALL SECTIONS MUST BE FULLY COMPLETED ON BOTH SIDES OF THIS APPLICATION

MAIL TO:
CN 252
TRENTON, N.J. 08646-0252

REGISTRATION DETAIL

A. Please indicate the reason for your filing this application.
(Check only one block)
☐ Original application for a new business.
☐ Application for a new location of an existing business
☐ Amended application for an existing business.
☐ Moved previously registered business to new location (UTF-C can be used in lieu of CIS-1)
Give name and NJ Registration Number of existing business.

☐ Other · please explain _____

B. FID # ☐☐ - ☐☐☐☐☐☐☐   OR   Soc. Sec. # of Owner ☐☐☐ - ☐☐ - ☐☐☐☐
☐ Check Box if applied for

C. Name _____
(IF INCORPORATED · give Corp. Name; IF NOT· give Last Name, First Name, MI of Owner, Partners)

D. Trade Name _____

E. Business Location:
(Do not use P.O. Box for Location Address)
Street _____
City _____ State ☐☐
Zip Code ☐☐☐☐☐ - ☐☐☐☐
(Give 9-digit Zip)
(See instructions for providing alternate addresses)

F. Mailing Name and Address · (if different from business address)
Name _____
Street _____
City _____ State ☐☐
Zip Code ☐☐☐☐☐ - ☐☐☐☐
(Give 9-digit Zip)

BUSINESS DETAIL

G. Beginning Date For This Business In New Jersey _____ / _____ / _____ (see instructions)
month   day   year

H. Type of Ownership (check one):
☐ NJ Corporation   ☐ Sole Proprietor   ☐ Partnership   ☐ Out-of-State Corporation
☐ Limited Partnership   ☐ Other · explain _____
O/C _____
NCT ☐

I. New Jersey Business Code ☐☐ (See instructions)

J. County / Municipality Code ☐☐ ☐☐ (See instructions)

FOR OFFICIAL USE ONLY
DLN   B-_____
CORP # _____

K. Will this business be open all year?   ☐ YES   ☐ NO
If NO · Circle months business will be open:
JAN   FEB   MAR   APR   MAY   JUN   JUL   AUG   SEPT   OCT   NOV   DEC

L. Telephone Numbers: Contact Person _____   Title _____
Daytime: ( ) _____ - _____ Ext _____   Evening: ( ) _____ - _____ Ext _____

M. IF A CORPORATION, complete the following:
Date of Incorp. _____ / _____ / _____   State of Incorp. ☐☐   Fiscal month ☐☐
month   day   year
Is this a Subsidiary of another corporation?   ☐ YES   ☐ NO
If yes, give name & Federal ID# of parent _____

N. Provide the following information for the owner, partners or responsible corporate officers. (If more space needed, attach rider.)

NAME (Last Name, First, M I)	SOCIAL SECURITY NUMBER TITLE	HOME ADDRESS (Street, City, Zip)

OWNERSHIP DETAIL

Signature
of Owner, Partner or Officer _____   Date _____

Title _____   BE SURE TO COMPLETE REVERSE SIDE

Fig. 4–6. A Sales Tax Application Registration Form. Front side.
Courtesy State of New Jersey, Division of Taxation.

Each Question Must Be Answered Completely   CIS-1 (Pg 2)

1a. Will you collect New Jersey Sales Tax and/or pay Use Tax? .... ☐ Yes ☐ No

GIVE DATE YOU EXPECT TO MAKE YOUR FIRST SALE .... Month____ Day____ Year____

b. Will you need to make tax exempt purchases for your inventory
or to produce your products? .... ☐ Yes ☐ No

2. Will you be paying wages, salaries or commissions to employees working in
New Jersey and/or to New Jersey residents working outside New Jersey? ...... ☐ Yes ☐ No

GIVE DATE OF FIRST WAGE OR SALARY PAYMENT ...... Month____ Day____ Year____

3. Will you be the payer of pension or annuity income to New
Jersey residents? .... ☐ Yes ☐ No

GIVE DATE OF FIRST PENSION OR ANNUITY PAYMENT ... Month____ Day____ Year____

4. Will you be holding legalized games of chance in New Jersey (as defined in
Chapter 47- Rules of Legalized Games of Chance) where proceeds from
any one prize exceeds $1,000? .... ☐ Yes ☐ No
NOTE: N.J. Lottery proceeds not included

5. Do you intend to sell cigarettes? .... ☐ Yes ☐ No
IF YES, please indicate your license requirements (see instructions).

☐ Retail (over-the-counter) (OTC)   ☐ Distributor (DIS)
☐ Vending Machine (VND)   ☐ Manufacturer's Rep (REP)
☐ Wholesaler (WHL)   ☐ Manufacturer (MFG)

6a. Are you a distributor or wholesaler of tobacco products other
than cigarettes? .... ☐ Yes ☐ No

b, Are you a retailer subject to the compensating use tax as defined under
the Tobacco Products Wholesale Sales and Use Tax? (see instructions) .... ☐ Yes ☐ No

7. Do you intend to sell or transport motor fuels? .... ☐ Yes ☐ No
IF YES, please indicate your license requirements (see instructions).

☐ Retail (RTL)   ☐ Distributor (DIS)
☐ Wholesale (WHL)   ☐ Special License "A" (SPA)
☐ Transport (TRN)   ☐ Special License "B" (SPB)
☐ Jobber (JOB)

8. Is your company engaged in the refining and/or distributing of petroleum
products for distribution in this state or the importing of untaxed petroleum
products into New Jersey for consumption in New Jersey? .... ☐ Yes ☐ No

9. Do you own or operate a facility, vessel or public warehouse in New Jersey
that receives, stores or manufactures chemicals or petroleum products? .... ☐ Yes ☐ No

10. Are you a manufacturer, wholesaler, distributor or retailer of
"litter-generating products"? (see instructions) .... ☐ Yes ☐ No

11. Are you an owner or operator of a sanitary landfill facility or a
solid waste facility in New Jersey? .... ☐ Yes ☐ No
IF YES, indicate D.E.P. Facility # and type (see instructions).

12. List any other New Jersey State taxes for which this business may be eligible (see instructions).

13. Type of business   ☐ 1. Manufacturer   ☐ 4. Construction
                        ☐ 2. Service   ☐ 5. Retail
                        ☐ 3. Wholesale   ☐ 6. Government
Principal product or service _____

Fig. 4–6. A Sales Tax Application Registration Form. Reverse side.
Courtesy State of New Jersey, Division of Taxation.

Chapter Highlights

- Product costs might include, but are not limited to such items as overhead, raw materials, freight, packaging, labor for production, marketing, and sales.
- Rent, utilities, salaries, insurance, and depreciation are generally included in product overhead expenses.
- Tools, equipment, furniture, and fixtures are some of the business assets that must be considered when calculating depreciation.
- You can avoid employment taxes and fringe benefits if you use contract labor rather than salaried people.
- Even though your craft business is self-owned, you must consider charging for your own labor when calculating product costs.
- A cost formula: Total cost of goods sold = Cost of material + Cost of labor including personal and family labor + All other business expenses.
- A rule of thumb for setting the selling price of craft products is to double your cost for a 100% markup.
- Always try to obtain the best possible price for your products.
- You may price above competition if your product is exclusive, convenient to the purchaser, has limited availability, is positioned for special markets.
- Selling a selective product only to a specific market in a special price range is called price lining.

CHAPTER 5

Market Research Techniques

Why Market Research?

Market research has proven to be a useful tool for businesses of all sizes, new or established. It can pinpoint what products people are looking for. If the research is specifically directed, it can also provide you with insights into how structural, design, price, and other product changes might affect your sales.

The process of collecting information, analyzing the data, and then projecting decisions based on the results is what market research is all about. Information can be gathered in a number of areas.

You want to know about the *size of the potential market* for your line of craft products. Based on the price of the items you are trying to sell, you would want to know about the *income level of the potential buyers* in the market area. A low income area, for example, would probably not be a good place to direct your selling efforts for expensive wall clocks or costly non-essential items, but might be a good area for inexpensive Christmas novelties.

The marketplace changes rapidly. *Tastes, interests, habits* and other variables fluctuate greatly over time. You need to know about these changes, and whether they affect your product line or marketing plan. Handcrafted decorative ceramic ash trays, as an example, would not hit the top of charts in an era when cigarette smoking is on the wane. On the other hand, handsomely-crafted yo-yos might sell well if your research indicated a high income bedroom community for business executives.

A *knowledge of your competition* is always valuable. Research can indicate the absence or presence of competition in your market and the degree or activity of this competition. It could also alert you to the nature of the competition that you might have to face. Suppose, for example, that you are producing handcrafted ceramics and pottery marked up to provide you with a modest profit. If you know that the area is loaded with competitors marketing cheap, foreign ceramic ware, you might want to consider a more stable and fruitful market area.

Among the most important barometers that you can use in market research are the *economic trends* in the target market. The economic indicators include unemployment figures, business and personal bankruptcies, property foreclosures, marketplace negativism, and other signs of the times. People who are unemployed tend to protect their remaining assets, and buy few, if any, items beyond necessities.

Knowledge of economic conditions in various areas is important if you follow a show route. If, for example, the choice is to participate in a week-long craft show in the northeast during a recession, as opposed to an exposition in the far west or the south where the economy was more stable, the wise choice might be to consider selling at the western or southern show.

Market research can also tell you if you are getting a *reasonable share of the market*. If there are several craftspeople in your market area selling products similar to yours, you should be aware if your marketshare is more, less, or the same as theirs. If you find that your sales are consistently lower than your competitors', you should learn why. It may be your booth, or the way you exhibit your craft products. It may be your sales style or your marketing program.

Sometimes, your market research will tell you that although your product is well made and attractive, it just *doesn't seem to meet the demands or requirements of a specific market*. You might want to consider changing either your product or your market area.

Price in the marketplace is always a consideration. Your market research should let you know whether your craft products are priced compatibly with the demands of the target market. You do not want to overprice or underprice your products, or, as indicated previously, attempt to sell a high-priced product in a market that normally purchases only moderate- or low-priced merchandise.

If you return regularly to the same show, shop, or other venue to sell your craft products, you should have a concept of what your *customers like and dislike* about your products, and indeed, about your entire selling operation. Market research can help you learn this.

Your market research can help you make sensible business decisions. You no longer must depend on "seat of the pants" judgments, hunches or possibilities. Fig 5–1 shows a summary of some reasons for conducting market research.

Market Research

Some of the areas you might be interested in researching include:

- Customer satisfaction or dissatisfaction with your current product line.
- Effectiveness of your advertising, publicity, and promotional campaign.
- Best media choices to reach potential consumers with the story of your products.
- Consumer responses to a new craft product that you intend to market (test marketing).
- Consumer responses to a "recycled" craft product that you intend to re-market (test marketing).
- Research of the market availability for your current craft line.
- Trends in the economy and the marketplace and the potential effect on your business.
- Evaluation of competitive business practices and advertising techniques.
- Projections of market demands for your craft product line.

Fig. 5–1. There are a variety of reasons for conducting a market research project for your craft business. The key word is DISCOVERY. There are things you may wish to learn about your product, your potential customers, the market's reaction to your craft item, and many other areas. Market research can help you uncover the information.

Simple Market Research Techniques

There are many internal and external sources of information available to you.

Use Your Own Records and Experience

If you have been in business any length of time, and you have kept accurate records, these records offer a wealth of internal information. Analyzing the number of pieces of each craft product you have sold year by year is a start in the research process. Some of your craft items will have sold better than others. Craft fairs in certain market areas may have been more or less lucrative than others. Certain periods of the year will show higher volume than others. High-priced items may have shown better sales than lower-priced items, or vice versa. This collective information from past experience goes into the research pool to help make future decisions.

Outside Information Sources

There are also many external sources of marketing information readily available to you at no cost. The government at all levels publishes tremendous amounts of material. Federal, state, and local government agencies regularly report on all types of business activities. Census data not only gives population numbers, region by region, but also many relevant facts about the people living in each area, broken down by zip codes. You can develop profiles of people living in specific zip code blocks, including their income levels, ages, family size, and many other demographic factors.

Craft trade associations and trade journals are also excellent sources of market research information. These organizations and magazines provide information specifically related to the craft industry.

Local libraries contain many sources of market research information, as do government publications and agencies. If you cannot locate what you are seeking, the staff of your state and federal representatives will frequently be of help.

The files, or "morgues," of newspapers are another source of selective information. Chambers of Commerce, utilities, and banks have market data that you can tap. If you live near a college offering business courses, you might consider contacting the head of the business department for sources of marketing information. You will probably also find the college library well stocked with business resource material.

Look to the business pages of your area newspapers as viable sources of business trends, business start-ups, mergers, and failures; mall openings and promotions, and other items related to your area. Larger newspapers and business magazines provide additional market information, but all of it may not be relevant to your needs.

Commercial organizations also provide all types of market research information for a fee. If the data you require is not available, and you believe it is worth the cost, these firms can research. The names and addresses of these research gathering companies are listed in telephone directory yellow pages.

How to Gather Research Information

Doing Your Own Research

You can check the available sources listed for market research data, and you can also seek out market information yourself.

Attend Shows or Fairs—Attend craft shows or fairs as a consumer and ask relevant questions of the exhibitors. Pay particular attention to the way booths are designed or products are exhibited, noting which booths draw best. You can research the price structure of products that compete with yours. You might count the number of people visiting particular types of booths, and also determine the age and type of people who show the most interest. This is gathering market information.

The Survey or Interview—In each of the following methods, you select a small group of people for your research from the total market population. In the research field, the entire population is known as the universe. The research segment you will be working with is known as a sample. If you are working with a reasonably large market area, one hundred people can be a reasonable representative sample. To develop a random sample, you might use every tenth name on a list, or every fifth name in the telephone book, for example.

- You can develop a brief questionnaire for people who visit your booth or your shop or who have been mail order buyers, or a random sample of potential buyers. Questions should be brief and very clear. Make it easy for the respondents to return the questionnaire. If you want to increase the response, you might offer a small gift. Some companies include a postage-paid envelope, a coin or new dollar bill with their request letter and the questionnaire.

- The telephone can also be used for your market research. You will have to develop a relevant questionnaire that can be answered rapidly. The calls should be made at a time convenient for the research respondents.

- Personal interviews are still another effective technique for a product market research project. Using this method, you would develop a brief questionnaire, go into the community in which your market is located, and select individuals to interview at random from a specific universe.

In carrying out the interview for your craft products, you should set a number of goals and objectives.

You want the information you receive to be accurate. You want to be able to complete the process rapidly. Your time is valuable and so is the time of the individuals you are questioning. You want the process to be cost-effective. Research work is a time consuming process, and time is money.

It is a good practice to test your questionnaires on several people before actual putting them to use so that any difficult questions can be reworked or eliminated. If you feel that your questionnaire is not giving you the information you want, seek help from someone with experience in preparing questionnaires.

Using Focus Groups

Focus groups offer another avenue for market research. These groups generally provide subjective as well as specific information. Commercial focus group implementers are expensive, but you can set up your own group if you learn the technique.

The responses you receive tend to be more relevant because you have better control of the questions asked. The controlled venue—where and how the meeting is being held—is also an advantage. A direct mail research piece can be thrown away. A telephone interview can be terminated. The focus group keeps all of the participants in one place during the process.

The way a focus group works is that a group of people, generally about a dozen, are gathered together in one room for a short period of time. At the meeting, the focus group leader poses a number of selected questions to the assemblage. The questions are designed not only to elicit information about a specific product, but also about motivations to purchase, attitudes about selling approaches, prices, product attributes in general, and any other relevant information. The participants are led by adroit questioning to discuss the issues from their personal perspectives.

The responses that are developed as a result of the focus group meeting can be evaluated with all of your other research material. The ground rules for setting up a focus group meeting are not complex.

- Pick out twelve to eighteen people who share an interest in the subject in which you are doing the research. If your craft products happen to be a line of children's toys, you might select young parents. You might place a small classified ad in your local newspaper seeking volunteers for your focus group.
- Select a meeting area that is neutral. Your place of business, for example, would not be suitable. The room should be large enough to be comfortable, but not so large as to be intimidating.
- The focus group should run about one to one and one-half hour. If it goes longer, people become restless, and responses may not be useful or accurate.
- Plan the time for the focus group session with your participants in mind. If the group consists of mothers with elementary school-aged children, they may only be available at hours when the youngsters are in school. If the participants' children are preschoolers, you may have to make babysitting arrangements at the focus group meeting site. Focus groups can also be held during the evening or on weekends.
- You may have to pay a small honorarium for focus group participants, or give each participant a gift of one of your items.
- There are professionals who effectively moderate focus groups. While you might conduct the focus group yourself, it is not generally a good idea because it is difficult to distance yourself emotionally from your product. This personal involvement can skew the response, and you will not get objective information.
- A focus group reacts best to questions which stimulate more than superficial responses. If you are using an experienced focus group

moderator, you should give him or her the questions you would like answered. These will not necessarily be the questions which will be asked, but will be used to develop subjective parameters for leading the conversation. If you are leading the group, make every effort to control your voice, facial expressions, and body language so that you do not inhibit open, honest response.

- If possible, record the focus group meeting on video- and/or audiotape so that you can review the data at your leisure. If this is not possible, have someone take accurate notes.
- If it is within your research budget, plan on conducting two different focus group meetings to further validate the results.

Using Market Research Data

Once you have gathered your research material, the next step is evaluating and making use of the information.

- Begin by asking yourself what has made your craft product and your company successful in the past. Then determine how much of your research bolsters your experience.
- From your research, extract those pointers that can be factored into your present operation to make it function even more effectively. For instance, you might have determined that additional staffing at your booth during a craft fair could impact favorably on sales. On the other hand, the cost of salary, food, lodging, and transportation for the extra people from your home area might eat up the profits. Additional research might show availability of good part-time salespeople in the show area. It may pay you to seek out and train these people in your sales methods.
- It is just as important to pinpoint areas in which your operation is successful as it is to understand any possible weaknesses. The areas of success will show you, for example, which are the most effective selling procedures.
- Your research may uncover new sales or marketing opportunities. Evaluate these options to see if they fit in with your current business. For example, if you are currently marketing pins or scarves, the addition of a line of matching earrings might open up a new market. This would be especially important if your research indicated that the areas in which you sell are populated heavily by teen-

aged females, and colorful, unusual earrings were the latest fad for this group.

- Part of your research will concern itself with your competitors. How do their operations affect your sales? If your marketing research shows some definite patterns of change in the way competitors conduct business, should you too consider similar changes, or should you hold to your present patterns? A competing craft vendor, for example, turns out a line of products similar to yours. The vendor uses a less expensive raw material and sells the product for less. You know that the product will have a shorter life span than yours. You must decide whether to meet the price, use a poorer quality material, or develop a marketing campaign that focuses on the superior material you use.

- Your market research data may help you develop a marketing plan incorporating the information you have learned.

- Most businesses set goals. The goals may be in the area of product sales, growth, or any number of other objectives. Market research helps make these goals and objectives realistic. For instance, if you are currently selling *X* number of a certain type of craft product, you may want to set *X plus 100* as the goal for the following year. Ramifications of business growth can affect your decisions. Additional equipment, space, and personnel may be necessary to reach the new goal. Market research will help you determine whether the cost of these expenditures will be absorbed by new sales.

- Always set a timeframe for evaluating results. Keep a careful check on the progress of new projects and always be prepared to make changes quickly to take advantage of sales opportunities or to stem the flow of nonproductive expenses.

A Market Research Design Plan

A research design plan for your craft business should include the following steps.

1—*Define the problem you want to resolve.* This will save time, effort, and money. Ask: Has there been a dropoff in business? Are there plans for the introduction of a new craft product? What pricing levels will produce the best results? What about expansion into other markets? How is this operation affected by competition? What can be learned from competition? Include any other questions you want to answer.

2—*Set goals* for your research. Clearly define what you expect it to accomplish. Do not set impossible tasks or search for undefinable answers. Be pragmatic.

3—*Start your research by identifying the type of information that you need.* Some important sources of this information are discussed in this chapter. Determine any limitations of the survey. Clearly identify the sample group that you expect to research. If, as an example, your craft product will only be sold to parents with children aged 3–8, there is little point to surveying an older adult population with teenagers.

4—*Plan your research, allocating the required time and money* to the project. A great deal of the information can be obtained using only an expenditure of time. Some of the information will have a cost factor.

5—*Spend time on the preparation of your survey, or list of questions.* Keep the survey material as brief as possible. Make sure that the questions are unbiased and easy to answer. If the answer to one of your questions requires a complex response, break the question into a number of sections.

6—In preparing a survey questionnaire, *consider the use of multiple choice and checkoff questions.* This performs two functions. It makes it easier for the respondents to answer, and it makes it simpler for you to tabulate research results.

7—If you mail questionnaires, always *include a cover letter with your survey.* A well-written letter encourages a larger survey response. An attractive, professional looking questionnaire may also bring in a better response.

8—*Always set deadlines* for yourself to complete the research project and for the individuals who will be responding to your survey material.

9—*Initiate the research project.* Begin and complete your program within a definite timeframe. If you permit the project to lag, circumstances and time will affect the results.

10—*Take time to analyze all of the information* that has been collected so that you can use it to make some sound business judgments rather than relying on hunches and second-guesses.

11—*Put the relevant research information to use* in your business. Don't place it on the shelf to gather dust.

Fig. 5–2 shows a guide for market research listing these items slightly differently for easy reference.

Market Research Guide

a) Clarify the research problem. *Focus on the prime difficulty* that you want to resolve through market research. Do not attempt to seek solutions to a broad spectrum of problems.

b) *Recognize the importance of the problem* and its relationship to your business. You should be aware of exactly how the results of the research will help your business.

c) *List your reasons for the market research* project. Detail the purposes, expectations, and limits on the time and expense that will go into the market research project.

d) *Learn as much as possible about problems similar to yours.* Learn about existing solutions. This information may be in your own files or available in existing market research material or literature.

e) From this very basic research, *start considering ideas and potential solutions that may be useful* in resolving your own business problem.

f) Once you have a more concise idea of the areas in which you wish to focus your research, *determine the full scope of the information you require.*

g) Make a decision about *how and where you will locate the information.* Trade associations, industry journals, government records and libraries are just some of your resources.

h) Make a decision about *how you will analyze the data.* Be sure that the system you use is unbiased.

i) *Launch the full market research project.* Gather all available information, ideas, suggestions, comments, etc. in an orderly fashion. Analyze the data when it is all collected.

j) *Develop a set of solutions and conclusions* from the market research to resolve your business problem.

k) *Prepare a written report* so that you have a record of your work for future reference.

Fig. 5–2. In order to get a clear picture of many business processes like market research, it is often practical to detail your view of the subject in writing. This gives you an opportunity to review the information before making any decisions. This guide was designed to assist you with the process.

Chapter Highlights

- Market research is a procedure that you can use to determine what consumers in the marketplace expect of your craft products. It can also provide you with information about how to improve or upgrade your product line and your sales.
- Economic trends in your area of market interest can be tracked using research techniques.
- The survey process used in market research may tell you if your product is receiving a reasonable share of the market.
- There are two types of research sources, internal and external.
- Some research information can be located in trade journals, trade associations, and federal, state and local government reports.
- Another tool for market research is the survey or interview.
- Surveys rely on questions asked of individuals by mail, via telephone, or in personal one-on-one interviews.
- A focus group brings together a group of people from whom you can illicit subjective as well as factual responses.
- A focus group, or any individual surveyed, responds best to a well-developed format of questioning.
- It is important for you to set goals for your craft business. Goal-setting and market research can complement each other.
- Always define the problem you are interested in resolving before you start a full-fledged market research program.

CHAPTER 6

Marketplace Positioning

Perceptions

Individual consumer thoughts are difficult to pin down. Some are obvious and others nearly imponderable. Nevertheless, these thoughts become the buying considerations of the normal consumer. They are recognized in marketing as *perceptions*. When a number of these perceptions are grouped together, they become *collective perceptions*. Each product in the marketplace has a perceptual relationship to others. That is, we tend naturally and automatically to compare. These collective perceptions play an important role in marketing craft products.

One of the important segments of the *marketing mix* is *positioning*, that is, targeting your product to respond to perceptions as well as needs.

We have previously discussed the factors that should be considered in product development and pricing. Both will contribute to the decision of where and how to position your product as well as how to package it. It is important, however, to understand that the reverse is also true. The very same product at the very same price that is a ho-hum seller in one position can be a hot seller in another, and vice versa.

It is obvious that even for professional, major marketers, the process of positioning requires an understanding of consumer perceptions. A number of thoughts may enter the consumer's mind as he or she views a product. Overriding questions include: What will this do for me? What will people perceive about me when I use or give this product? Secondary questions help answer primary questions: Who made this craft item? Is it backed by a reputation for turning out quality products or a warranty against defects? How does it compare in price and quality with competing items? Would the person for whom I am buying the product prefer this craft item or be pleased or more impressed with another product? Would I like to own this craft item? Will it increase in value over the years? Does the person who wants to sell me the craft product take pride in it?

The perceptions created by answers to these unspoken questions are affected by how your product is positioned. What is important to recognize is that positioning affects consumers who are making purchasing decisions. It provides them with a system of comparing products in the marketplace.

While you can enhance perceptions of your product with effective promotion, advertising, brochures and the other communications and marketing tools discussed throughout this book, the decisions you make about positioning your product will affect these processes as well. For example, if you are positioning your product for the church and school craft fair market, using slick, four-color brochures creates a perception that your product is overpriced. On the other hand, the well-designed, quality-paper, slick brochure in the boutique or gallery market enhances the perception of product value.

The Rite of Positioning

Assume that you have accepted an invitation to a large social gathering. What will you wear? Something conservative or outrageous? How will you get there? By public transportation or by sleek limo? You arrive on the evening of the event and enter the room. Now you have a series of choices to make. You have to find a suitable place for yourself somewhere in the room. You may opt for a table in a corner or for a busy ringside table where you can easily greet and be greeted or a spot in the center of traffic flow, to see and be seen. You may find it more appropriate to circulate throughout the room. You might decide to mix with the young professionals attending the party or with their distinguished elders, or you might single out the creative people like yourself—the musicians, artists, craftspeople, the writers, or even the critics.

During the entire process, you have positioned yourself, deliberately or otherwise, so that people seeing or meeting you for the first time develop some perceptions about you. These perceptions may affect their future relationships with you. Your packaging, your positioning in location, and your place in the social structure might be perceived in varying ways. Some might say that your choice of the high density sections of the room show that you are active and outgoing: the selection of smaller, quieter, out-of-the way sections give an opposite impression. The choice of mobility from one group to another tells another story, just as your choice of clothes.

The story you tell about yourself by the way you dress, the people you associate with, the places you frequent, the degree of affluence you project, and the messages you communicate create perceptions. Political pollsters are fond of saying that perceptions are the true realities, and successful marketers agree.

Product movement from producer to buyer is in many ways analogous to the above example. When a potential customer sees a craft item that you have produced, certain internalizing processes take place. Where the product is seen affects the viewer's perception; how the product is packaged and displayed also send messages to the customer, just as its price and the company it keeps.

Although many craftsbuyers are impulse purchasers attracted to the sheer creativity, workmanship, or beauty of the product, others seek out crafted products for themselves for businesses, for family members or friends. Some people are one-stop shoppers doing the bulk of their buying in department stores or through catalogs; others frequent craft shows large and small, artisan workshops, boutiques, and galleries. For some people, the higher the price tag, the higher the perceived value; for others, the well-publicized signature heightens the value; still others seek out outlets for quality products at discounted prices.

Positioning your product in the marketplace has a significant effect on your sales.

Positioning Your Craft Product

Although the consumer may not recognize it, positioning means that a basis for comparison has been developed. *Your job as the marketer of your company's line of craft products is to guide potential consumers so your product naturally takes a dominant role.* From the buyer's point of view, the positioning of your craft product reflects his or her perception of the value of your product in relation to similar products.

Positioning by Place

A leatherworker we knew did her first craft show at her son's school holiday fair "because it only cost $25 for a booth." Her exquisitely-worked, supple leather bags were well worth their three figure price tags but she did not sell one. Nor did she make a sale with her gorgeous designer belts priced upwards of $35.

However, risking the expense of a kiosk in the lobby of an office building with a large number of women climbing the career ladder, she found she could not keep up with the demand. The deliberate decision to position by price and place enabled her to develop a cottage industry with other craftspeople participating in her increased production needs.

Another, and equally creative, leatherworker preferred to stay in the craft fair market and retooled his production for lower priced items—eyeglass cases with velcro-attached belt loops, compartmentalized checkbook covers, simple belts in sturdy leathers with a choice of buckles, passport cases, barrettes and ponytail holders, and leather earrings. While he sold leather bags, he was able to price them lower because he used basic designs with less time-consuming detail and less costly leathers. Maintaining a year-round workshop show and sales room and, currently, a growing number of traveling show booths, he, too, has successfully positioned his products for a general, moderately-priced marketplace, and realized good profits.

You position your product by place when you make the decision to sell it from your own workshop wherever you might be, or from a shop in a crafts community like Woodstock or Sugar Loaf, New York, where tourists are attracted by the assemblage of many artists and craftspeople. You position your product by place when you decide to sell from a shop in a tourist area like Cape Cod, or Waikiki Beach. Your product is positioned by place when it is sold from a gallery, a museum, or a craft cooperative.

You can position by place when you enter a juried show rather than a mall show; or select a library fair rather than a book shop to sell your wares.

It is possible to choose several positions. For example, at least one vendor in Waikiki's Kuhio Mall craft cooperative shop sells his wares to tourists for most of the year, but participates in craft shows catering primarily to residents of Oahu during the pre-holiday season. His prices at the craft shows are approximately ten percent less than those in his shop because he doesn't believe show customers should pay for his shop overhead. He sells out at each of the shows he enters and builds a year-round following for his shop.

When we talk about positioning your product, we are looking at it in terms of creating or fixing its place in the market. It is important to emphasize that you can position your product by place, price, unique characteristics, benefits, target niche, sales location, and many other considerations.

Positioning by Price

Price and place positioning frequently go hand in hand. People are more likely to accept higher-priced merchandise in elegant settings. Companies like Godiva Chocolate, Rolls Royce, and others recognize this relationship. Their advertising is generally in the slick media; their packaging and promotion is upscale, and their shops and showrooms are located in high-income areas.

People expect more bargains at flea markets, expect to pay more in more upscale settings, and tend to do more comparison shopping in department stores. Marketers can take advantage of these expectations by using flea markets to move out-of-date products, irregulars and seconds; upscale settings for their newer, pricier products; and intermediate marketplaces for products which meet the competition in price/quality perception.

Positioning by Differentiation

Another objective might be to differentiate or distinguish your line from all others. If you are to position your product by differentiation, for example, you must develop credible or meaningful differences between it and similar products in the same marketplace.

In any instance, your objective in positioning your product should be to give the consumer as many reasons as possible to perceive your product favorably in comparison with others. Incidentally, competitive products do not have to be identical with yours in composition or style to vie for position. All they have to do is to compete for consumer perception.

Positioning by Multiple Uses

Suppose that your handcrafted product is an attractive, expensive, large ceramic serving dish. A competitor has produced an attractive, moderately-priced ceramic serving dish with a handle that permits it to be used as a decorative wall hanging. Your competitor has positioned his or her handcrafted product in at least two ways: first, on the basis of pricing, and then on the basis of multiple use. You may decide, nevertheless, that you will position your product in higher-priced, single-use market which you believe is large enough to absorb your production. This may or not be a realistic positioning decision, but it should at least be a deliberate one.

If your craft product is a food specialty, you might position by sight, taste, odor, testimony as to the number of years in business, reproduction of awards won at food fairs, etc. If your product is similar to others in the marketplace, you might try positioning by building a perception of quality and longevity. If you are in a price-conscious market, you may have to position by price. This can be accomplished simply by lowering your profit margin, or creatively by packaging a number of your products together and selling at a special price, or couponing. A coupon provides a discount to the purchaser if a product is bought within a certain time period.

Or, you might position your product for catalog, mail-order, or direct-mail sales; for sales in exclusive restaurants, hospital gift shops, or gourmet shops.

Positioning by Specific Time or Place

Finally, just as you can position by filling a specific need in the marketplace, you can position by selling at a specific time or in a specific place. If, for example, your product line is concentrated on hand-carved duck decoys, you might position your products at a sports show, at general craft shows prior to the duck hunting season, or before Father's Day; as well as at Christmas and Chanukah shows where gifts may be purchased for sports enthusiasts. You might also position your products at a country show or in a decorators' market. Or, you might target your sales to shops and boutiques in duck-hunting regions.

Product Segmenting

You can also position your craft product by selecting a *segment or segments of a potential market.* Your craft product can be designed or adapted to meet the needs or requirements of a select group of customers. You might also select a specific market, and then attempt to reach this target market with a specialized advertising and/or promotional campaign. This approach may eliminate the need for changing or readapting your product. Common baking soda used for leavening in quick-bread baking, although certainly not a craft product, provides an excellent example of this advertising and promotional technique. This product is targeted to multiple market segments including cooks for cooking and baking, homemakers for deodorizing and cleaning, and the over-the-counter market for medicinal purposes. Each market segment receives a complete and different message. The original use of baking soda as a cooking and baking product remains solid. Baking soda's position as a fine refrigerator deodorizer is well respected; its use as a antacid has a solid following.

One of the disadvantages of this approach to positioning is that duplication of the product by a competitor using the same techniques of advertising and promotion places the competitor at the same positioning level.

Niche Marketing

Niche marketing is another name for attempting to position your craft product in specialized markets. In the Pennsylvania Dutch Country and in Hawaii, for example, some quilters have positioned their products exclusively thus becoming known for costly bed coverlets made with traditional designs. Others, however, specialize in equally costly, contemporary or original designed quilted wall hangings or spreads. The famous Aloha stadium in Hawaii, catering primarily to tourists, features several booths targeting the typical grandmother tourist. The booths specialize in inexpensive, machine-quilted, traditional Hawaiian pineapple- or leaf-patterned infant items such as crib, carriage, and pillow covers, baby buntings, bibs and coveralls.

Some quilters position their products for the kitchen, offering placemats, napkin rings, appliance covers, and tea cozies. Still others craft their quilting for the fashion market with bedroom slippers and boots, bed jackets, robes, vests, or outerwear. Many quilters add profits by targeting the do-it-yourselfer and the wishful thinker. For the former, quilters offer kits of varying sizes; for the latter, postcards, posters, and pamphlets illustrating the best quilts in their collections.

Some quilters, just as some ceramicists, sculptors, metal-, or woodworkers, find their niche in the industrial, business, or public-sector markets. They solicit architects, designers, decorators, and consultants for commissioned—that is, made to order—pieces, many with pricetags of five or six figures. Banks, insurance companies, colleges, and other organizations who require pieces large enough to make a statement in spacious lobbies, corridors, or hallways are prime targets. These targets require a more sophisticated approach in solicitation, a highly-professional presentation, and a totally businesslike expression of credibility, accountability, and responsibility in addition to talent. If you can meet these standards and like the idea of crafting just a few major works each year, this is an area to look into.

Niche marketing requires a more than casual analysis of people's perspectives. A memorable case in point is that of a baby food product. Supermarket checkout surveys indicated that many senior citizens were buying baby foods and junior foods because they were easily digestible, posed no problems with dentures, and were packaged in one-serving portions.

"Wouldn't sales increase if we packaged these foods in a senior line?" the marketing executives asked. They did, but the sales didn't increase. Seniors refused to buy the products because it identified them with perceptions they did not want. At least when they bought baby food, the perception could remain that it was for grandchildren. Had the marketing experts understood the senior market, they might have spared the company this costly experience in positioning.

Niche positioning is frequently a marketing strategy that gets a jump on competition. It should be carefully considered as you develop your product, not only in terms of potential niche market size, but also *in terms of comparative returns on your investment in time, talent, and materials.* Fig. 6–1 and 6–2 show craft products targeted to niche markets.

Fig. 6–1. Craftspeople can position their products in a variety of ways. One method is to design a product for a particular market. In this instance, the craftspeople targeted bird lovers and conservationists as a primary market. *Courtesy American Pie Company.*

Fig. 6–2. Positioning takes many paths. For example, postage stamp enthusiasts are prime prospects for this craftsperson's product. Using postage stamps as a base, this individual weaves a specific stamp into an unusual framed picture story. Each stamp/story is totally different. The products are marketed at craft shows. Special orders are available. *Courtesy Pete Prince.*

Locating Poorly Served Markets

Positioning can also mean locating a market that is *poorly served or underserved* by other marketers. Your craft product may be particularly adapted or adaptable to an ethnic or minority market and may only require proper product exposure. Checking these markets for festivals and fairs, popular magazines, newspapers, and cable programs, and accepted commercial enterprises serving these markets may open a very special niche for you.

The teenage market may also be poorly or under-served by competitors. A craftswoman we know who used to spend her weekends doing mall sales took advantage of teenagers' penchant for personalized pocket and purse accessories, book covers and carryalls. First, personally or by phone and later by direct mail, she contacted junior and senior class officers, offering the class treasury commissions for mass orders. Her business has grown to the point that she only does mall shows to test new products.

Positioning Questions

There are a number of questions that will help you position your operation and your products. Some of them are:

- What position do I want for my product in the marketplace? Do I want to sell to the upscale market, the mid-range market, a special market segment, or the overall consumer market? Are there opportunities to reach these markets now, or must I begin building toward this market position?
- Can I adapt my product or my promotion to a specific market niche which is un- or underserved?
- What competition can I expect to face if I am to retain a fair share of the market? What competitors will I have to outclass, outprice, or outmaneuver to take a strong market position?
- Do I have sufficient advertising and marketing dollars to launch a campaign strong enough to hold my market position?

Figure 6–3 shows some of the choices the craftsperson can make on possible positioning decisions.

Positioning Choices

The following are some of the techniques available for your craft product. You can position by:

- Price
- Quality
- Value
- Exclusivity
- Durability
- Guarantee
- Age
- Income

- Investment Potential
- Product Life (Longevity)
- Uniqueness
- Decorative Qualities
- Uses
- Credit Availability
- Gender

Fig. 6–3. There are a variety of choices to position your craft product in the marketplace. Some are conceptual, and cost-free, while others have a price tag. A number of positioning techniques can be used at the same time either to aid sales or to reach different consumer audiences.

A Positioning Caution

If you do not develop an effective method to position your product in the marketplace, you may find that potential consumers will do the product positioning themselves. This process can be almost automatic, and leave you with a product that may carry the stigma of low price, low end of the line, filler item status, or other hard-to-dispel labels. To turn things around, you may have to start the positioning process all over again with a product design change, new packaging, and a different promotional campaign.

Chapter Highlights

- Defined consumer purchasing considerations in marketing are known as perceptions.
- When a number of consumer perceptions are grouped together they are called collective perceptions.

- One of the important segments of the marketing mix is positioning. In the marketplace, positioning presents a variety of possibilities, depending on your product.
- It is possible to position your product by selecting a segment of a market and targeting your efforts in a particular direction. You may also position your product to meet different market objectives.
- You can position your product by perception, by place, by price, by packaging, by general target market, and by specific market mix, as well as many other considerations.
- In some instances, your product line can be positioned to serve an underserved or poorly-served market.
- It is always important to develop an effective positioning posture. If not, the process may fall to consumers and you will find it difficult to change their perceptions.

CHAPTER 7

Packaging Your Craft

The Importance of Packaging

Competition for the consumer dollar is fierce. Every business day of the year nearly thirty new products hit the marketplace. Each of these products vies for a share of the market. Your competitors are also some of the businesses and their advertising agencies who crank out thousands of public relations, advertising, and sales promotions messages each day in an effort to grab the consumer spotlight for their products. The ability to meet this competition is one of the goals of a planned marketing campaign. In later chapters we will discuss promotional techniques to help you do this. This chapter focuses on packaging and how it can enhance product sales.

Packaging can serve to protect and position your product, to identify it, to advertise it, and to help sell it. *Packaging* generally means a physical wrap or container, card, bag, or box in which an item is packaged for display, protection, shipment, or storage. Packaging, however, can also have another meaning. A packaged deal, for example, gives the potential buyer the perception of added value or special benefits. The average purchaser likes a packaged deal when buying a gift for a friend or relative. A pre-packed craft product resolves not only the problem of gift selection but also the problem of presentation.

Many craft products, especially those sold at craft fairs, are turned over to the purchaser without any packaging consideration. The articles are brought to the show booth in bulk and bagged as sold. Some craftspeople wrap in newspaper and hand the product to the buyer in a used plastic or paper bag. Other vendors, in varying degrees, consider packaging only for products to be sold in shops, galleries, and boutiques.

Benefits of Packaging

Packaging for a craft product offers a number of benefits. It can, of course, protect breakable or delicate items like pottery, glassware, or handmade dolls. In some instances, the primary function of packaging may be to make the product easier and more convenient to handle. It may also be used as a protective vehicle for storing the product in mint condition or shipping it safely.

Packaging may also be used to identify a particular product or product line and its designer or producer. There are times when an identifying name or product brand cannot be put directly on the item itself. Identification on the packaging box, pouch, bag, or even on tying ribbon may be especially useful in this instance. Product identification through packaging becomes an extension of the promotional or advertising process. A case in point is the shiny, light blue box or shopping bag with the simple Tiffany logo. The box, the wrapping, and the bag have become well known to the gift recipient for whom they spell class and elegance. The distinctive packaging also serves as a walking billboard.

Differentiating one product from another can also be accomplished by packaging. A color or shape consistently used in the packaging process can serve as a means of separating one product from a similar one. There are, for example, many types of ketchup on the market. Heinz's distinctive bottle shapes have come to serve as instant identification for the majority of consumers.

Distinctive packaging may also call attention to the products and enhance their perceived value. Creative packaging may provide the force that effectively helps your product stand out in a display.

Compare for a moment a diamond ring packaged in a small plastic zip-top bag with one in a silk-lined velvet, suede, or leather jewelry box. Consider rows and rows of beautifully-crafted earrings or necklaces hung from hooks on a display board, and a few samples of the very same pieces, each resting on a tasteful silk or satin pouch. Which do you think can carry a higher price tag? Consider the child's toy peeping out of tissue or tinsel in a slick shopping bag; or the silk scarf gracefully folded in a clear plastic box girdled with a stretch silver or gold cord and bow, as opposed to toys on the table and scarves slung over a hanger. Which do you think will have greater impact on the potential shopper? Which do you think bespeaks greater value?

What Kind of Packaging?

We have mentioned wrappings, tissues, cords, ribbons, pouches, boxes, and bags. There are also shredded papers, silk or other fabric envelopes, flat or folded cards, balloon and bubble wraps, and more. There is sufficient variety in each category to meet your specific objectives; that is, to add the benefit you feel is important. Within each category, there are standard variations in size, shape, color, and quality. If your needs are sufficient, and you are willing to pay the price, there are also suppliers who will produce uniquely-designed or shaped containers for your products.

At the Dole Plantations in Hawaii, gifts of many types can be sealed in new, authentically-labeled Dole pineapple cans. This enables tourists to buy gifts manufactured in many parts of the world as legitimate souvenirs of Hawaii.

If you believe that your product sales might be increased by canning, you, too, can buy the necessary equipment and supplies from firms dealing with commercial food processors or from companies supplying the needs of home canners. If, on the other hand, you believe your sales might grow from packaging that allows total visibility of the product, you might consider balloon- or shrink-wrapping equipment.

If visibility is an objective, you could also consider a box with a clear plastic window or one entirely fabricated of clear plastic. Is visibility the prime objective? Consider how each design and each type or kind of plastic, flexible, rigid, poly, acrylic, fiberglass, styrene, lucite, etc, affects the consumer perception of product value.

It is important to consider not only size, but also packaging strength, shape, and color requirements. You may want to think about how the packaging will lend itself to various display possibilities. You may also want to consider the potential of package reuse for the customer, especially with modern trends toward recycling. The delicately-printed lavender boxes that once held Louis Sherry chocolates have become prized, pricy collectors' items. Many other gift boxes have been recycled as stationery holders, pen and pencil cases, button boxes, and repositories of varied and sundry other items. Each time they are used, they are reminders of the product and the producer, as well as meeting conservation goals.

Product package design and size should also be considered in terms of convenience of storage, transport, and display. This is especially important if you are doing a lot of shows or if your showroom and storage space is limited. Whether packaging material folds flat or whether boxes fit within each other are considerations not to be ignored.

Costs of Packaging

No matter what type of packaging you use beyond the newspaper and recycled plastic or paper bags and boxes, packaging will add to your costs. If packaging is a necessity, these costs must be considered along with production costs. However, effective packaging, as we have noted previously, may allow you to increase the selling price of a product by adding to the buyer's perception of value. Packaging costs should be weighed against the potential for producing additional profits.

There are two distinct types of packaging. One places each individual item for sale in its own separate container. The other packaging process is known as *bulk packaging*. This process is usually used for shipping to a store, gallery, or other sales outlet. A number of the same products are packed together in one packaging unit with enough insulating material, shredded paper, styrofoam peanuts, foam, bubble wrap, or the like to keep the individual pieces from damaging each other or being damaged. When the products arrive at the sales point, the bulk package is opened and the individual items are placed for sale.

Products may be packaged in various types of containers, some of which we have mentioned above. Selection should take into consideration the various possible uses for the packaging. A light cardboard box might be used for display and light storage, but might not be strong enough for, and usually cannot be used for, shipping. A heavy corrugated container, on the other hand, might be used for shipping and storage, and, if properly designed with a coated stock cover might be appropriate for display of certain products.

If you can afford to, it is generally cost effective to have your name and logo emblazoned on your packaging. If you are ordering in limited quantities and find the cost of individualization prohibitive, you can order, at a comparatively low cost, multi-purpose labels that can be used to identify your box. If you are having packaging imprinted, it generally does not add significantly to the cost to have salient product details printed on the sides of the box. These might include product name and address for re-orders, directions for use, warranties or guarantees, and other useful consumer information.

Printing can be done in black or one or more colors, or metallic ink. It is more expensive to use two or more colors or metallic ink, and still more expensive to use full color. In some instances, the packaging manufacturer will prepare the artwork and printed material for your packaging for a fee. If not, you will have to provide camera-ready art.

Purchasing Packaging

Containers for packaging can generally be purchased in lots of 100, 500, 1000, and upward. There is usually a minimum order. Like most products, the more you purchase, the lower the price per piece.

Container companies manufacture boxes to order and also have stock boxes in a broad range of sizes. Stock boxes are containers for which dies are available. Usually a supply of stock sizes is kept on hand. These factors act to keep prices down, so it makes sense to check a number of sources to locate stock-sized containers for your product.

Most manufacturers and distributors will supply catalogs of their products and will send samples to legitimate customers. This helps you try to adapt stock boxes to one or more of your products. If samples are not available without charge, it pays to pay a reasonable fee to make sure that you will be ordering what you want to receive.

Some suppliers are also sources of filler and protective material. White plastic foam "peanuts" come in a number of different shapes to be used to fill in open packaging space. Bubble-wrap, a plastic wrapping material composed of sheets of trapped air bubbles of varying sizes, may be purchased in sheets or rolls.

Some sources of packaging materials are listed in the appendices of this book. You can locate other sources in the Yellow Pages or in trade magazines.

Chapter Highlights

- A good package for a craft item can mean a positive identification for your product.
- Packaging has the capacity to enhance product sales by developing some additional buyer interest in the item.
- From a consumer's standpoint, some products can be differentiated by using specific types of packaging.
- Packaging is also used to protect a product during its storage and shipping.
- When selecting packaging, it is important not only to select the proper size but also determine the strength of the box and its shape.
- There are two distinct types of packaging. They include individual and bulk packaging. In the first process, individual products are placed in single boxes. In the latter, a number of products are packaged together.
- If possible, identify your product, company name and address, and instructions for product use on the packing box.
- Boxes are usually purchased in lots of 100 pieces and up. The larger the quantity purchased, the lower the per box price.
- A stock box is a box that a manufacturer regularly carries as part of the company's inventory.

CHAPTER 8

Selling Your Craft

The bottom line of all product marketing programs is the actual sale of your craft items. The tools and techniques that are discussed throughout this book have been designed to alert and expose potential consumers to your craft products. If you have done the job effectively, potential customers will know about and want to purchase you product.

Direct marketing is one sales direction, and will be covered at more length in Chapter 11. Selling your product in the marketplace, one-on-one, is the technique that will be covered in this chapter.

The Show Route

Craft shows abound in all sections of the country. They are put together by professional show promoters or volunteer fund raisers for not-for-profit organizations. Some move their shows to warm weather climates in the winter months, and reverse the process during the summers. Others specialize in certain sections of the country and run their shows only in these areas. Some of the shows are run in malls while others are held outside under open skies in fields or parking lots.

In some instances, promoters rent halls as venues for their craft expositions. At other times, working with a community group, they may organize a street or city fair with craft booths dominating the event.

Churches, synagogues, fire departments, schools, and many other community groups also sponsor craft shows.

Craftspeople almost always pay for the privilege of exhibiting at these craft shows. They pay for booth space, and the number of days that they attend a show. Prices may range from $10 per day for space in a parking lot show sponsored by a local community group to hundreds of dollars per day for space in a metropolitan exhibition hall craft show sponsored by an established promoter.

A booth or exhibit space can be almost any size, depending on the show venue and the promoter. The 8 × 10 booth, for example, is the most common size provided by exposition supply companies. These supply companies rent the structural piping, colorful backdrops, and dividers that form booth layouts for hotels, convention and exposition halls. If a craft show is being held at an inside strip mall, the hall space may be limited, necessitating long, narrow booth space, or some other variation.

There are a number of national craft trade journals that provide you with the locations and other pertinent information about craft shows throughout the country. There are also regional newspapers and newsletters that carry similar information on a more local basis. Show information includes the name, date, and location of the event, and the name, address, and/or phone number of the show promoter. In some instances, the show space charge is provided.

The information is usually printed well in advance so that you can schedule the shows to suit your needs and plans. Solicitation ads from community groups and promoters about forthcoming craft shows are generally found in local newspapers, either in the display or classified sections. Sometimes there are press releases in the arts, leisure, or entertainment sections. It is also possible to place your name on mailing lists for show applications from selected promoters.

Juried Craft Shows

There are a number of ways to gain entry into a craft show, no matter where it is scheduled to be held. At some shows, a craftsperson can participate merely by requesting an entry form for the show and paying the entry fee. As long as there is room in the show, the promoter will accept the vendor.

Juried shows, however, work differently. Every craftsperson who applies does not automatically get into the show. Juried shows usually require that the craftsperson supply photographs, slides or transparencies of the work that he or she intends to display at the event. These are viewed and "judged" by the promoter or a committee seeking to elevate the quality of the show for the benefit of all vendors.

Promoters choose to jury shows for a number of reasons. The most important, as we have noted, is to assure the quality of the exhibits. Jurying also helps the promoter limit the number of similar types of crafts in a show.

Some show promoters require a jury fee to accompany each application. This may or may not be returned if the craftsperson is rejected for entrance into the show. The jurying system can be simple, requiring only one-person approval for acceptance or rejection, or more complex. At some shows, a number of craft experts working together as a panel make the decisions.

While the intention of the juried show is to maintain a standard of quality exhibits as well as to limit the number of similar crafts, the system can and does eliminate certain craftspeople. This can occur if the slides or photos do not illustrate the product effectively, if the jury panel has personal prejudices against certain types of crafts, or if the panel's vision of the show precludes various works.

If you intend or are asked to participate in a juried craft show, always send in your best photographs or transparencies. If you have any doubts about them, use a professional photographer. Also remember to follow instructions for the jurying process exactly. If rules state that you need three slides of your craft and one of your display, do exactly that.

Show Competitions

Some shows offer an added incentive to craftspeople exhibiting at events. These incentives may be sponsored by the show producers or area craft organizations. Craft show incentives can take the form of competitions with prizes in varying medias such as ceramics, leather, jewelry, fabric, and the like. In many instances, the prizes are colored ribbons or medals which denote prize position, for example, 1st, 2nd, or

3rd place in a section. At other times, a cash award or gift accompanies the ribbon or medal.

Some organizations arrange for purchase prizes, that is, an assurance that area businesses, museums, or individual collectors will buy certain prize-winning pieces.

The important thing about an award won at a competition is not so much the value of the cash or gift, but the fact that a prize was won. The award, which in effect says: "Your craft product is the best!", provides a publicity peg from which news releases can be generated. If a photograph is taken when the award is presented, copies should be used in your press kit. If the prize has been awarded at a prestigious craft competition, it can increase the value of some of your other craft items.

Exposition Hall Shows

For many craftspeople, it is often much simpler to exhibit craft products in an enclosed exposition hall. The booth, the exhibitor, and the craft products are not at the mercy of the weather. Electricity, lighting, and a water supply are available on request, though there may be a charge for these extra services. The promoter makes space assignments in the hall for the individual craftspeople and is responsible for public relations for the event—advertising, and drawing visitors, viewers and buyers.

Generally, there is a modest admission charge for the public to view the show. These fees go to the promoter to pay for hall rental, advertising costs, security and cleanup people, and other expenses involved in the effective operation of the show.

Some show promoters give each visitor with a sheet, leaflet, or booklet listing the names of craft show exhibitors and their exact positions and booth numbers in the hall. For easy reference, the list may even be divided into types of craft products. There are often maps in the booklets to guide the visitors around the hall. Sometimes the addresses of the craftspeople are provided in the booklets. This is particularly useful to craft exhibitors if show visitors want to place future orders after the event is over.

Some craft show promoters go to great lengths to help craftspeople sell their products. They recognize that successful, satisfied craftspeople will return to their shows in the future. At one show, craft prizes were awarded hourly in drawings held for show visitors. The promoter bought the prizes from vendors at the show. At another show, long tables were placed to divide the booth area. The tables were surrounded with a security rope. Any craftsperson exhibiting at the show could place one of his or her products on the table in the enclosure along with a name card, booth number, and price. Show hall lights illuminated the area.

Craft shows in exposition halls usually have specific hours for set up, close down, and operation. Booths must be set up and ready before the show opens, and may not close down until the official end of the event. Craft vendors are required to have their booths manned during all show hours.

In states requiring sales tax collection, craftspeople must follow state sales tax regulations.

Signed contracts between the promoter and the craftsperson prior to the show date are generally required. The contract specifies the charges for the show, date, and location. It may also detail the items that will be exhibited as well as outline show rules and regulations. Many contracts also contain a clause which holds the promoter harmless from any liability.

Outdoor Craft Shows

Large outdoor craft shows sponsored by promotion companies usually use the same guidelines as exposition hall shows. They require craftsperson contracts and adherence to any state sales tax regulations. Specific craft booth areas are designated by the promoter, and craftspeople are expected to abide by the rules stipulated.

There are a number of specific differences between the two types of shows. Some outdoor craft show promoters arrange for a camping area for their crafts vendors. These are sections set aside on the property where craftspeople can set up tents or place their camping vehicles for the duration of the show. There is usually also a great deal more parking space for show visitors available at outdoor events. At most shows, parking is free. If the parking area is located any distance from the main exhibition area, some promoters provide jitneys or buses to and from the shows. Exposition hall craft shows, especially in large cities, depend on parking garages and lots. There is generally a charge for parking.

Vendors are more prone to put on demonstrations of the techniques of producing their craft items at outdoor shows. This may be because there is usually more aisle space available. Exposition hall craft shows often set aside stage space, apart but near the booth area, for vendors interested in exhibiting production techniques.

One of the greatest detriments to an outdoor craft show is the weather. If it rains, attendance drops. If the weather becomes terribly hot, potential visitors prefer the swimming pool. Some craft show promoters resolve some of the risk by providing huge exhibition tents in which multiple craft booths are laid out. Many craftspeople travel with their own small tents, tarps, or protective awnings so that they are not at the mercy of inclement weather.

Mall Shows

Mall shows are similar to exposition hall events. In some instances, they are put together by a show promoter, while at other times, mall management handles the event. The shows generally require a contract between the craftsperson and the promoter, and there is a charge levied for booth space. The craftspeople at the mall shows, like other craft events, must adhere to local state sales tax regulations. They are obligated to remain at their booths during mall hours and are subject to normal mall rules.

One of the large differences between the two types of shows is the potential traffic pattern. Although a promoter or mall management may advertise a mall show, the really heavy flow of show viewers and potential customers is heavily dependent upon the normal mall traffic flow. If the mall stores are involved in holiday advertising or special promotions, a strong flow of consumers should be expected. If there is no outstanding mall promotion in progress, the traffic pattern will be normal for the particular time of the year in which the show is being held.

Another difference between an exposition-type craft show and a mall show is that many consumers come to an exposition hall craft show anticipating making purchases. The mall craft show, to many shoppers, on the other hand, is just another activity available at the mall. They usually come to a mall to make selective purchases or to window shop at the venue. If they see craft products of interest, and they have expendable income, they may make purchases.

Prior to both mall craft shows and exposition hall craft shows, many craftspeople often self-promote. They send informational cards or letters to former customers and/or special mailing lists advising the recipients that they will be at a specific craft show. The cards sometimes can be turned in at the craft booth for a 10, 15 or 20% discount on any craft merchandise purchased at the event, or for a free gift.

Country, County, and Community Fairs

Country, county, and community fairs are generally held in areas such as religious hall basements, veterans meeting halls, or county fair exhibition buildings, schools, or other public or quasi-public structures. Frequently, the craft show is just a part of a larger exhibition or show, festival, or fair.

Community members of the sponsoring organization usually serve as show chairpeople for fairs of this kind. These individuals often make the original contact with the craftspeople, provide contracts, send out instructions for the fair, lay out booth space. and oversee the program on the day of the event.

You should be cautious about local fairs, in fact, you should make judgments about all of the craft events at any venue before you sign up for space. Your judgments as to whether to participate should be based on a number of factors:

- Is this a first time event?
- What type of advertising and promotion is planned for the show?
- If the craft show has run in prior years, what were the attendance figures over the past three years?
- How many craft vendors will be at the show selling the same or similar product?
- Is there a convenient way for you to unload your craft products at your booth?
- Are there any union or special charges that must be paid in addition to the craft booth fee for unloading or loading your products at the booth, or for any other special services?

- What type of restroom facilities will be available at the show?
- Are easy-access parking facilities available for your vehicle during the show?
- If you sign up for a booth at an early date, will you be given any space preference?
- Will electricity, water, or other services you need be available?

Show Selection Guidelines

A craftsperson needs to follow certain guidelines for all types of shows as well as country, county, and community fairs. Before you commit yourself to spending a great deal of time, energy, and important budget dollars participating in a particular craft show, consideration should be given to a number of elements. Once these factors have been investigated, you should be able to make an effective decision about which show or shows to select for your marketing efforts. The following are some practical guidelines that you can use in your search for this information.

- Always read the promoters' contract rules and regulations carefully to be sure that your craft products fit all the show requirements. *(If you do this, you will not be disappointed by being shut out of a show at the last minute.)*
- Determine from the available records of past shows the projected attendance of the craft show in which you wish to participate. *(If a promoter refuses to reveal attendance information about previous shows, it may be advantageous to pass up the show.)*
- Try to learn as much as you can about the projected audience of a show. Determine the average income level, age level, type of audience (e.g., upscale professionals, senior population, etc.), and type of region in which show will be conducted (e.g., many new homes, old homes, single family houses, apartments). Try to judge whether your craft product will be attractive to the purchasing audience. *(Once you become familiar with the potential marketing segments, you can then make intelligent pricing and product decisions.)*
- Whenever possible, get a count of the total number of exhibitors expected at the craft show. *(This may be a fair indication of the show's potential.)*

- Find out how many of the craftspeople at the show will be marketing the same craft item that you produce. *(You may have to develop some creative marketing techniques to match and beat the competition.)*
- Before signing up for the event, try to establish, exactly where on the show floor your craft booth is to be situated (Fig. 8–1). Will it be placed at a row end, in the center of traffic, directly adjacent to the show entranceway, off by itself, etc.? *(If you know the placement in advance, you can (a) send cards out to potential customers with the booth number; (b) make special decorating arrangements to attract viewers based on booth placement; and (c) develop special marketing techniques to increase the flow of customers to your booth.)*
- If you use a "follow the sun" (northern areas in summer/southern areas in the winter) pattern of craft show exhibiting, make sure to have a complete listing of all shows in the country well in advance so that you can make a wise routing selection. *(Many shows fill up rapidly so you may want to make your decisions early.)*

Designing a Craft Show Booth

Your craft booth should be attractive, durable, simple to set up and break down, and easy to transport. Booths can be simple or elaborate in design (Figs. 8–2 and 8–3). Some booths just use one or more tables covered with cloths. Others may be built or constructed out of a variety of materials including wood, metal, PVC pipe, glass or a combination of products. You can also purchase ready-made booths from manufacturers who specialize in this type of construction (Fig. 8–4).

The booth must also be capable of displaying your products in an attractive manner that calls out for customers not only to browse, but to buy. When you set up your booth, try to do it in a manner that can protect items from potential theft. If you are a jewelry maker, you might want to display your more expensive items in closed glass cases. Seconds, irregulars, and outdated products may be displayed to the sides of the booth where oversight may be more difficult.

Most shows now specify that vendors use fire retardant cloths for their booth. These can be purchased in many stores or easily sewn up from fire retardant material bought in local fabric stores.

Many promoters may also specify the color cloths that you use on

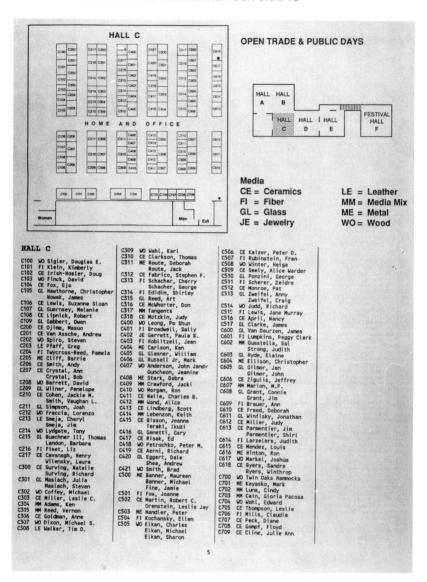

Fig. 8–1. It is always a good practice to know where your booth will be positioned on the show floor prior to the day of the event. In this way, you can prepare your booth and your approach to attracting potential customers in advance.

Fig. 8–2. Booth displays can be simple or ornate. A great deal depends on the market and the audience expected to attend the show. *(Courtesy Skyline Displays Northeast, Inc.)*

your tables. In arena shows, some promoters may also require carpeting for the floor of your booth.

Most craft items appear at their best when viewed under lights. Sometimes you will be exhibiting in outdoor areas where day light floods the booth. However, when exhibiting indoors, auxiliary lighting is extremely important (Fig. 8–5). Clip-on lights, spotlights, and other creative lighting options will provide effective lighting for your booth. Remember to check your lighting from all angles to make sure you are not creating glare spots. Also remember to bring a number of long lengths of electric cord in case you are not close to an electrical outlet. Multi-outlets, and electrical tape to cover electric cords so that people will not trip over loose wire are also often necessary. You might want to check in advance to see if halogen lights are being used in the exhibit venue. This type of lighting has a tendency to cast a green coloring over your products. It can cause color distortions, or completely wash out some product colors. You may want to make arrangements to use a canopy over your display area to handle this problem (Figs. 8–6 and 8–7).

Booths can be designed or laid out in a number of ways depending on

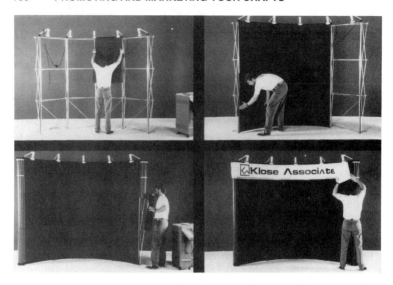

Fig. 8–3. Try to select craft show booth display units that are attractive, easy to erect and break down and simple to transport from show to show. *(Courtesy Professional Displays, Inc.)*

available space and your product (Fig. 8–8). Booth design is also determined by the type of show. Some shows, for example, provide draped exhibit booths. In others, you may want to use screens around the back or sides. There are booths with modular walls, and booth layouts that have only a one-time use. These are made of disposable material and discarded after the show. Special modular pedestals allow set-up and breakdown convenience. Made of heavy cardboard or plastic, these display units fold and stack for storage and provide multiple exhibition possibilities.

Some crafts lend themselves to being set up on one or more tables which are parallel to the aisle viewers will be using. Others can be displayed on lattices, small screens, steps made of boxes or wood, etc. Be creative. If for example you make puppets, you might display them in a frame similar to that of a puppet theater. Other aids such as turntables (Fig. 8–9) can also enhance the image of your crafts.

U- or L-shaped booth designs allow viewers to enter the booth area. More display space is provided by these styles because tables or

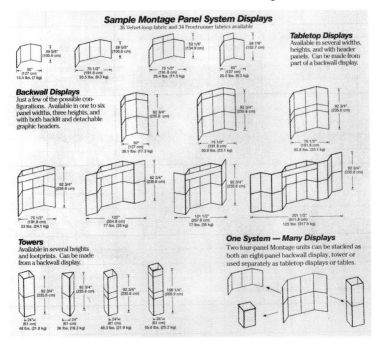

Fig. 8–4. Panel displays allow the craft exhibitor to make a number of different booth display arrangements. *(Courtesy Skyline Displays, Inc.)*

other display pieces are placed along the back wall, one or both side walls, or in combination.

Try to have an area of your booth where customers can talk to you about your product. It is also helpful if there is a place where your buyers can write a check comfortably.

All booths should have signs indicating your name and address. These should be large enough so that customers can read them from the walkway.

Consignment

There are many other ways to sell your craft products. Craft shows and craft fairs are just one option. Consigning your crafts to a craft or gift shop, boutique or department store are other choices. *Consigning*

Fig. 8–5. There are many times when a craft product stands out as a result of proper display lighting. When electricity to the booth is not available, battery-operated display units can light up the job. *(Courtesy ON DISPLAY)*

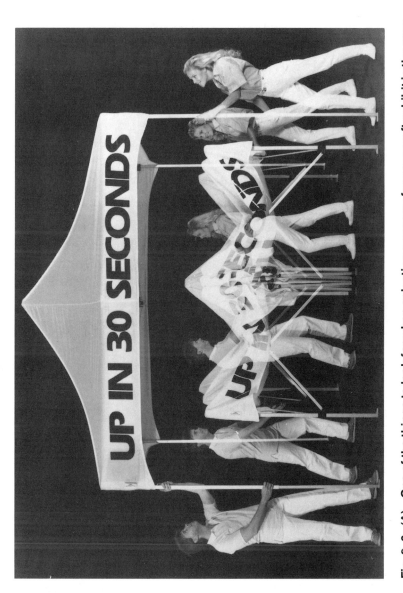

Fig. 8–6. (A) One of the things to look for when selecting a canopy for your craft exhibit is the ease and speed in which it can be put in place. *(Courtesy KD Kanopy)*

Fig. 8–6. (B) As canopies have to be transported from craft show to craft show, weight and ease of packing are important when making a booth canopy selection. *(Courtesy KD Kanopy)*

Fig. 8–7. Easy-to-erect canopies are available to craftspeople in a wide range of sizes and shapes. *(Courtesy World Shelters, Inc.)*

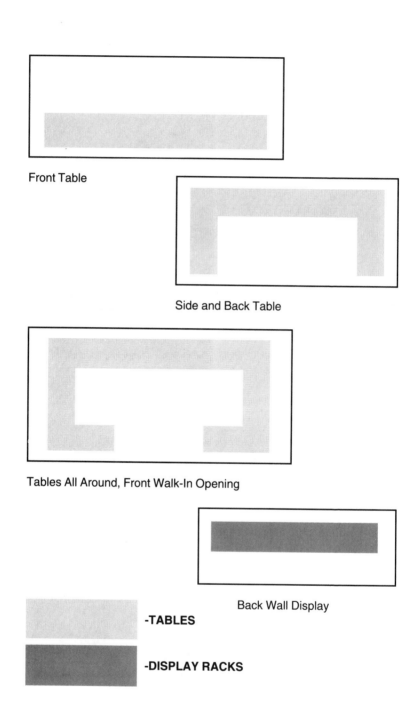

Front Table

Side and Back Table

Tables All Around, Front Walk-In Opening

Back Wall Display

-TABLES

-DISPLAY RACKS

Fig. 8–8. Booth layout options.

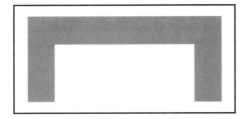

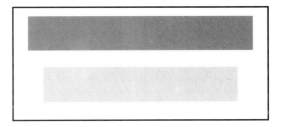

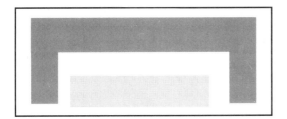

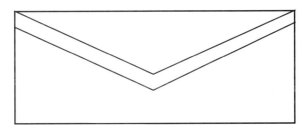

Fig. 8–8, cont.   Booth layout options.

Fig. 8–9. Effective displays for craft products can mean increased sales. Powered by electricity, this turntable display unit can highlight a craft item. *(Courtesy ON DISPLAY)*

means that you offer a product to the shop to sell on speculation. If they sell it, you are paid for it. If they do not, you get your product back and receive no payment.

Each shop has different rules, regulations, and policies regarding pricing, length of time an item stays on display, etc. In some instances, you tell the shop what you expect to receive for each item. They then add on their markup. In others, the shop will determine what they want to pay you for the product. If you agree, they will take your item on consignment. They can then sell it for any price they wish. When your product is sold, the store will give or send you the agreed-upon money. In most instances, expect the shop to take from 33 to 50% of the retail selling price of your product in payment for the consignment service.

You should get a signed receipt for the products you leave with the store on consignment. The receipt should describe the item, indicate the monetary arrangements and any other terms of the transaction.

There are a number of things that you should check before leaving your products on consignment. Find out how long the store has been in business. Also make sure that the shop is insured against fire and theft. You can check with the Better Business Bureau or other such source to pick up background information.

In many instances, storekeepers are willing to accept products on consignment only because they do not have sufficient capital to stock their store adequately. At other times, the store owner may not be willing to speculate on the demand for your type of craft product, preferring to test the market with your consignment pieces before purchasing.

Gallery Shows

Placing your craft products in a gallery can open up a number of marketing possibilities for you. If it is an established gallery, it may provide a long-term stable market for your product line. Your items will be displayed in the best possible way, because once a gallery assigns space to an item, the expectation is for the exhibition area to produce an income. A gallery also provides a longer period of consistent exposure for your product. At a show or a fair, the event concludes in a day or a week, and consumers are no longer exposed to your craft product. The opposite is true of gallery exposure where a changing group of customers moves through the shop on a consistent day-in/day-out basis.

There are a number of different financial arrangements that may be made with a gallery. A system similar to the consignment process may be worked out where you leave your craft items at the gallery at no charge. The items are displayed and payment is made after the sale. The gallery may also purchase your craft products outright. In each of the previous instances, the method of payment, including exact percentages and payment period, is agreed upon ahead of time. Another payment option is known as the guaranteed sale. You settle on a price for your craft product with the gallery owner. Your craft item is displayed in the gallery. If the product does not sell within a specified timeframe, you agree to repurchase the craft item from the gallery for the original price.

In order to develop interest in your craft products and therefore potential sales, the gallery promotes, advertises, and conducts special invitational showings or exhibitions of your line. The invitations are sent to the gallery's customer list, the art press, and to a list prepared by the individual whose work is being shown. The craftsperson is usually expected to attend the program on the opening day of the exhibition to mix with the people who have been invited. The opening day of the show may include a cocktail party or reception.

You should know in advance if you will be involved and responsible for any personal expenditures for the gallery showing or exhibition of your craft products. The length of time the gallery show will run, and any other matters relating to the exhibition, should be clearly understood before initiating the program. Most important, you should know exactly what percentage the gallery will take for selling your craft product, or what financial arrangements are to be. If possible, it is beneficial to have all of these operational details outlined in writing.

Tie-Ins

Opportunities sometimes present themselves for a tie-in between your line of craft items and certain products produced by a manufacturer. The *tie-in* provides the manufacturer with a promotional tool, and gives you the opportunity to sell multiple quantities of your craft products. For example, if you make baby bibs, you might contact a baby food company like Gerber, or if you turn out wooden nut bowls you might seek out a distributor of nuts like the Planter's Company.

To become involved in the process of enhancing sales through tie-ins, it is necessary to have an operation that can produce products in quantity. The production must also be consistent.

Product tie-in possibilities are everywhere. You have only to consider the possibilities as they relate to your product line and make contact with manufacturers or their advertising agencies. A letter or personal visit can explain the process you suggest to the marketing or sales department or to the agency account executive.

If you do develop a tie-in with a company, make sure you have all of the financial arrangements detailed in contract form. For example, you should delineate the amount to be paid by the company for your products, the payment schedule, the responsibility for postage and handling for sending your craft item to the customer, and any other pertinent detail.

Wholesaling

Another option for marketing your product is selling to retail outlets. These include specialty shops, boutiques, department stores, or chains. You should recognize, before you go in this direction, however, that the price you receive for your products will be lower than if you sold them yourself. This is because you will be *wholesaling* or selling in quantity, to the store. The store, in turn, will add a markup to cover sales expenses and profits. The good part about selling to retail stores and wholesaling is that you have the opportunity to sell in quantity. Before contacting the buying departments of the stores, review Chapter 4, *Pricing Your Products,* to determine cost and markup information. If you decide that you want to market your craft products through retail stores, start by locating the potential outlets for your product line. These can include gift shops, department stores, boutiques, and specialty shops. Get a list of stores by looking in the Yellow Pages of the phone book. You can usually find phone books for other geographical areas in the library if you are interested in selling in other locations. Call the targeted stores to find out who the store or department buyer is. You can then either try to set up an appointment by phone to meet with the buyer, or contact the individual in writing to make an appointment to show your line of merchandise.

When you meet with the buyer, be prepared with samples, your product price structure, and possibly bank references. You should also find out in advance what all financial arrangements will be if you do get an order. Do you have to pay shipping? When can you expect payment? When is your order due? Getting this information ahead of time can save problems later.

Once again, be sure that you can meet production dates and standards. Many firms will refuse an order which arrives even a day late and will penalize you for products which are not considered perfect or as agreed upon.

Most of the special sales techniques discussed in this chapter have advantages for a craftsperson. Consignment sales, gallery sales, and wholesale sales of your product offer opportunities for you. These options free you from the time-consuming process of selling your products piece by piece. It allows you to spend more time creating and turning out craft products. The disadvantage is obvious. The profit margin for each craft product is considerably less because the gallery owner, consignment shop, or specialty store has overhead and must make a profit on each sale.

Chapter Highlights

- Crafts shows are usually organized by show promoters whose purpose is to make a profit, or community organizations who use the event as a fund-raiser.
- Craft shows can be held in halls, exposition areas, community build-

ings, city streets, parking lots; in fact, any suitable area that can comfortably hold a gathering of booths and show visitors.

- Craftspeople usually pay a fee for the privilege of renting space at a show and exhibiting their products.

- Juried craft shows usually require that the craftsperson supply one or more photographs, slides, or transparencies of the work that is to be displayed at a show. In some cases, photos, slides or transparencies of your exhibit also required.

- Promoters use juried shows to assure the quality of an event, and to limit the number of similar types of crafts.

- Some craft show promoters run competitions at the shows and award prizes for different craft categories.

- Almost every show promoter, conducting craft shows at any type of venue, requires craftspeople to sign a show contract.

- Many show promoters arrange for camping-out areas for their craftspeople at outdoor craft show events.

- Craft shows conducted in malls are usually sponsored by a show promoter, or someone from mall management.

- County, country, and community fairs use religious hall basements, veterans meeting halls, county fair exhibition buildings, and other community locations for craft shows. They may also rent spaces at malls or other venues.

- Craft booths should be attractive, durable, simple to set up and break down, and easy to transport.

- All booths, no matter what craft product they are exhibiting, should have signs identifying the craftsperson by name or business name.

- Your craft products can be taken on consignment by a shop, boutique, etc. When the product is sold the consignee receives a percentage of the selling price and you receive the balance.

- A gallery can display, highlight, and introduce your craft product to the buying public.

- A tie-in provides a manufacturer a promotional tool, and gives the craftsperson the opportunity to sell multiple quantities.

- Craft products can also be wholesaled to retail stores; however, the craftsperson must expect a smaller profit.

CHAPTER 9

Promotional Craft Marketing Tools

Developing Promotional Programs

Promotional tools serve to draw attention to your craft products. The techniques involved in promotion can inform potential customers not only about the existence of your work, but also its features, design, structure, uses, cost, and, most important, the qualities that make it desirable.

Some promotional tools give potential buyers a point-of-purchase, hands-on, close-up look at your product, while other tools communicate your product and its attributes through art, photography, print, or video.

Effective promotion can be costly. It is, however, possible to maximize the effectiveness of even a limited budget by creatively using low- or no-cost promotional vehicles. This chapter will discuss a range of promotional options to help you make the most of the dollars you spend.

Promotional Opportunities at Craft Shows

There are many promotional options open to the craftsperson. Some are inexpensive to launch, and others come with a hefty price tag. Some are easy to implement, while others take a great deal of preparation. Some merely take the thought and effort of making the most of every opportunity.

The craft show booth is a case in point. As we noted in the previous chapter, shows are held in shopping centers or malls, churches, schools, arenas, halls, fields, and fairgrounds. They are often held in conjunction with fairs, festivals, and other special events. They offer opportunities to move your craft products, not only to those people attracted generally to the show, but also to those whom you invite specifically.

Some shows have special hours or days set aside for wholesale buyers to preview the wares and make bulk purchases or place orders with the individual craftspeople. If you can and want to sell wholesale, it is worth spending the money to mail postcards or flyers to appropriate wholesalers in the region, giving show dates and times, your booth number, and any special offers. It is important to deal with buyers in as businesslike a way as possible, knowing your production schedules, possible quantity discounts, payment requirements, as well as the answers to any of their specific questions. Many buying relationships initiated at shows result in continuing orders and sound business growth.

For the wholesale buyers and for the throngs who crowd the aisles, there are activities that you can engage in to enhance sales. It may sound simplistic, but it should be recognized that the objective of exhibiting at shows is twofold: first, to get as many of these show visitors as possible to stop by and see your booth, and then to convert as many of these viewing visitors as possible into product purchasers.

Success in selling your craft products at a fair, show, or event depends on a number of factors. Each, to an extent, is dependent on the other. If all of the factors are in synch, you can reasonably expect to have a great show.

Display Booths as Promotional Tools

The major factors affecting your sales include *booth design, booth location*, the *craft products* you exhibit for sale, the *actions or activities conducted* at your booth, the *attitude of the individual or individuals working at your booth*, the *attendance* at the show, and the *timeframe* during which the show is conducted.

Booth Design: Some booths practically tell people to walk by and ignore them, while others are an invitation for viewers to visit. Design your booth so that it is colorful and inviting. Use lights, balloons, banners, backdrops, etc. to pique interest. Leave space so that people can comfortably see your products. Make your booth stand out from its neighbors and its competitors no matter where the latter are located in the show. Use signs effectively. Have them pose interesting questions to which people might want to learn the answers. Experiment with different layouts to see which might be more inviting than the standard draped table. A U-shaped arrangement, for example, draws people out of the aisle and into the booth. Try to design or purchase a booth layout that is simple to erect, easy to dismantle, not too heavy, but is also attractive, easy to maintain, and adjustable to varying show sites.

Consider using wall displays, grid hangers, clotheslines, painted pegboards, mirrors, oversized vases or baskets, an antique or unique eyecatcher, or other decorative pieces that may enhance your product display or offer the viewer better perspectives. Consider, too, the pull of registering for a prize drawing, or the sign that calls out, "SHOW SPECIAL" or "SALE".

Booth Position: You can usually get the best choices by registering early for a show. Show sponsors generally assign space on a first-come/first-served basis, although many steady vendors are booked into the same spot year after year. Remember that where-ever your booth is located, if you have a product that people want, they will seek you out. Prime exhibiting spaces are different for everyone. Most sponsors will respect your request not to be placed next to someone selling the same or similar products. If you have a choice, after studying the show layout, request a space that places your booth in the main traffic pattern flow. Corner booths offer visibility from two sides, but are frequently more expensive. If your products are large, the corner location may be more advantageous than a double booth, regardless of the higher cost. If you are placed in what you feel is a less advantageous area, try to make up for it with a creative, attractive booth that calls attention to your exhibition.

Craft Products: Bring only your most attractive products to exhibit and sell. Make sure that you have a sufficient quantity on hand for the event so that your booth does not look sparse. Less costly products, overruns, end of runs, discontinued items, and irregulars should be displayed separately to the front and on only one side of your booth. If you showcase your valuable products to limit theft, make some display for customers to touch and feel.

Do not just lay your products on the exhibit table. Set up an interesting, eye-catching arrangement. Create steps out of wooden blocks or simple cardboard boxes and cover them with designer papers or fabrics before laying out your products. Invest in appropriate drapery materials, table coverings, and display cases. An expensive-looking display makes your product look pricier. A cheap-looking display detracts from product value.

There are several schools of thought about whether pricetags should be placed on every product and whether these price tags should be visible to the buyer. In most instances, buyers appreciate being able to see the price of articles on display. Many viewers overestimate the cost of unpriced items. If there is heavy traffic at a booth, some people will not wait to ask the price. On the other hand, having a potential buyer ask about the price gives you an opportunity to engage in one-on-one selling: to talk about the piece, how it is made, how it compares with others of varying prices, etc. Generally, if all of the products for sale in a specific section of the booth are priced the same, a sign will suffice. Showcased jewelry with varying prices is frequently individually pricetagged but the tags are reversed so that the prices are not immediately visible.

If you know that there will be certain questions asked about your product line, prepare a flyer or brochure that answers these questions. If there is space in the booth, use signs to highlight any special features of your product. Words like "original design," "washable," "imported fabrics," "handmade paper," "lead-free glazes," and others that draw attention to your work, should be highlighted.

If possible, use your product at the show. If you are selling jewelry, wear it. If your product is a pipe, keep one in your mouth. If you are selling handpainted silk scarves, drape one over your shoulders, around your waist, or tie it in a fanciful bow or ascot around your neck. If you are selling a lamp, show it lit; toys which can move should at least periodically be put into motion. Whatever the product, show as many ways to use it as possible. Baskets can hold magazines as well as dried flowers, an assortment of rolled socks as well as onions, small toys as well as office supplies.

If you take orders for your craft products, have a photograph album of sample products available for customers to look through and select from.

Booth Activities: In the International Marketplace in Waikiki, scores of vendors sell similar items, most frequently handstrung seed pearls, coral beads and other semi-precious stones. At some booths, vendors sit and string beads, creating necklaces and bracelets for sale. Despite the similarity of their work to that at most other booths and kiosks, these vendors attract larger crowds and make more frequent sales. People who come to craft fairs and shows enjoy seeing things happen. They like to watch a product being created—sewn, painted, carved, or otherwise constructed. Watching the process adds a dimension of interest and a perception of value.

A demonstration at the booth is one of the best ways to draw people. If you plan on working on your product at the booth, make sure to lay out the space so that the maximum number of people can watch you at the same time. Arrange to have help at the booth to answer questions and sell while you are demonstrating. Always have a supply of flyers, brochures, or business cards available so that potential buyers know how to contact you. Put the name of the booth and its number or location on the flyers so that an interested consumer can find you after he or she has completed a tour of the show booths.

If you plan on working on your craft, alert the show promoter. When a newspaper, radio, or TV interviewer is looking for an interesting story at the show, you are an obvious candidate. Some promoters issue printed demonstration schedules or use a public address system to announce when the activity is taking place. Others post schedules on bulletin boards or blackboards.

Check before showtime to make sure that electric, water, or other services you will need are available and working for your booth. If, for example, you require electricity to power a saw or sewing machine, you want to make sure it is in place when you need it. It is a good idea to check with the show promoters when you register for the show to determine what, if any, restrictions there are on demonstrations.

Some promoters set up separate demonstration areas so that show aisles are not congested by viewers. As a bonus, some promoters offer reduced booth fees for demonstrating vendors.

Exhibitor Attitude: The attitude of the individual working at a craft booth plays an important part in the success of the venture. A person who squeezes into a back corner of the booth, reads a book, and seldom looks up does not create much of a buying incentive. A smiling, friendly salesperson who invites questions, and speaks to passing showgoers can actually generate business. A simple smile or hello goes a long way, and a viewer drawn into conversation about a product is more likely to be drawn into a sale. "Are you looking for a gift?" or "That's an interesting tie (or pin, or scarf, or color, or whatever) you're wearing!" or "Do you collect. . . . ?" or "Have you been to this show before?" or "Please feel free to browse," or "Let me know if I can help you," or other similar phrases are good for openers.

While most people do not appreciate an overbearing salesperson, many people like to talk with someone about the craft products they see. Some want to learn more about the product. Some want to know why an item is a good buy. Recognize that there are people who honestly feel that they can produce a similar product at home. Handle them in a friendly fashion, too.

Show Attendance and Time Frame: If attendance at the show is good, you and other exhibitors will generally enjoy satisfactory sales. If attendance lags, your sales could conceivably suffer. Attendance is affected by the weather, external events, and many other causes. Insufficient promotion and publicity can also cause attendance problems. While show advertising is a responsibility of the show sponsor or promoter, many craftspeople boost attendance by letting past buyers and potential customers know where they will be showing. There is a payoff in sending promotional cards, letters, and flyers to a selected mailing list. These communications pieces should give show date, time and place, and, if possible, the show booth position. Some cards note special offers, discounts, or bonus gifts, introduce new products, or picture outstanding pieces. If you have time, the impact of the mailing is heightened considerably by a handwritten note, no matter how brief. "Hope you're enjoying your last purchase," or "I hope you'll stop by," or "I think you'll enjoy seeing this," or similar lines often cause people to come out even in poor weather.

The time of the year also affects attendance and sales. The pre-Christmas-Chanukah periods draw the greatest numbers of viewers and buyers. The periods before Valentine's Day, Mother's and Father's Days, and June weddings and graduations are also times of heightened buying activity. In tourist areas, however, attendance is greatest during "the season." In warm climes, the season is generally winter when snowbirds flock to the sun. In Scottsdale, Sedona, and Jerome, popular craft centers in Arizona, the season runs from December through March, for example; while on Cape Cod or in the New York State Catskills, the season starts on July 1 and is over on Labor Day.

Show sponsors frequently schedule events year-round, varying their rates for special times of the year. Even if your initial budget is limited, it may pay to consider the higher-priced dates which offer the greatest audience potential.

Promotional Photographs

One of the easiest, and probably the quickest, promotional techniques is to make available color *photographs of your product.* These photographs can, of course, become part of your sales album. They can be and frequently are also printed in large quantities as post cards. One side of the card contains the photo, and a section of the reverse side of the card is used to describe the craft item. There is usually also space on the reverse side to announce a forthcoming craft show, and space for the mailing address and a postage stamp.

If you use this technique, choose a photograph that clearly displays your product. Make sure that the background does not distract from the product. Lighting is important, too. Be careful that shadows do not hide or distort any important product features. Decide whether the photo is to be used in a horizontal or vertical position. This is important if you are laying out a postcard.

Always remember to put your name, address, and telephone number somewhere on each craft photograph. Generally, this information is printed on the reverse side of the print. If applicable, also include the name of your craft item. People tend to keep your product photograph for periods of time. The contact information is important to purchasing decisions.

You may want to consider using a professional photographer to take the product photo of your craft item to insure a more professional reproduction. Expect to pay a one-time creative fee for this service. Always secure a price estimate before you start a job.

There are two ways to make copies for customer distribution. You can have photographs reproduced in small quantities on photographic paper in any photo studio, or you can use specialty photography shops who will mass produce photographs in quantity at a substantial savings (see supplier list). There are different qualities and weights of photographic paper. If you are considering mailing the prints, keep paper weight in mind. Standard photographs sizes are 3-½ × 5 inches, 4 × 6 inches, and 8 × 10 inches. The size you select depends on the use to which you will put the photos, and also how intricate or detailed your product is. Be sure the size of your photo is sufficient to show features clearly.

An alternative to photo studio print reproductions is the printing process shop. The photograph of your craft product can be reproduced by the thousands in full color on plain paper at a very reasonable cost per unit. There are also shops that specialize in quantity reproduction of color postcards. The initial preparation of the photo for 4-color printing (color separation) is a one-time charge that you will have to include in your costs.

Printed Promotional Items

Brochures

A photograph can provide excellent visual identification for your product. If you also want descriptive space to talk about, and sell your product or products, you should consider a *product sheet, leaflet,* or *brochure.*

Brochures can be simple or complex, plain or ornate. The components will usually include:

Photographs: One or more photos can be used to illustrate your product. Make sure the picture is very clear and well-composed, and illustrates the important features of the item or items you are promoting.

Copy and Contents: Prepare all of your copy carefully. Detail all of the product highlights and consumer advantages and uses. Be descriptive but not too wordy. Be credible in your claims. Do not overuse effusive adjectives. Include the name of your company, address, telephone and FAX numbers in your brochure. This information is vital for consumer contacts.

Design: A brochure should be designed to be eye-catching. Your brochure will probably always be in competition for public shelf or viewing space. The more attractive the brochure, the more attention it will receive. If you are not a graphic artist or using one to design the brochure, spend some time looking at the effective pieces others have used, or study graphic art textbooks at your local library. If the brochure is to be placed in a rack or holder, make sure the top-quarter of the brochure contains the important information about your product. Until it is removed, this is usually the only section that can be seen in a brochure holder.

Colors: A single color or several colors of ink can be used to print your brochure. Using more than one color raises the cost. Full color photographs also add to the cost. If the brochure is to be used alongside your product as a handout, you may want to match the product colors. If your products are identified by a logo in a particular color, you may want to carry that through. If the piece is to be passed out by the thousands at exhibits and shows and you want to keep costs down, a one-color print job may suffice. In some instances, for limited purposes, a single-color print job may be enhanced by the use of pasted-on full color photos.

The color of the paper should also be considered. Buffs, ivories, greys, and pastels are all available as are the new "hot" colors. Depending on the quality of the paper, colored stock may not add substantially to the costs. Colors of paper and ink should always be coordinated.

Paper: If the brochure is to be printed on both sides, use a heavy enough paper so that the printing on either side does not "bleed," or show through. Keep mailing costs in mind when selecting paper for your brochure, remembering that you must also consider the weight of a letter or note, order blank, and any other material to be included in the mailing.

Folds: Brochures can be folded a number of ways. Most brochures are designed to fit a #10 envelope (standard business size) because of the availability. Larger or odd-size envelopes can be costly to purchase and mail.

An 8½ × 11-inch piece of paper, for example, can be turned into a three-panel brochure. Each panel of this brochure would be 3⅔ × 8½ inches. The folds could be from top to bottom, from side to side, or accordioned. Two-panel, four-panel, and irregular paneled folds can also be used.

Size: In addition to sizing brochures to fit available, cost-effective envelopes, it is necessary to determine where the brochures are to be displayed. There are standard-sized brochure display holders, and standard-sized spaces on display racks (Figs. 9–1 and 9–2). In most instances, they are designed to hold standard 3⅔ inch, two- or three-panel brochures.

Deadlines: Set a schedule for the completion of all job parts with

Fig. 9–1. Brochures are excellent marketing tools. In order to be effective, consumers must have easy access to these informational pieces. A display rack is an ideal method to provide this access. *(Courtesy Color Optic Displays, Inc.)*

the print shop and any other suppliers, such as artists and photographers.

You may want to use the services of a layout artist and copywriter to prepare your brochure. Most print shops offer these services, or they are available through the Yellow Pages or as referenced by other craftspeople who have used their services. No matter whom you call upon to layout, write the copy, and print your brochure, you will have to provide the basic product information. Make sure it is complete, and

Fig. 9–2. Brochure display racks ensure that your craft product brochures are adequately displayed to the public. When designing brochures make sure that they are standard-sized so that they fit standard display racks. *(Courtesy Photo Optic Displays, Inc.)*

make sure that anyone who performs work for you gives you a satisfactory product. If you do not think a design concept or copy portrays the image you want, work with the artist or writer until you are satisfied. Make sure that these people understand your customer and your market areas.

After the copy and design concept are complete, it is a good practice to get a response to them from a number of people to make sure that they convey the image, ideas, and information that you want.

Flyers

While the *flyer* is less complex and less costly than the brochure, its basic use is similar. It is usually one page of product information prepared on inexpensive paper, and is most often used where heavy promotional distribution is required.

The flyer is prepared in much the same way as a brochure. Copy, photography, and layout are required. Paper selection and printing ink colors must be chosen, and printing quantities have to be determined. Flyers can be mailed, but generally they are handed out, or picked up at fairs and show booths. Flyer preparation steps include:

- Develop and write product copy.
- Take photographs or make line drawings. Prepare to use this art to supplement product copy.
- Select artist to layout copy. Choose printer. Some artists will take care of all the production and specification tasks for your job.
- Select paper and ink colors for flyers.
- Decide printing quantity.
- Set printing deadline with print shop for job completion.

Newsletters

Newsletters can provide an effective means of one-time or periodic communication between craftspeople and the purchasers of their products. Newsletters offer an opportunity to sell additional new products to past buyers, as well as selling to new customers.

Newsletters can be produced in single page, two-page, or four-page sections. If more than four pages are desired, each additional segment must be prepared in four-page units. The standard newsletter page size is 8½ × 11 inches. Most newsletters are printed with one color ink, usually black, on white paper, although almost any paper color or printing ink may be used. Photographs, singly or in quantity, black and white or color, can be placed in the newsletter.

If you have a computer with desktop publishing capabilities and a laser printer, you can produce a professional-looking promotional newsletter yourself. If you do not have computer capability, you will have to go to a graphic artist and printer to turn out a similar job.

The format for developing a newsletter is similar to that used for producing a flyer or brochure except that more material must be written to fill the pages, and much of this material should be informative or educational. You could discuss the raw materials you use, the special techniques of craftsmanship, and the history of the item. You might use a piece on your background, training, credentials, honors, etc. A column might be devoted to unique uses for the product. Photographs of the production process and the finished product can also be used. An order blank can become part of the newsletter.

In its open position, a four-page newsletter is usually 11 × 17 inches in size. If the newsletter of this size designation is folded in half (to 8½ × 11), then into thirds, it can be mailed in a standard #10 envelope. Many newsletters of this size are designed as self-mailers, that is, they do not require an envelope. The equivalent of one column (one-third to one-half of the page, depending on the folds) is left blank on the outside when the piece is folded. The return address is placed in the upper lefthand corner of the special section of the newsletter. The individual to whom the newsletter is being mailed is placed in the center of the section, and a mailing stamp is placed in the upper right hand corner.

Couponing and Incentive Promotions

Discount Coupons

You probably have been on the receiving end of *discount coupons* or *special incentive promotions*. These offer the potential buyer lower prices or additional merchandise if a purchase is made within a certain time period. Food purveyors, drug companies, restaurants, large chains, and specialty stores, etc., use couponing most frequently.

Coupon offers also have been used effectively in craft promotion. We have previously mentioned the postcard with a product photo on the front and a promotional offer on the back. The offer may be a 10 or 15% discount if the product is purchased at a forthcoming fair. The date, place of the show, and booth number is printed below the discount offer (Fig. 9–3).

If you are planning an enveloped promotional mailing, you may want to consider enclosing some form of discount coupon. A similar coupon can also become part of a newsletter. Coupons may offer straight percentage discounts, or an incentive for the consumer to pur-

---

SAVE 10% - SAVE 10% - SAVE 10% - SAVE 10%

**DISCOUNT COUPON
FOR
SPECIAL CUSTOMERS
OF
BLUE GRASS CERAMICS
MONTROSE, PA**

Visit us at Booth #103 at the Great Falls Craft Fair, Philadelphia, PA on September 30. Receive a 10% discount on all purchases. This discount coupon cannot be used with any other promotion. Only one discount coupon may be used with a purchase.

Fig. 9–3. Discount coupon. Discount or special incentive coupons can be used to promote interest, attendance and sales at a craft show. They may also be used as promotional tools in a direct mail campaign. The coupon should be designed to urge the consumer to respond. Any rules of of the promotion should be clearly explained on the coupon itself.

chase a second product, for example, at half-price. There are many other variations on the discount/incentive theme.

Make sure that all purchasing requirements are clearly spelled out on the discount coupon. The most common rule would be that the coupon cannot be used in conjunction with any other discount or incentive. The special promotion, incentive, or discount should also have a closing date printed on the coupon.

Incentive Promotions

The *incentive marketplace* offers another promotional outlet for the craftsperson. It is a particularly good market because in many instances, the incentives are used as gifts or awards to limited numbers of individuals or small groups so that large product quantities are not required.

An incentive is an award presented by a company to an employee for outstanding service or special achievement. The award is usually an item of quality and may be just a little different than run-of-the-mill store products. The incentive award may be something for personal, home, or business use.

Many companies in your local area may have incentive award programs. You can solicit these companies directly in person or by direct mail. There are also incentive magazines in which you may advertise your product.

Craft Seminars

Teaching people craft production and design techniques is another promotional tool with possibilities for enhancing business growth.

To begin with, craft seminars and workshops serve as a publicity peg. They provide a solid reason to send out press releases and feature stories to the press, radio, and television media. In the body of the seminar article are opportunities to talk about your craft product line. See Chapter 10, Publicizing Your Craft Product, for more extensive information on writing a press release. Your press release may stimulate coverage of the actual seminar or pre-seminar interviews. There are additional opportunities to talk about and receive press coverage of the seminar when its concludes. The printed articles about the seminar can be used background material for your press kit.

Teaching a craft seminar also stamps you as an expert in the eyes of the community and potential buyers. In addition to the promotional benefits, seminars can provide a source of income. A woodcarver we know not only sold handcarved wooden signs to business people in his community, but he gave evening woodcarving lessons to interested individuals from far and wide. Although the risk existed for the woodcarver to put students into personal competition, the spread of his "master carver" reputation through the classes far outweighed the risk.

There is a great deal of information that you can provide in a seminar setting. If, for example, you are a potter, the talk might be purchasing raw materials, and the secrets you've learned working with glazes and kiln temperatures, or you might demonstrate various production techniques.

Seminars can be promoted in newspaper classifieds or life and leisure sections. Attractive flyers or posters can be developed for community bulletin boards. Craft shops selling related supplies are usually happy to pass out seminar flyers—it can mean the sale of raw materials to seminar participants.

A craft seminar can be conducted in your studio if there is space, and students are limited in number. If larger quarters are required and student attendance warrants, public space can be rented.

Videotapes

Go into any video shop and you will find a supply of how-to videotapes on almost every conceivable subject. A how-to video on your product can be useful in promoting your product, and may also produce additional income. When the how-to tape is ready to place on the market, it can serve as a publicity peg. A news release can be sent out describing the tape. See the section of Chapter 10 describing news release preparation. You can send sample copies of the tape to selected editors who may write a feature article about you, your craft product, and the videotape.

While you can use a video professional to create your tape, someone who is proficient with a camcorder can frequently do a credible job. A commercial video can cost upward of $1,000 a minute to produce. A camcorder version can be completed for several hundred dollars, depending on how much editing is required.

A how-to videotape requires the preparation of a script. If you follow the steps you would normally take in producing the product, verbalizing, and writing down each step, you will have the basis of your how-to script. Make sure that the words you use are easy to pronounce. Do not talk too rapidly. Make sure that the verbal flow is smooth.

If you require help in remembering your lines as you move along in the taping, write out the script on large boards, and have someone keep changing the boards as the videotaping progresses. Editing of the tape can smooth some glitches, but if you make mistakes that are too obvious, repeat the section. Be sure that there is sufficient light so that the viewer can clearly see you at work. Closeup lenses should be used to catch the detailed work.

After all of the craft how-to work has been described and videotaped, the raw unedited tape will have to be edited into a final master copy. Arrangements can usually be made at a local television studio for an editing person to help with this process. They will assist you in selecting the best portions of your tape, and add titles, music, and special effects. Expect to pay an hourly charge for this editing service.

The completed master of your how-to videotape will be used to make duplicate tapes. There are video "dupe" houses that can rapidly produce duplicate tapes in mass quantities at a modest cost per tape. Depending on your requirements, these houses can also supply cardboard or plastic jackets for each tape, and prepare promotional and identification labels with or without photographs for each jacket. While you are waiting for the tapes to be duplicated, you may want to design and have promotional posters for your videotapes printed. These will describe your tape and be used at points of distribution in stores and video outlets.

You can also use an artist to design your videotape labels and promotional posters, and also to manage the production of them for you. It will generally take more time to have materials printed than to duplicate the tapes, so plan accordingly and make a schedule.

Once the tape duplication is completed, you will have to develop a price structure for each tape and create a distribution system. The stores will expect to make a profit on each tape sold, so this cost plus your own profit must be built into the price. Possible outlets include craft and hobby shops, as well as video distribution outlets. The video departments of stores are also a distribution possibility. To sell your videotapes to any of these large outlets, you will have to reach through to the buyers at the main office of the chains. You can also contact local video stores on an individual basis.

Your how-to videotapes can also be sold by direct mail to your customer list, to specially-purchased mailing lists, or at your booth at craft shows.

Chapter Highlights

- Promotional techniques are methods that can be used to alert potential customers to your products.
- While promotion can be costly, creative low-cost or no-cost promotional vehicles can be effective marketing tools.

- Craft show promotion is one of the most effective promotional vehicles.
- Product sales at craft fairs can be affected by booth design and position, the craft product, booth activities, the individuals selling at the booth, show attendance and timeframe.
- A craft show booth should be colorful and inviting.
- When exhibiting at a craft show, give consumers an opportunity to make a product judgment by inviting them to handle your product.
- If it is permitted at the show, demonstrate the way your craft item is made. It will usually draw an audience and potential purchasers.
- A smiling, friendly salesperson who invites questions and speaks to passing showgoers can generate business.
- A good color photograph of your craft product can be an excellent promotional tool.
- If you plan on using a craft product photograph, make sure that your name, address, and phone number are on the photo, usually on the reverse side of the print.
- An alternative to studio photo prints is a color offset printing of your photograph.
- Brochures provide space to promote your product. A number of your products can be shown in one brochure.
- A promotional flyer is less complex and less costly than a brochure, but its basic communication use is similar.
- The newsletter format as a tool to promote your craft product offers a great deal of sales, informational, and communications space.
- A discount coupon can often activate a potential customer to make a purchase.
- An incentive is an award presented to an individual for outstanding service or special ability. Craft products can make excellent incentive awards.
- In addition to bringing in an income, a craft seminar can generate publicity for your craft product.
- How-to videotapes can be sold by direct mail to your current customer list or to a specially-purchased list of interested craft buyers.

CHAPTER 10

Publicizing Your Craft Product

This chapter, dealing with publicity and public relations, could fall under the heading of the previous one on promotional craft marketing tools. The decision to create a separate chapter is based on budgetary considerations. All promotions have a price tag. Sometimes they are inexpensive, and in other instances, high ticket items. An important criterion for selecting a promotional program or technique is *cost*, or how it will affect your marketing budget.

Since publicity is free, in the sense that there is no charge for media space or time, it warrants separate treatment, and different techniques are involved.

This chapter will tell you how and where to generate free publicity for your product and yourself. It is entirely possible to obtain a great deal of newspaper, radio, and television exposure at no cost. The secret is to provide print, radio, and television media people with interesting, worthwhile storylines and photo opportunities. In other sections of this book, publicity pegs are discussed. A *publicity peg* is simply a hook on which to hang your story. The hook is designed to create subject interest and reach out to the reader, listener, or editor.

People often confuse advertising with public relations and publicity. You pay for the advertising time or space in which your message appears in newspapers, radio and television. Public relations and publicity messages are unpaid news or feature stories carried by the media. Readers, and rightly so, recognize that *advertising is self-promotion.* It is what you say about yourself. On the other hand, publicity can be, and often is, what editorial people say about you.

You do not pay for editorial publicity space. Readers or listeners have come to understand this, and recognize that what appears in editorial space is *what others say about you.* It adds credibility to your message because a third party, the editor or program director, is in effect endorsing the message.

Publicity is an integral part of public relations. "Public relations," says the Public Relations Society of America, "is a management function which evaluates public attitudes, identifies the policies and procedures of an individual or an organization with the public interest, and executes a program of action to earn public understanding and acceptance." With this definition in mind, various research techniques are used to determine public attitudes. Products may be designed to satisfy the attitudes or needs of the buying public, and publicity or public information is one of the tools used to communicate to this public.

The functions outlined in the above PR definition are activities many of us automatically perform when we market ourselves and our crafts. Formally or informally, we begin with research and evaluation of the public's attitude toward our work. We try to adjust our operation and products to meet the demands of the marketplace better. We communicate with the target public through publicity and other means to achieve product awareness, acceptance, and sales.

Getting Press

In the parlance of the information profession, *getting press* means having information about your craft product published in the print media, or listened to or viewed over the airways on radio or television. The techniques and tools used to accomplish this are not complex, and require only a moderate amount of attention. Editors, news directors, and show producers consistently are looking for timely and interesting pieces.

You begin a publicity campaign by targeting your audience. Select newspapers, radio, and televisions stations that have the format and the audience that you feel lends itself to your craft product or its story. Target media who will have a genuine interest in your news releases, feature stories, trade press articles, photos, press conferences, and press kits. There is little sense in sending a press release to a heavy metal music magazine, or an astrology journal about your new craft product for children unless it relates to heavy metal or astrology. The editor will have little interest in the product and your release will end up in the wastebasket, your time and postage wasted.

You might, however, consider sending information about your product to media who may not be on the same "wavelength" if you can develop a special story lead. For example, consider the possibilities of sending a story about your handcrafted toy truck to a national trucker's magazine. Develop your article from the editor's standpoint using an interesting and relevant upfront lead or peg. Perhaps the editor will recognize that most of the readers have children or grandchildren for whom the toy might be appropriate. The publicity peg might be a story about toy trucks through history. This certainly ties in with the trucking industry, and many editors look for slightly different angles to fill their magazines. To research background for your story, you might contact the toy industry association. You might also discuss your production techniques, your use of safe paints, and the variety of toy trucks you have available. A product photograph might complement the story. Whatever your product is, you can come up with similar angles to gain placement in special media.

The Press Mailing List

Your *press mailing list* is best developed with two objectives in mind. You must determine both the type of potential buyers you are seeking (the people), and your target market (the area). You can develop a local press mailing list yourself from the telephone business pages and your own general knowledge of the area. If a more extensive press mailing list is required, it can be bought from a mailing list company.

Mailing list organizations are discussed in Chapter 11, *Marketing Your Craft by Direct Response*. The required media names can be purchased in selected quantities by region. The lists are composed of daily newspapers, weekly newspapers, radio and television stations, including cable, city by city. The lists are sold on index cards or on labels for direct application to mailing envelopes.

The names and addresses of a number of list companies are available in the supplier section of this book. They may also be located in telephone or business directories.

Special Mailing Services

There are also publicity distribution agencies who will mail your prepared news release along with the news releases of other companies promoting their products. Their mailings are targeted to selected media lists such as weekly newspapers, dailies, radio and television stations. You can control mailing quantities and select specific sections of the country where you want to target your release. Your release is printed in a format that permits many of the newspapers to remove it from the distribution service mailing and paste it into the pages of their paper.

The process is similar to the card packs and piggy-back mailing services where you pay a charge for the distribution but not for the postage. Charges are based on the size of the news release and the number of media receiving your information.

Publicity Tools

There are many tools you can use to publicize your product. Each has its particular strengths and applicability to specific purposes. The following are some major publicity tools that might be used for your craft product marketing.

- News releases
- Trade press articles
- Feature stories
- Photographs and photo captions
- Press kits
- Press conferences
- Interviews

The News Release

The most popular means of communicating with the press is the *news release*. You use it to tell your story about your product as you want it to be read and seen. You can send the article to as many media sources as you want.

In the body of the news release, you place all of the information that you want to disseminate that might be of interest to the reader. If the information is useful to the editor of a paper or magazine, or news director of a radio or television station, the release may be used in full or part. Or, the release may trigger enough interest so that the editor or news director follows up with a special angle interview or feature.

News Release Format—Before planning the contents of your news release, consider the normally acceptable size and format of the release. The majority of editorial people prefer to see news releases on 8½ × 11 inch white paper, although 8½ × 14 inches is also acceptable. Releases should be typed or computer-generated. Handwritten copy is generally unacceptable. The information should be typed double-spaced, and a margin of at least one inch should surround the release copy.

The top lefthand section of the page should have *release date information*. This lets the editor know whether the information is *for immediate release*, or whether the release has a *specific date for release*. The top righthand portion of the news release page tells the editor where the information comes from and *who to contact for additional information*. The line generally used is: "For Additional Information, Contact:".

A *headline* or *caption* precedes the main body of the release. In a few words, in **BOLD CAPITAL LETTERS,** the headline or caption attempts to capture and explain the subject of the release. The actual copy begins with a designation that alerts the editor to the place where the news release originated. For example, New York, NY; Cleveland, OH; Los Angeles, CA.

At the end of a news release, a pound sign (**####**) or the designation (**- - -30- - -**) tells the editor that the copy has concluded. If the news release information requires additional pages, the word (**more**) follows the release copy on each page to be continued to tell the editor that another page of information follows. The second page begins with a page marking and a repetition of the original news release headline. Editors prefer one-page releases. They also cut stories from the bottom up, so the most important copy should come first in your release.

News Release Structure—Answer the questions *who, when, what, why,* and *where,* and you will have all of the necessary information to prepare your news release. Think of any situation that you may encounter in your craft business: attendance at a craft show in a series of cities;

a story about a new craft product you have developed; a product discount or incentive program you have put into place; a move to a new location; a new partner, associate or senior employee in your craft business. These situations, and many more, will provide you with media story opportunities. Figs. 10–1 through 10–4 will provide you with detailed information on the preparation of news release formats. Fig. 10–5 is an example of a craft fair news release.

Trade Press Articles

Trade press articles are publicity stories about your craft product that are targeted to specific trade magazines. The trucking trade journal we mentioned previously is one of hundreds of similar magazines devoted to a single trade, industry, or profession that may use your stories or press releases. The secret to article acceptance is to make the story highly relevant for the readers of the magazine.

Creating a news release or feature story for a trade journal takes similar preparation to developing a story for most other media. The news release, to be useful as a trade article, would have to be "flushed out" or lengthened. For article status, trade journals usually require a larger quantity of copy than is normally found in news releases.

When writing an article for trade journals, use the who, what, when, why, and where questions to develop the story line. Look closely for a peg-type story lead. If you have examples of individuals in the specific trade, industry, or professional field who have purchased your work or speak highly about its effectiveness for a particular purpose, include the information in the story. Do a "wrap-up" or conclusion to the story that ties together all of the article's details.

The same story, with a new lead and proper copy alteration, can frequently be used for publicity purposes by a number of different trade journals. We once wrote an article about a particular type of heating unit. It was first printed in a heating trade journal. It then appeared, with some copy alteration, in a milk production magazine that required an article about heat for sterilization. It ran, again with copy adjustment, in a laundry trade journal that required an article about a dependable heat source for washwater preparation. In this instance, publicity about the heating unit was effective because it reached potential customers in each type of magazine.

New Product Announcement
News Release Format

Special Considerations:

1. Does the product represent the addition of newly-available technology or is it a replacement?
2. What benefits or advantages are offered (to whom) by the product, e.g., cost savings, time savings, comfort level, enjoyment etc.?
3. Is this product the first or only one on the market, or is it available elsewhere, and if so, for approximately how long?
4. Is product owned in conjunction with any other company or group?
5. Have the funds for the product development come from any special source, e.g., grant, gift, or organization?
6. To what audiences or public should your announcement be targeted? In what media?
7. Who should make the announcement, e.g., craftsperson, partner, president of company, etc.?
8. What special objectives do you want to achieve with the announcement, e.g., image building, marketing, education, etc.?
9. Does the product announcement offer the opportunity to make any additional points about your company or craft products?
10. Is descriptive and/or explanatory information available?
11. Does the product lend itself to, or require, a series of releases or collateral advertising?

Major Facts To Be Included:

1. Company name, equipment name, and model number.
2. Popular or generic name of product.
3. Company name if different from the above, for better recall or identification, for marketing or image-building purposes.
4. Name and title of spokesperson making announcement.
5. Benefits and advantages of the product.
6. Individuals, groups, who might reap benefits.
7. Cost of product or investment in product if significant.
8. How people can use or take advantage of the product.
9. Description of how product works, how it differs from previously available products, etc.

Optional Additional Information:

1. Related products in the line.
2. Anecdotal material or quotes from customers.
3. Background on relevant information.
4. Future plans and objectives of company.

Fig. 10–1. This outline can be used to prepare news release information about your new craft products.

Appointment Announcement
News Release Format

Special Considerations:

1. What is the level or stature of the appointment, i.e., top management, middle management, or staff?
2. Is it a promotion or move from within the organization or from another organization? Is it a reappointment or reelection?
3. To what audiences or public should announcement be targeted? In what media?
4. Are there any areas of sensitivity in the appointee's background, the selection process, or staff or public perceptions?
5. Are there any points to be made in addition to the straight announcement?

Major Facts To Be Included:

1. Full name of appointee.
2. Appointee's community.
3. Title or position.
4. Name and title of person announcing appointment.
5. Description of position or responsibilities.
6. Date appointment effective or duties assumed.
7. Relevant career or employment history.
8. Educational background.
9. Special achievements, honors, awards, publications, etc.
10. Professional, civic, and other relevant memberships.

Optional Additional Information:

1. Appointee's spouse and children, if any.
2. Appointee's special interests, hobbies, volunteer activities.
3. Quote(s) from appointee relating to position, hopes and objectives, institutional programs or plans, etc.
4. Quote(s) from person making announcement.
5. Description of institution, special programs, etc.

Fig. 10–2. This outline can be used to prepare news release information about new appointments in your company.

Event/Promotion Announcement

News Release Format

Special Considerations:

1. Is this a new event or a repeat of a previous one? Can event be given a catchy, memorable name?
2. Detail the objectives of the event, i.e., image building, community education, etc.
3. To what audiences or public should announcement be targeted?
4. Can a series of releases be scheduled effectively, i.e., basic calendar announcement, special aspects of event, growing response to event, photo captions, etc.?
5. Are there other agencies, organizations, individuals, or events which can be involved in the event to minimize negative feedback or maximize positive response?
6. Can benefits be derived from a post-event recap release?

Major Facts To Be Included:

1. What, where, when, who, how much, and for what should be stated as briefly and clearly as possible in two or three sentences in the lead paragraph.
2. Name of sponsor.
3. Spokesperson for sponsor, i.e., president, craftsperson, etc.
4. Description of event and unusual aspects, if any.
5. How and where to get event tickets, if these are necessary.
6. Deadlines if any.
7. Where to get additional information.

Optional Additional Information:

1. Description of company sponsoring event, its activities, services, plans and objectives, achievements, etc.
2. Detailed information on event; biographical information on performers, craftspeople, etc., if any; reviews of previous performances or events; statistics on numbers of participants, preparation hours; history of event, etc.
3. Biographical information on participants.
4. Human interest aspects of events, e.g., humorous aspects, etc.

Fig. 10–3. This outline can be used to prepare news release information about events that you plan to hold.

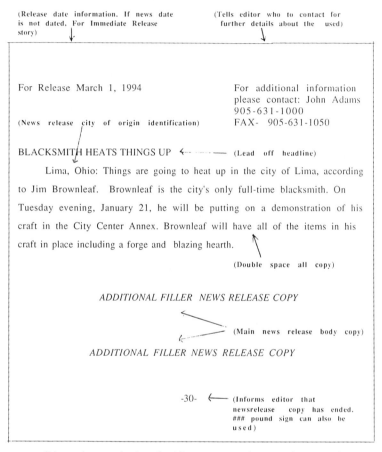

(Release date information. If news date is not dated, For Immediate Release story)

(Tells editor who to contact for further details about the used)

For Release March 1, 1994

For additional information please contact: John Adams
905-631-1000
FAX- 905-631-1050

(News release city of origin identification)

BLACKSMITH HEATS THINGS UP ← (Lead off headline)

Lima, Ohio: Things are going to heat up in the city of Lima, according to Jim Brownleaf. Brownleaf is the city's only full-time blacksmith. On Tuesday evening, January 21, he will be putting on a demonstration of his craft in the City Center Annex. Brownleaf will have all of the items in his craft in place including a forge and blazing hearth.

(Double space all copy)

ADDITIONAL FILLER NEWS RELEASE COPY

(Main news release body copy)

ADDITIONAL FILLER NEWS RELEASE COPY

-30- ← (Informs editor that newsrelease copy has ended. ### pound sign can also be used)

(Always leave a border of white space around news release copy.)

Fig. 10–4. Sample copy of news release.

Feature Articles

Feature articles in the right magazine, or magazines, can create a great deal of interest and publicity about you and your product. They can boost your product sales beyond all expectations and can be the key to having other media editors seek you out for publicity interviews and articles. A *feature article* is usually targeted to a wide, general-interest audience, while a trade journal piece focuses on a rather narrow readership.

THE RIVER REPORTER

JULY 4, 1991

★★

Check out Honesdale for the 4th — and the summer

★★

Robert W. Starkey

Contributed Photo

Starkey exhibit at Summerhill

BETHANY — Impressionist landscape artist Robert W. Starkey will have a showing of recent pastels and oil paintings from July 6 to 20 at the Summerhill Gallery on Ash Street in Bethany. The public is invited to the gallery reception from 2:00 to 5:00 p.m. on Sunday, July 7 to meet the artist and enjoy some refreshments.

Starkey moved to his home and studio at Lakewood in 1988 to pursue his artistic career full-time. For 13 years previously he was a painting, printmaking and drawing instructor in independent schools in New Jersey.

Working both small (10 by 12 inches) and large (6 by 6 feet), almost all of Starkey's current works depict the lively rolling farm and forest scenes of northern Wayne County. The style he employs is impressionism, which uses a colorful patterning of brushmarks.

The early French impressionists often painted "en plein air" (on location) as does Starkey, who creates much of his artwork outside, whether in a hayfield or at the edge of a river. The changing seasons, and nature's variety of colors is his prime source of special interest to him.

All of his works are for sale, ranging in price from $100 to $500. There are also does commissions, usually of views of favorite locations suggested by his patrons.

Starkey will also be an exhibitor on Main Street in Honesdale on Saturday, July 6, where he will display his smaller oils and pastels, as well as his PIN-ITINGS, which are small, wearable works of art.

For more information call 717/448-2856.

Audubon Craft Fair on July 20 and 21

By VONI STRASSER

HONESDALE — "Quality Crafts" is the hallmark of the sixth annual Audubon Craft Fair from 10:00 a.m. to 5:00 p.m. on Saturday and Sunday, July 20 and 21 in the Wallenpaupack High School gymnasium, two miles southeast of Hawley. The show is sponsored by Northeast PA Audubon Society.

All exhibitors have been juried using high standards of selection and screening, and only original and unique handcrafted items have been accepted. Artisans represent a wide variety of crafts, with only one or two in each category.

Parking is free, and entry is $1.

One interesting fact to note is the number of artisans that are married couples. Some of the couples have the same craft, sharing in the design and development of their wares, while others attend craft shows together but create their own art work to demonstrate and sell.

Sam and Polly Glading of Montrose are two such people. He is an outstanding tinsmith working with 19th century designs, turning out such items as old fashioned Christmas sleigh plans holders and Paul Revere lamps. He will demonstrate his tinsmithing along with the selling of his unique creations.

She is a quilter, whose prize winning quilt "The Flower Garden" took a high award in international competition at The Museum of American Folk Art in New York City. Displayed at Manhattan's Pier 92 this spring, the quilt is now on exhibit at Lincoln Center through September. She will have some of her quilts at their booth.

Another interesting couple are Tom Turzo and Mary Scheffer of Penn Argyl. He is a blacksmith and will work on his forge in a tent outside the craft fair doors. She is a spinner and weaver and will ply her old fashion crafts in a tent along with her per angora rabbit. They will be the only artisans in outside items, but it is certainly and to the color and appeal for "fair goers" even before they enter the show.

One more couple share in the making of their craft. Brenda and Jim Aucker of Bloomsburg make candle and beeswax products, and will have an apiary with them at their booth. Herb and Joyce Hays of Shippensburg, also new this year, make handmade baskets copied after many interesting New England designs. Marianne and Clyde Kealer again join the fair with their country craft wood items and hand dipped candles.

The craft fair would not be complete without Kathy Latournous and her father Ray Latournous, who are always a highlight of the show. People come from far and near to see their beautiful etched glass and attractive booth that features Kathy working on her stone cutting wheel.

Mother-in-law and daughter-in-law teams do work Roseanne and Lillian Puchalski of Moscow labor together in harmony. Roseanne does decorative painting and Lillian a well respected teacher in her craft, and Lillian does all types of woodworking.

Additionally, an exciting new exhibitor this year is the Ray Family from Rockville, MD. They create beautiful handcrafted jewelry from nature that has been electroplated with silver and gold. Helen and Allen Weichman of Roeders bring the very popular and sought after Groundhog Blues Pottery. He will work on his potter's wheel all during the two day fair.

Plenty of action in Wayne County during July 4th week

STROUDSBURG — Visitors to Wayne County will have much to keep them busy during the popular Fourth of July vacation week.

Festivities start with a big Independence Day parade in Hawley complete with floats, fire engines, soldiers, antique cars and more. The parade starts at 12:00 noon.

Hear the big band sounds of Ron Baldwin's Larand 16-piece swing band at Settlers Inn in Hawley on July 6, or boogie to a marathon '50s concert featuring the Del-Vikings and the Harptones in Honesdale on July 6. A quieter pursuit is the Dorlinger-Suydam Wildlife Sanctuary in Hawley, with classical music performed by the Annapolis Brass Quintet on July 7.

Bring the family on an old-fashioned train ride aboard the Stourbridge Line from Honesdale to Hawley on July 6.

For more information about summer events in the Poconos, call the vacation bureau at 717/424-6050.

Fig. 10–5. An important marketing tool for your craft exhibition or craft show participation is publicity. Usually the show promoter or gallery owner generates and sends out press releases to the area media. It is possible to generate your own publicity by developing a "publicity peg" about your craft product to interest an editorial writer in the item.

A feature article usually runs approximately 1000 to 1500 words, but may be longer. Similar to news releases and trade journals, the feature article is dependent on the five W's—who, what, why, where, and when—for its basic inspiration. Feature articles usually have a strong focal point, and the article expands around the area of interest.

While you would generally send a news release without any preamble or covering letter to the editor of newspaper, or to the director of radio and television programs, you would send a *query letter* to a magazine editor before submitting an article or feature story. The query letter spells out what you intend to write about, gives highlights of the story, perhaps provides a sample paragraph or two of your writing style and the story's content, and asks the editor whether there is any interest in the story. If you want to make sure of an editorial response, be sure to send a stamped, return-addressed letter with your query letter.

Graphic Representations

The old adage, "one picture is worth a thousand words," is still valid in public relations. It makes eminent good sense to try to get publicity photographs and captions of your craft products placed in the media. In today's active society, with the mass of stories and advertising appearing daily in all forms of media, it's easier for potential buyers to see and be attracted by good publicity photos and graphics than it is for them to read articles.

Not only are photographs used for publicity purposes, they and other forms of graphics, can also be used effectively to enhance your brochures, flyers, and other promotional pieces. Properly enlarged, sometimes to poster size or larger, photographs and graphics can also be used to good effect to publicize and decorate your craft show booth. **Working with Photographs**—The rules for effective photographs are essentially the same as for written material. The photo has to be a built-in publicity peg. It must be appealing, tell a story, and be of good quality for it to stand out among the many photographs competing for editorial space.

There are a number of distinct types of publicity photographs. There is the *black-and-white photo* (or *halftone*) where all objects in the shot have similar color gradations. Newspapers, trade journals, and magazines use black-and-white photos. *Color prints* pick up all of the colors in the scene being photographed. Some newspapers and most magazines and trade journals can duplicate these prints in full color. Where newspapers do not care to use color, a color print can be converted to a black-and-white photo during the newspaper or magazine printing process. *35mm color slides* are another photo alternative particularly useful for television productions, but they may be used for other reproduction purposes as well. The best sizes for publicity photographs for use by the media, black and white or color, are 5 × 7 inch or 8 × 10 inches. Photos can be printed with a glossy texture or with a matte or dull finish. Glossy photos are best for reproducing in the press. Matte- or glossy-finished prints can be used in booth displays.

A decision must be made, usually at the time a photograph is taken, whether the print will be horizontal or vertical. Some newspapers or magazines prefer one type of layout to the other.

Photo Techniques—Once you have taken a publicity photograph, although there is no way to change the scene or action, there are ways to make changes in the photograph.

Your publicity photograph can be cropped. This procedure either cuts off a portion or portions of the picture or changes the proportions of the entire picture. The procedure is usually accomplished in a photo processing shop and can actually put a dramatic spin on the picture.

Your publicity photographs can be reduced or enlarged. No matter what size the photo negative is you start out with, prints either smaller or larger can be made from the negative.

Your publicity photos can be airbrushed. If certain details in your photograph require removal or highlighting, or even adding to, a skilled photo processing shop technician can airbrush select effects onto the photograph.

Your publicity photos can be retouched. If there are any obvious blemishes in your photograph, a touch-up artist can correct the problems on either the print or negative.

Publicity Photograph Hints

- When you plan a publicity photograph, it should express a message to the viewer.
- Make your publicity photograph eye-catching. Do this by moving around the subject and taking photos from different angles and positions.
- Always check the background and areas surrounding the people or items you are photographing for anything which distracts from the

central subject in the photo—clutter, unsuitable objects, unrelated people or objects, etc.

- Do not allow the people you are photographing to stare at the camera. Editors call these "firing squad shots," and they don't like to use them. Have the people doing something animated so that your photo takes on lifelike qualities.
- Try to limit the number of people in your publicity photo. A mass shot may lose its editorial attraction.
- Locate a reputable photo processing house that turns out a professional job on time.

Photo Captions—A photograph without a caption may find itself half a picture. The picture tells the story; the written caption beneath the photo explains the story. Photo captions should be brief and to the point. The caption should explain the picture and direct the viewer to look again at the picture with deeper understanding.

Other Publicity Graphic—There are other graphic resources in addition to still photography that have publicity applications for the craftperson. The video recorder and the videotapes produced by this equipment can be used for your publicity purposes. Local, and even major, television stations can and frequently do show these tapes or segments of them.

The subject matter and editor interest rules for videotapes are similar to those for news releases. The subject must be interesting, and offer a strong publicity peg for editors to consider your tapes. The tapes are particularly useful to news editors if they tie in with a news event, a trend, or a fad, but they often are used for their intrinsic value in changing the pace of a program, or introducing the viewers to new concepts.

A publicity videotape, professionally put together, showing you working on several features of your craft product might interest a station producer or editor. This is especially true if the show's producer must preview an area craft show that has not as yet set up.

Press Kits

Your *press kit* should be a collection of communications and publicity material about you and your craft product. It is an information source for editors. It provides editorial people and show producers with good background material. It gives these people an opportunity to get to know about you and your product in the convenience of their own office.

A publicity press kit has a number of components. It begins with a *folder* in which your material is held. The folder should be sized to fit conveniently into the editor's file drawer. A standard 9 × 12-inch folder with your company name typed on the tab is best for this purpose. For convenience, the exterior of the folder can have your name, address, and telephone number as well. Inside this folder should be a *photograph* or photographs of your product or product line, a *background piece,* or fact sheet, about your craft company and yourself, and a *news release* about the product or event you are publicizing. The kit might contain a *question and answer sheet* that can provide editors with answers to some of the commonly-asked questions about your product or business.

When preparing a press kit, make absolutely certain that the information you are providing is accurate. Avoid turning the information in your kit into a commercial pitch for your product. Use professionally-produced photographs that an editor can reprint. Out-of-focus dark prints that do not tell a story end up in the editorial garbage bin. Provide the editors with enough information so that they can pick out and develop a story line. Try not to overwhelm them.

When you provide your publicity press kits to editors, include a letter explaining why you are sending the information. If the data is just for background information, indicate this fact. If you are introducing a new product with the press kit, let the editor know this when you send the kit. If you can develop any specific relevance between the information in your kit and timely events or editorial focus, include this in your letter.

Press Conferences

A *press conference* is an event to which you invite media people so that you can tell them about the introduction of a new product or program. Although many companies schedule these media events, you should be cautioned that unless you have something really important to talk about or introduce, the effort can be disappointing. Editors and reporters are busy people who are usually working under a deadline. In addition, they receive a large number of similar invitations through the year and thus can easily become jaded. It often requires an extremely important event to get them to attend such a conference.

You are really obligated to ask yourself if a press kit with a new product photograph, background sheet, and a news release about the newest craft product in your line will not do the job as well. It certainly will be a lot less expensive.

One company public relations department, recognizing the difficulty of gathering together a large group of editors for a press conference, decided to hold its "conference" in the individual editors' offices. They delivered to each editor a press kit with all of the background material, the new product news release, and a hot cup for coffee, a packet of instant coffee, sugar and cream substitute packets, and a generous slice of cake.

If you decide that a press conference to introduce your new product can be an effective approach to your publicity effort, there are ground rules that can make the conference easier to put together and successful.

- Start by developing a list of the media people you want to invite. Make sure that you have the correct names of the people from each newspaper, radio or television station.
- Try to select a timeframe that is best for as many of the media people as possible. Each area is different, so check in advance. Generally, the early part of a day is the best time for most media people.
- Extend the press conference invitation in writing. Provide the date, time, and place of the conference, and clearly indicate the reason for the conference. If a special speaker is to be involved in your program, provide the name and background. Make sure that you put a contact name and a phone number in your invitation so that the editorial people know who to respond to. Send the press conference invitation out at least a week to ten days before the program.
- If you decide on refreshments, which can be simple or elaborate, note this information on your press conference invitation. Refreshments can be an expensive addition to your conference.
- Follow up all press conference invitations with a re-invitation telephone call the day prior to the program.
- Set up the conference area properly. Unless your workshop is easily accessible and can accommodate those you expect, select a room in a motel or hotel that is convenient to reach by public transportation or personal car. Make sure that property has parking. Provide seating for all members of the press. If you are expecting television cov-

erage, leave space for camera equipment. Check in advance for electrical outlets and room lighting. If the room is large, make arrangements for a microphone.

- Timing is important. You cannot afford to let a conference begin late or drag. It must start on time and end promptly. It is best to let the audience know in advance that the conference will have a specific time limit.
- In order for your press conference to be effective, do not discuss the subject of the conference with reporters before the program begins. Editorial people can become extremely annoyed if they feel a competitor is receiving information to which they do not have access.
- Make sure that all of the media people present at the conference receive a copy of your press kit, including news release.
- You should keep a list of all of the media invitations sent out, and a list of the people attending the conference. When the program has concluded, make sure that all of the media people who did not attend receive a copy of your press kit, including news release.
- Leave time at the conclusion of the press conference for a question and answer period. If your press kit has a question-and-answer sheet, a great many of the questions may automatically be answered.
- If there are any questions that cannot be answered at the press conference, keep a list of the questions, and the names of people requesting the information. Respond personally to these individuals as soon as possible after the conference with your answers.

Interviews

In another chapter, the subject of talk show interviews is discussed extensively. If the opportunity arises to appear on a television or radio interview show, or to be interviewed by a newspaper editor for an article, accept the challenge because it can mean exposure for you and your craft product.

Interviews come in other ways, too. A news release, for example, can generate a call from the press. Sometimes, the request for an interview arises serendipitously. When you are exhibiting at a craft show, a reporter at the event may become interested in your product, and request an interview. At a gathering or party, the discussion may turn to creativity and your work as a craftsperson. A reporter also at the event may seek you out for an interview. Friends and associates may also suggest to their media friends that you would make a good subject for an interview.

When you receive a request for an interview, there are steps you should take to help make the interview a positive experience.

- Most reporters enjoy preparing and writing an interview story. It provides copy for their paper, and an opportunity to learn something completely new and different. Always remember that you are the expert on the subject, and that the reporter or interviewer is trying to gather as much story information as possible.
- *Always prepare for an interview.* Bring written material with you for the interviewer to use in preparing the story. If you have an opportunity, learn what type of paper or program the reporter works for, and try to review some past stories by the interviewer.
- *A relaxed attitude produces a better story.* If you can come into the interview relaxed, in most instances, the interviewer will respond in an equally relaxed manner and the interview will run more smoothly. Preparation is a major key to relaxation.
- *Answer as many questions as you can* in a short, concise and direct manner. Don't expound on theories or offer convoluted responses. If the interviewer leads you off into unfamiliar waters, try to bring the questioning back to the subjects with which you are familiar. If you cannot answer a question, offer to provide the interviewer with the information as soon as possible, and do so.
- Interviewers usually like *facts.* If you can provide this type of information, bring it with you to the interview, preferably in writing, and supported with sources. They also like human interest angles if you can give them briefly and in interesting fashion.
- *Don't fabricate responses.* Always tell the truth. If an interviewer should trip you up with even one small falsehood, the rest of your interview will be suspect.
- *Be wary of "off the record" responses.* Many interviewers and reporters will stick judiciously to their word and not use off-the-record information. On the other hand, long interviews, deadline pressures and work on other stories can cause confusion in a writer's mind. The information may be used in error. The easiest rule to follow is if you don't want to see your words in bold print, or hear them on a radio or television playback, do not say them.
- If an interviewer calls by phone and catches you unprepared, indi-

cate that you are in the midst of a project, and offer to call back within half an hour. During the interviewer's first call, however, try to learn the direction of the interview and perhaps some of the questions the reporter wants answered. This should give you enough background and time to gather your information before responding.

- If your interview or story comes out satisfactorily, you may want to seek permission from the reporter, newspaper, radio or television station to reprint or reuse the article or tape. It can be useful for your press kit, or when seeking other interviews.
- After the story appears, always send the interviewer or reporter a follow-up thank-you note.

Working with the Press

There are a series of steps that you can take to develop and maintain a good working relationship with the press. Try to include as many of the following activities in your press relations program as you can.

- Maintain a helpful attitude. Editorial people are trying to do their job just as you are.
- Most reporters have a limited amount of time in which to gather and prepare their stories. They work on deadlines and generally appreciate as much background material as possible.
- Try to provide interesting information for the story. This is what the reporter and the readers or audience are looking for. Consider the way a well-balanced story appears, and provide a sufficient amount of information for the reporter to develop such an article.
- Think about your media interview as an opportunity to let people know about you, your product and your business in as favorable a light as possible.
- Spend time preparing for an interview. Gather together as much information as you can.
- Learn about media deadlines in your area, and any of their specific requirements. It can work to your advantage.
- Try to develop a friendly, working relationship with members of the media even before you send them press material. When they do receive news release material from you they may be more responsive.

Chapter Highlights

- Advertising space in which your message appears must be paid for. Editorial space devoted to publicity items is free.
- Publicity is an important and integral part of any public relations program.
- Most of us automatically perform public relations activities as part of our everyday business functions.
- A publicity campaign is initiated by targeting an audience.
- Press mailing lists may be developed from your own records and customers, or may be purchased from list houses.
- There are organizations who will distribute your news release, along with others, to specific media lists.
- Some of the major publicity tools include news releases, trade press articles, feature stories, photographs, press kits, press conferences, and interviews.
- The basic ingredients of a news release are developed when answers to who, what, why, when and where are provided.
- A news release or feature story depends on a "peg" to generate editorial and/or reader interest.
- Feature articles usually run from 1000 to 1500 words. The stories may be shorter or longer depending on the particular media requirements.
- Good publicity photographs enhance your opportunity to have stories about your products placed in the media.
- When taking a publicity photograph, always have it express a message to the viewer.
- A basic press kit consists of a folder containing your name, address, and telephone number, background information, photograph, and news release about the new product or event.
- A press conference is an opportunity to invite a group of media people to meet in one place and learn about the introduction of your new craft product or a special event in your business.
- If you are to be interviewed by the press, it is important that you are prepared with all available information and facts about your product.
- In all work that you do with the press, always try to maintain a helpful and friendly attitude.

CHAPTER 11

Marketing Your Crafts by Direct Response Methods

The most direct route that you can use to reach large numbers of potential purchasers is to communicate with them one-on-one. Aside from face-to-face selling, this is best accomplished using a *direct response technique*. For many years, direct response selling was commonly called *mail order*. The name change results not only from the many carriers who now deliver purchases, but also from the many different types of techniques to which buyers respond. Whereas previously the United States mail was the primary carrier for offering and ordering products, today offerings also come by radio, television, fax, and phone. People can order by phone and fax or mail and receive delivery by Federal Express, United Parcel Service, and other carriers who compete with the postal system.

Direct response marketing includes, but is not limited to, such methods as direct mail, direct response publication advertising, postcard advertising, card pack advertising, cooperative ads, free-standing inserts, catalog sales, and telemarketing. While all of these methods can be used for craft marketing, each has distinct applications.

Advantages of Direct Response

Among the advantages of direct response marketing is the ability to target messages accurately to selected groups of potential craft buyers. Control of all marketing expenditures can be achieved by limiting quantities to specific markets or limiting the number of markets targeted. An important economic advantage of direct mail is that a number of products can be promoted in the same mailing package. The direct response package, brochure, leaflet, or catalog can feature one or many product offers.

The direct response advertising process can also provide you with a fairly rapid reaction to your mailing package. In a relatively short time, you can determine whether your solicitation is successful or requires adjustment.

The Changing Product Response Scene

Years ago, most people traveled to stores of all types to buy their staples, luxuries, and gifts. Today, with most adults working, there is less time to attend to shopping chores.

Other factors also affect people's shopping habits. These include heavy traffic patterns on highways, crowded shopping centers, and, in some urban areas, fear of being victimized in inner cities.

The use of "free" telephone numbers (800 calls) has simplified the ordering process, and home delivery services have become quick, convenient, and relatively inexpensive. There has also been an increase in disposable income for certain segments of the population. Disposable income means dollars that individuals and families can spend on products other than necessities.

Perhaps the biggest boon to the direct response/direct mail industry has been the credit card, which allows consumers to purchase products easily without resorting to an instant outlay of cash. The advent of the computer, which provides almost instantaneous information about products and prices for the consumer, has also contributed to the growth of the direct response industry.

Craft Products as Direct Response Items

Handmade craft products are adaptable to the direct response market, particularly products that stimulate repeat or multiple orders. A craftsman from whom we had bought baby quilts each time we saw him at a show in our region now travels a different route. Periodically, however, he sends us his latest price lists and we place an order for quilts for all the babies we anticipate among friends and family.

Most craft items are unusual in one way or another, and are not easily available in any store or outlet. Craft products are almost always consumer-useful, and of good value. By the very nature of the individual item-by-item craft production process, handcrafted items are not always easy or convenient for potential buyers to locate. These factors help make craft products good, marketable direct response items.

Modern packaging, bubble wrap, foam, plastic nuggets, etc., makes it possible to ship even the most delicate crafts safely. There are carriers who will handle packages, large and small. Moreover, most buyers are conditioned to picking up postage and handling charges so that these costs do not have to be absorbed by the craftsperson.

Types of Direct Response

When you see a product advertised in your newspaper or a magazine and place an order for it, within a certain period of time, you can expect it to be delivered to your home or office. This is known as a *one-step direct-response* purchase. *The request and response are direct.*

Suppose, however, that the product is a high-ticket item and you want to learn more about it before making a decision. You might fill in a coupon requesting more information, or you might write to the address provided in the ad asking specific questions about the product. Within a week or so, a brochure or spec sheet will be delivered to your home or office, or you will receive a call from a salesperson. If you like what you see in the brochure, or learn during the phone conversation about the product, you will place an order. Within a reasonable time, the product will appear at your doorstep. This is known as a *two-step purchase.* The *request, initial response, and followup move forward as two separate actions.*

A technique that some companies, such as book and record clubs or telephone space-sale operations, have built into their direct response campaigns is the so-called *negative option.* Even though this system may be a boon to the seller, it often generates negative feelings in consumers. In this technique, a sales letter or other direct marketing device is sent to the consumer announcing a flow of products to be sent and billed automatically, *unless the consumer reacts and says to the direct marketer: "I don't want you to send your product to me."* The responsibility for action rests on the consumer who receives the direct marketing package.

Direct Response Techniques

While there are many theories, formulas, and experiential philosophies, direct response marketing is not an exact science. A great deal depends on such factors as the type of information package or inserts used; the time of the year, and even the day the message is received and read; the number of times the buyer is exposed to the message; competitor input; and simple trial and error.

The following techniques are some of the major direct response methods that have been used by product marketers, large and small. The degree of success in using any of the techniques for your product depends a great deal on testing and evaluation.

It is sound practice to use a test sampling before investing in a major campaign. The time that this may take will generally be justified by improvements to the package made as a result of the sampling. If, for example, you plan a product solicitation mailing to 20,000 names, select 1000 for your test mailing and await the consumer response. If you are working with a number of lists, choose your sampling from within each list.

Another test technique is to use two different variations of your offering to small segments of the planned mailing to see which pulls the greater response. Keep an accurate log or record of the results achieved from each test mailing, and *evaluate the responses.* If they are satisfactory, you can continue your direct mail campaign. If the orders are sparse, you should carefully review your package and make changes that you believe will positively affect the outcome of the larger mailing.

Direct Mail Direct Response

The *direct mail direct response* is the sending of a product offering to a specified group of people, chosen to have a good probability of being potential customers for the product. The two major components of a direct mail program are the *mailing list* and the *mailing package.*

The mailing list contains the names of the potential purchasers of your craft product. These lists may be bought from list houses, or developed from people who have shown an interest in your product at shows, in your shop, or at other venues.

When selecting a list from a list house, you can be highly specific about the type of people you want on the mailing list. For example, you can purchase lists of people who have bought craft products from other sources, or people who subscribe to specific magazines, or support or belong to specific organizations. You can buy list of people who have spent specific amounts of money on gifts or other items. If your craft item is a warm weather product, your list selection can target only people from certain warm weather states. If you are unsure of the type of list that might best suit your needs, list company representatives can be helpful.

Test Mailing Packages—Testing your mailing packages can save you time and money. It will provide you with a systematic way to determine the response climate before expending a major effort or monetary outlay. The testing technique requires only that you experiment with a sample portion of the major mailing or other selected direct response method. You are simply "testing the waters." Although direct mail lends itself more readily to testing techniques, the method with variations can also be used with other direct response programs. Figs. 11–1 and 11–2 suggest some information you might consider in a direct response program, and show some list categories available.

The Mailing List—Mailing lists are usually purchased for *one-time use* in quantities of 1000 names. This means that the names can only be used for one mailing. If you plan on additional mailings, arrangements must be made with the mailing house. List prices run $35 to $50 per 1000, with higher prices for names on specialized lists. There is generally a minimum quantity of names that must be purchased per order, or

Why should you buy our lists?

- **If you need new prospects.** Don't spend your valuable time searching through directories for leads. We can provide the prospects, for only pennies per name, so you can concentrate on *selling.*

- **If you want to reach your market economically and quickly.** Use our lists for direct mail or telemarketing, and generate more sales at a fraction of the cost of personal calls.

- **To update your existing files.** Even if you maintain your own prospect database, we can provide you with verified new names from the most current telephone directories.

- **If you want to deal with an honest company.** We believe in 100% honest representation of our services. We'll give you the facts about our lists - good or bad - so you can make an educated decision.

- **If you want fast service and guaranteed satisfaction.** Ordering lists from us is quick and painless. Our customer service representatives are knowledgeable and ready to help with your order. Plus, 95% of all orders are shipped the next working day - an industry record.

  We also offer a **Money Back Guarantee** on any order up to $150, no questions asked. No other list company will offer a guarantee like that. We do - because we're confident we can earn your continued business.

What should you expect from our lists?

- **100% accuracy?** This is simply impossible, due to all the changes in the business world. Our lists are updated continuously from the new telephone directories, and are telephone-verified as well. They're the best business lists available anywhere, but they're still not perfect. You will still find a small percentage of errors and "out of business" names. However, 5-10% undeliverable names is not uncommon, especially in industries with high levels of turnover.

  To help reimburse you for undeliverable names, we do offer a generous **postage refund guarantee.** Please see page 77 for details.

- **We can't qualify every name.** We compile our lists from the Yellow Pages, and then call every business to verify and collect additional information. But we can't guarantee that every name is valid; for example, if a company is listed under "Computer Dealers," we can't guarantee that they actually sell computers (although **most** do). We must rely on the Yellow Page classifications as they appear in the phone books.

- **Don't expect to "get rich quick".** The list is only one factor in the success of any promotion. You must also have a good product, competitive pricing, quality service, an attractive mailing piece or effective telemarketing script and so forth. You won't get rich overnight by using our lists; but if you use them properly, you will increase your sales and profits.

Why are we telling you this?

We want to be honest and provide you with the facts *before* you buy our lists. That way you'll know what to expect. After all, we want you to be a satisfied regular customer - not a "one-time" customer.

Fig. 11–1. Table of Contents from a company's list sales booklet indicating the variety of lists available, and other customer information. *(Courtesy American Business Information)*

a minimum dollar amount. The names are sent to you on labels, called *Cheshire labels* that can be affixed to envelopes or brochures by special machines. If you want self-adhesive labels on special sheets (usually 33 labels to the sheet) or on index cards, you must request them specifically and you may pay an extra charge.

Consumer - Crop

Description	Qty	Names	Code
Consumer Purchasing Services	940	160	729912
Contact Lens Specialist - Optometrists	310	240	80420101
Contact Lenses, Prescription	14,010	9,350	59959901
Container Mfrs, NEC, Wood	540	510	2448
Contract Haulers	200	50	42139903
Contractor - Nonresidential Buildings	18,440	11,290	1542
Contractors - Highway & St Cons	1,910	580	16119901
Contractors - Indl Buildings & Whses, NEC	9,850	4,390	154199
Contractors - Industrial Buildings & Whses	14,670	9,100	1541
Contractors - Multifamily Units	166,990	57,950	1522
Contractors - New Single-Family Houses	25,690	9,660	15219901
Contractors - Remodeling & Additions	67,550	24,410	152101
Contractors - Repairing Fire Damage	7,150	2,500	15210104
Contractors - Single-Family Houses	138,980	79,870	1521
Contractors - Single-Family Housing, NEC	25,690	9,660	152199
Contractors' Materials, Whis	13,270	5,480	50820302
Contributors	—	6,408,000	—
Contributors, Political	—	2,801,000	—
Contributors, Religious	—	1,999,000	—
Controlling Instruments, Whis	1,180	290	50840701
Convalescent Equip & Supplies, Retail	4,880	2,380	59990902
Convalescent Homes	2,040	110	80599901
Convenience Stores	16,000	3,890	541102
Convention & Show Services	7,130	1,980	73890301
Converted Paper Products, NEC	40	10	267999
Conveyor Systems, Whis	2,560	990	50840801
Conveyors & Conveying Equipment Mfrs	1,430	1,320	3535
Cookie & Cracker Mfrs	490	390	2052
Cooking Equipment, Commercial, Whis	490	200	50460303
Cooking Oils & Shortenings, Whis	100	40	514901
Cooking Oils, Whis	100	40	51490101
Cooking Utensils, Retail	1,090	450	57190103
Copper & Copper Alloy Die-Castings	1,020	470	336401
Copper Foundries	910	800	3366
Copper Mills - Primary	130	60	3331
Copper Mills - Rolling & Drawing	250	210	3351
Copper Ore Mining	40	30	1021
Copper Products, Whis	380	160	505103
Copper, Whis	300	130	50510301
Coppersmithing	50	30	76991202
Copying Equipment, Whis	10,570	3,540	504402
Copyright Protection Services	110	50	73891304
Cordage & Twine Mfrs	350	320	2298
Cork Products, Fabricated, Whis	110	50	50990202
Corn Farms	50	20	0115
Corn Milling - Wet	140	110	2046
"Corporate Climbers" (Mid-management Execs on the Move)	—	530,000	—
Correct Time Services	1,370	130	73891002
Correctional Institutions	1,730	—	9223
Cosmetic & Beauty Supply Stores	1,590	410	599913
Cosmetic Stores	1,250	310	59991301
Cosmetics, Perfumes & Hair Products, Whis	2,010	620	512201
Cosmetics, Whis	1,420	470	51220101
Cosmetologists	880	30	72310101
Cosmetology & Personal Hygiene Salons	37,290	3,820	723101
Costume & Scenery Design Services	210	70	792206
Costume Design, Theatrical	80	30	79220601
Costume Jewelry & Novelties Mfrs	16,000	5,900	3961
Costume Jewelry Mfrs	15,250	5,210	39619901
Costume Jewelry Mfrs, NEC	15,250	5,210	396199
Costume Jewelry, Retail	30	10	56329903
Costume Rental	50	20	238903
Costume Rental	160	70	72990901
Costumes & Wigs, Retail	10,180	2,650	569902
Costumes, Masquerade Or Theatrical, Retail	2,970	1,420	56990201
Cotton Broadwoven Fabric Mills	1,480	880	2211
Cotton Broadwoven Fabric Mills, NEC	10	10	221199
Cotton Compresses & Warehouses	100	20	42219901
Cotton Farms	60	30	0131
Cotton Ginning	1,260	700	0724
Cotton Ginning Machinery Mfrs	150	70	35599005
Cotton Goods, Whis	230	120	51310105
Cotton Merchants	230	100	51590101
Cotton Merchants & Products	250	100	515901
Cotton Seed Delinting Services	30	20	07230102
Cotton Yarn, Spun	90	40	22810302
Cottonseed Oil Mills	130	90	2074
Counseling Services - General	12,650	6,280	832206
Counter Tops, Retail	3,250	1,480	52119904
Country Clubs, Private	10	—	79979904
Country Music Groups & Artists	110	50	79290103
Coupon Printing	20	—	27590304
Courier & Messenger Services	3,170	540	73891601
Courier Services, Exc By Air	4,650	2,850	4215
Courier Services, Exc By Air, NEC	50	20	421599
Credit Clubs - Indoor & Outdoor	1,840	670	799705
Court Reporting Services	4,820	1,830	73380201
Courts	1,420	840	9211
Courts - Federal	290	230	92119901
Courts - Local	670	470	92119902
Courts, NEC	980	700	921199
Covenant & Evangelical Churches	2,520	—	86610114
Crackers, Cookies & Bakery Prod, Whis	9,120	2,230	514907
Cranberry Bogs	50	10	01719903
Crane & Aerial Lift Services	3,350	1,390	73899909
Crane & Lift Equipment - Rental	990	380	73539901
Cranes, Hoists & Monorail System Mfrs	590	520	3536
Cranes, Industrial, Whis	3,010	1,240	50640802
Crankshaft Assemblies, Motor Vehicle	20	—	37140106
Creative Svc To Advertisers, Exc Writers	20	10	73360102
Credit Agencies - Federal	80	40	8111
Credit Card Central Collection Agencies	750	200	61539901
Credit Card Holders (Bank and Retail Cards)	—	41,567,000	—

Credit Card Holders

Originating from major credit bureaus, our credit card selections are available on over 41,000,000 consumer names. You may select Bank or Retail card holders — and further refine your selection by:

- Income
- Age
- Mail Responsiveness
- Card Holders with Phone Numbers

Description	Qty	Names	Code
Credit Card Services	40	10	73890903
Credit Institutions - Personal	59,490	24,830	6141
Credit Investigation Services	10	—	73239904
Credit Reporting Services	3,230	1,470	7323
Credit Reporting Services, NEC	170	—	732399
Credit Unions, Federally Chartered	11,540	5,530	6061
Credit Unions, Not Federally Chartered	470	430	6062
Crematories	3,440	230	72619901
Crisis Intervention Centers	2,150	210	83220302
Crop Cultivating Services	130	40	072104
Crop Dusting Services	2,210	160	07210302

Fig. 11–2. Page from list company sales booklet indicating variety of lists available. List contains description, quantity, contact name availability, and classification of each list by S.I.C. (Standard Industrial Classification). *(Courtesy Ed Burnett Consultants, Inc.)*

It is important to understand that list house brokers can provide you with all of the necessary information and list breakdowns that you require for your craft product mailing. You have only to provide your list requirements, or ask for the broker's assistance. A good list house will be happy to provide the services you require. In most instances, especially if you are selling a product that could be considered in competition with a company providing a mailing list, the list house will ask to see a copy of your mailing package for approval.

If you have developed your own extensive mailing list of purchasers, you may want to generate some additional income by selling your list. Mailing houses often are interested in purchasing lists representing specific buying publics such as craft product purchasers.

The Mailing Package—The mailing package that you will be using to generate business for your craft product will take time and work to develop. While there are a number of functions that must be fulfilled by a mailing package, it is possible for a single one-sided or double-fold sales card to do the job.

In most instances, however, the mailing package consists of a combination which includes, but is not limited to, an outside mailing envelope, a solicitation letter, a brochure, a product photograph, a discount or incentive coupon, an order blank, a return envelope, and perhaps some testimonial information praising your craft product. Consideration should be given to the total weight and size of the mailing package. A package that is overweight or oversized can raise costs excessively.

While there are professionals who can prepare the complete mailing package for you for a fee, it is altogether possible for you to develop it yourself.

Begin by planning the mailing. Know what product or products you want to sell. Write the copy about your product for your sales letter, developing all of the highlights and uses for the item. If testimonials are applicable, they can be included in your sales letter, or as separate items in the package. Even before you test mail your letter, have several people read it for clarity, typographical and spelling errors, and general impact. While it has been said that a committee could change the Gettysburg Address in a hundred different ways, it is worthwhile to consider the criticism of people whose judgment you value. If you have a brochure or photographs, you may want to make them part of the package.

The outside mailing envelope is the first thing potential buyers will see when they receive your mailing package. Check with your local postmaster about postal mailing regulations. You might use colored envelopes or print teasers on the outside to encourage the consumer to read on. Be cautious about oversized envelopes that require extra postage. The post office has definite requirements for size and barcoding of envelopes and postcards. If a direct mail service will be sending your offering, then you must work with the service to be sure that the mailing side of your piece is accurate. If the service is affixing postage with a meter, using a bulk-mail permit, or any other specific postal services, your piece must comply with the correct marking procedures, permit numbers, locations, etc.

You should develop product ordering information and order blank that gives all relevant information including postage and handling charges, credit card details if you accept these charges, applicable sales taxes, approximate shipping time, and guarantees or warranties. Order blanks can be on cards or sheets or on forms which become self-seal envelopes. They also can be printed on a wide envelope flap. Envelope companies and printers will show you samples of various types of outer and return envelopes, but these can be more expensive than including your form in other ways. Remember, the simpler you keep the elements in your package and the more standard sizes you use, the lower your production costs will be.

If you include a pre-addressed return envelope in your mailing, you can use either a postage-paid return envelope or one on which the buyer must place a stamp. Some direct mail people claim that return envelopes in a mailing package increase sales and that postage-paid return envelopes increase sales further. A postage-paid return permit is available to you for a fee from your local post office. In addition to the fee, you will be charged a per piece postage for every envelope that is returned to you. Check postal regulations and the amount of time necessary to obtain this type of permit. A deposit account is also required for this service.

Posting the Direct Mail Package—Once you have prepared the mailing package and selected your mailing list, you must decide how the envelope will be mailed. It can be sent first class, which is the way most regular mail is sent, or it can be mailed bulk rate. Bulk-rate mailing lowers postage costs, but requires that you bundle or tie the envelopes into packages or groups based on United States Postal Service regulations including zip-coding and other postal designations. The process can be time-consuming. Moreover, bulk-rate mail can be delayed. If time is of the essence, this can be a problem. If you do use bulk mail, be extremely cautious with mailings during Christmas and holiday periods and allow plenty of advance time. In addition to potential delays in delivery, non-deliverable bulk mail is not returned to the sender unless it is imprinted with "Address correction requested." If the address correction is forwarded to you, there is a per-piece charge in excess of first class postage.

Co-Op Mailings and Card Pack Direct Response

A *card pack* or a *co-op mailing* is a package combining offers from multiple vendors who want to reach the same market. This allows you to reach potential buyers at a much lower cost than if you were to mail to the same list yourself.

When you select a card pack mailing, all of your promotional information is developed and printed in the space allotted your product on a $3\frac{1}{2} \times 5\frac{1}{2}$ inch card. One side of the card has your promotional pitch and an order form or form requesting additional information, the other side a short promotional message and your return address. In most instances, the cards are postage paid, though some require a stamp. Color can be used to enhance your promotional message. Your card and 25 to 50 other cards are mailed together in a pack to a targeted list.

The limited space for your message on a postcard can be a disadvantage of the card pack mailing. A cooperative mailing of larger-sized pieces may be more appropriate. This allows more copy space for your message. A large number of non-competitive product promotional pieces are combined in a mailing envelope and sent to a selected list. Postage and handling costs are borne by the co-op mailing company.

Both types of shared mailings offer the advantage of lower costs. If you are considering them, however, it is important to know what other products will be promoted in the same package to make sure that they are not heavily competitive and that they will not detract from the quality image of your product.

Catalog Direct Response

A slightly different direct marketing/mailing process is *syndicate* or *catalog marketing*. In this type of mailing, you prepare the necessary promotional copy and supply photographs of your craft product line. The information is used as part of a catalog of products, mailed under the catalog producer's name.

When orders are received, the producer activates a *drop-shipping* arrangement with you. This means that the catalog company does not have to stock your products. You mail, or drop-ship, your craft products directly from your shop to the ordering customers as soon as the catalog company advises you of their orders. Under this arrangement, the catalog producer will either forward to you the full price received from the buyer and you will return an agreed-on amount, percentage, or commission, or the producer will keep the retail price and forward to you the previously-agreed-upon wholesale price.

Newspaper Direct Response

Newspapers offer craft producers a number of useful direct response options. Ads can include an order form, a coupon order, or a coupon requesting further information. Either *display* or *classified advertising space* can be used. *Free-standing inserts,* sections that are dedicated only to your product, can be inserted in the newspaper on the particular day in which you choose to advertise. Some larger papers also offer the opportunity to place your free-standing insert in certain editions of the newspaper. This permits you to target select areas with your direct response ad.

Display advertising space in newspapers is usually bought by the column inch. This is the space one inch in depth times the width of the newspaper column. Newspaper columns vary in size so that no exact size can be provided. Some papers, generally weeklies and smaller daily papers, sell display space by the page, half page, one-third page, and one-fourth page. This type of advertising is usually accepted in all sections of the newspaper. Classified advertising is generally relegated to a specific portion of the newspaper. In most instances, classified ads are purchased by the word or line.

You can have layout of copy and art produced at no charge by the newspaper's advertising department. You provide the information about your craft product and the newspaper's creative department handles the design and placement of your ad. You can, however, write your own copy and have the ad prepared by an outside agency or graphic artist, providing the newspaper with camera-ready art for your ad space. This gives you more control of the process and can provide a cohesiveness and consistency with your overall promotional effort. It is, of course, more expensive.

Advertising space preparation is similar to readying any other direct response program. You must decide on the copy and art or photograph that you wish to use for the ad, make sure that it fits into the budgeted space, select the date for the ad to appear, keep tabs on the responses received, and evaluate the results.

Many newspaper, radio, and TV advertising departments have *national rates* and *local rates.* The national rate is the charge for large accounts—major companies like automobile and beverage advertisers whose ad space is purchased through agencies who receive a media commission, usually 15%. Ads which are not placed through agencies usually receive the local rate. Rate sheets are available (Figs. 11–3, 11–4, and 11–5); contracts are generally required (Fig. 11–6).

Magazine Direct Response

Among the basic differences between magazine and newspaper direct response advertising is the timeframe. Major newspapers appear daily, while most magazines are issued weekly or monthly. This means that magazine ads will remain in the reader's hands for a much longer time period newspaper advertising.

Magazines also offer a much wider range of color and quality than do newspapers, and can be chosen to reach a more selective target market. They can, for example, portray your product better for the upscale market.

Many magazine ads can be bought *run-of-the magazine* or *split-run.* The split-run allows you to target or segment your direct response effort to specific areas or to limited numbers, while the run-of-the-magazine will place your craft product ad in every magazine printed. Magazines also accept inserts which are generally bound into certain positions in the booklet. Rates and timetables for these inserts are different with every magazine and available on request.

One of the newest magazine advertising techniques is the *advertorial.* This allows you to develop an advertising piece that looks like an editorial about your craft product. Although there is some notice that it is advertising, the material often appears to the reader as a product endorsement.

Magazine space is sold by the column inch, page, or fractional section of a page. Camera-ready art is expected from the advertiser. Magazines can produce the ads but often level a charge for the service.

Many magazines, like newspapers, have special classified sections

Classified Advertising Rates

CLASSIFIED DISPLAY
Open Rate — $4.40 per Column Inch

Consecutive Insertions:	Rate Per Column Inch	Savings from open rate
6 - 12	$4.18	5%
13 - 25	$3.96	10%
26 - 51	$3.74	15%
52 or more	$3.52	20%

CLASSIFIED READER ADVERTISEMENTS

Consecutive Insertions:	Rate per word	Savings from open rate
1 - 3	$.18*	—
4 - 7	$.17	6%
8 or more	$.16	13%

*Minimum Charge $3.06
$2.00 billing charge if payment not received within 10 days.
Blind Box Rate: pickup - $10.00; mail - $15.00

LEGAL NOTICES

Insertions	Rate per Line
First	.445
Additional	.365

Tabular rate: add $.08 per line to initial insertion rate.
Affidavit or Voucher- $2.00 each.

SERVICE DIRECTORY

Consecutive Months	Rate per column inch	Savings from open rate
3	$87.	24%
6	$147.	36%
12	$257.	44%

All Service Directories must be pre-paid.
Ads begin first of each month and are published in every issue.

NEW YORK STATE CLASSIFIED AD NETWORK

This unique program will allow classified advertisers to run a 25 word classified ad in any or all of New York State's three regions with one phone call to the Sullivan County Democrat. Now you can target your advertising to either the Western, Central or Metro areas of New York State or hit all three — including more than 180 Community newspapers and more than 3 million readers. One region is $80, two regions $145 and all three regions only $198. The only way to cover all of New York State with a Classified ad . . . It's so easy. For further information call the Sullivan County Democrat at 914-887-5200.

PUBLICATION DATES AND DEADLINES

Publication Date	Deadline
Tuesday	Noon Friday
Friday	Noon Wednesday

BILLS/CREDIT

Accounts must be pre paid until credit investigation has been completed.

2. Accounts 30 days in arrears will be refused until such time balance has been paid. A finance charge of 1½% per month (18% per annum) will be applied to all accounts with a balance of 30 days or more.
3. All errors must be reported within 30 days to insure proper credit applications.

PUBLISHER'S CONDITIONS

1. The Democrat reserves the right to edit, reject or cancel copy or illustrations at any time which does not meet its standards of acceptance.
2. All advertising in the Democrat must conform to local, state and federal laws.
3. The Democrat's liability for errors in publication or for wrong date of publication are limited to the cost of the advertising space involved. The Sullivan County Democrat shall in no case be liable for failure to publish, no matter what the reason for that failure.
4. The Sullivan County Democrat assumes responsibility for one days publication of an error. Credit will be determined on 1st insertion only. The advertiser has the responsibility to check the ad for accuracy and is responsible for subsequent days of incorrect publication.
5. Written cancellations of advertisements are necessary to assure cancellation.

9 COLUMN MECHANICALS

1 col. — 1 5/16″	4 col. — 5 13/16″	7 col. — 10 5/16″
2 col. — 2 13/16″	5 col. — 7 5/16″	8 col. — 11 13/16″
3 col. — 4 5/16″	6 col. — 8 13/16″	9 col. — 13 5/16″

Fig. 11–3. Classified advertising rates for a weekly newspaper.
(Courtesy Sullivan County Democrat)

Retail Advertising Rates

RUN OF PAPER DISPLAY
Open Rate — $6.08 per Standard Advertising Unit (SAU)

Consecutive Weeks: (1 issue per week)	Rate Per SAU	Savings from open rate
6	$5.77	5%
13	$5.47	10%
26	$5.17	15%
52	$4.86	20%

Minimum Ad size for discount rate is 3 SAUs.

BULK RATE
Open Rate — $6.08 per Standard Advertising Unit (SAU)

Units of Space Reserved Per Year	Rate Per SAU	Savings from open rate
250 Units	$5.80	4.5%
450 Units	$5.68	6.5%
650 Units	$5.50	9.5%
850 Units	$5.38	11.5%
1050 Units	$5.20	14.5%
1350 Units	$5.02	17.5%

CATSKILL-DELAWARE MAGAZINE

Page Size	Rate
Full	$415
2/3	$277
1/2	$208
1/3	$1
1/6	$ 70
Full Page w/Color	$515

TABLOID RATES

Page Size	Rate
Full	$399
1/2	$200
1/4	$100
1/8	$ 50

PUBLICATION DATES AND DEADLINES

Publication Date	Deadline
Tuesday	5:00 p.m. Thursday
Friday	5:00 p.m. Tuesday

Sample

General Information

PUBLISHER'S CONDITIONS

1. Advertisement orders for specific positioning within the newspaper containing the proviso "or omit" will not be accepted. Special page placement is available on ads of 1/4 page or more at 15% extra.
2. The Democrat reserves the right to edit, reject or cancel copy or illustrations at any time which does not meet its standards of publication.
3. The Democrat may decline to run further advertising for a contract advertiser whose account is more than 30 days overdue.
4. All advertising in the Democrat must conform to local, state and federal laws.
5. The Democrat's liability for errors in publication or for wrong date of publication are limited to the cost of the advertising space involved. The Sullivan County Democrat shall in no case be liable for failure to publish, no matter what the reason for that failure.
6. The Sullivan County Democrat assumes responsibility for one days publication of an error. Credit will be determined on 1st insertion only. The advertiser has the responsibility to check the ad for accuracy and is responsible for subsequent days of incorrect publication. All errors must be reported within 30 days of publication to insure proper credit applications.
7. Written cancellations of advertisements are necessary to assure cancellation.
8. Advertisements resembling news type must carry the heading "advertisement."

ADVERTISING POLICY

Inclusive in rates are standard composition and layout. Additional camera work, typesetting, reversals and art services are subject to extra charges. Ads with reverses or screens in excess of 25% of the ad's area will be surcharged 25% of the cost of the ad or $3.00, whichever is greater.

SPECIAL CHARGES

1. ROP color available upon request.
2. Preprinted sections, insert rates and requirements furnished upon request.

SPECIAL SECTIONS

List of annual special sections available upon request.

9 COLUMN MECHANICALS

1 col. — 2¹/₁₆''	4 col. — 8¾''
2 col. — 4⁵/₈''	5 col. — 11''
3 col. — 6⁵/₈''	6 col. — 13¼''

MECHANICAL REQUIREMENTS

1. Type page: six columns to the page. Image Area: 13⁵/₁₆''x21''
2. Ad depth over 18½'' will be billed at 21'' depth.

Fig. 11–4. Advertising rate chart for a weekly newspaper. The SAU (Standard Advertising Unit) is the column width of the newspaper times one inch deep. Weekly newspapers have different column widths. *(Courtesy Sullivan County Democrat)*

Advertising Rates

A. Rates for ROP Local Display Advertising

No agency commission allowed on rates printed on this rate card.

Weekly Minimum Contracts

Advertising space to be used within specified number of weeks from date of contract.
Advertiser must also meet weekly space requirements.

Rates Per Column Inch

Contract Size	52 Week		26 Week		13 Week	
Column Inches	Daily	Sunday	Daily	Sunday	Daily	Sunday
3	$12.84	$14.81	$13.52	$15.59	$14.24	$16.41
5	$12.50	$14.41	$13.16	$15.17	$13.85	$15.98
10	$12.32	$14.21	$12.97	$14.96	$13.66	$15.75
22½	$12.20	$14.07	$12.83	$14.80	$13.51	$15.58
45	$11.92	$13.75	$12.54	$14.47	$13.21	$15.24
90	$11.74	$13.55	$12.36	$14.25	$13.01	$15.01
180	$11.55	$13.33	$12.16	$14.03	$12.80	$14.77

Monthly Minimum Contracts

Advertising space to be used within one year from date of contract. Advertiser must also meet monthly space requirements.

Sample

Contract Size		Rates Per Column Inch	
Column Inches			
Annual	Monthly	Daily	Sunday
270	22½	$12.98	$14.80
540	45	$12.80	$14.59
1,080	90	$12.67	$14.46
2,160	180	$12.37	$14.10
4,680	390	$12.19	$13.91
9,360	780	$11.89	$13.56
18,720	1,560	$11.42	$13.04
28,060	2,338	$11.12	$12.70
37,400	3,120	$10.76	$12.29
50,000	4,166	$10.34	$11.80
60,000	5,000	$10.04	$11.47
70,000	5,833	$9.80	$11.18
80,000	6,666	$9.07	$10.36
85,000	7,083	$8.84	$10.08
90,000	7,500	$8.65	$9.87
95,000	7,916	$8.54	$9.74
100,000	8,333	$7.94	$9.05

Yearly Bulk Space Contracts

Advertising space to be used within one year from date of contract.

Contract Size	Rates Per Column Inch	
Column Inches	Daily	Sunday
135	$14.53	$16.59
270	$13.79	$15.74
540	$13.66	$15.57
1,080	$13.36	$15.22
2,160	$13.11	$14.94
4,680	$12.85	$14.66

Open Rate - Per Column Inch

Daily	Sunday
$19.26	**$22.15**

Fig. 11–5. Advertising rate chart for a small daily newspaper. *(Courtesy Times Herald Record)*

Sullivan County Democrat

RETAIL ADVERTISING CONTRACT

*The purpose of this contract is to offer lower ad rates to our quantity buyers
and quality customers*

1. The Advertiser will furnish the SULLIVAN COUNTY DEMOCRAT copy in such quantities and size as is necessary to complete this contract. The contract period will extend through the following dates: _____to_____.

2. The Advertiser agrees to pay the SULLIVAN COUNTY DEMOCRAT at the rate of $_____ per Standard Advertising Unit, subject to the conditions set forth.

3. a. **Weekly contract:** Minimum amount of space to be used under this agreement is 3 Standard Advertising Units to appear for _____ consecutive weeks, one issue per week.

   b. **Bulk contract:** Minimum amount of space to be used under this agreement is _____ Standard Advertising Units. The advertiser agrees to use space contracted for within the one-year contract period.

4. The Advertiser agrees to make payment monthly, on or before the 30th day of the month for all advertising used during the preceding month.

5. SULLIVAN COUNTY DEMOCRAT may terminate this contract without notice, if the Advertiser should fail to pay for said advertising as provided by paragraph number four.

6. SULLIVAN COUNTY DEMOCRAT may terminate this contract upon seven (7) days notice for any other cause considered sufficient.

7. All advertising is subject to acceptance by the SULLIVAN COUNTY DEMOCRAT. The Advertiser agrees that all advertisements are accepted and printed by SULLIVAN COUNTY DEMOCRAT upon the Advertiser's representation that said Advertiser is authorized to publish the entire contents and subject matter thereof. In consideration of SULLIVAN COUNTY DEMOCRAT acceptance of such advertising publications, the Advertiser will indemnify and save SULLIVAN COUNTY DEMOCRAT from and against any loss or expense resulting from claims based upon the contents or subject matter of such advertisements without limitations.

8. The Advertiser agrees that all errors in advertising must be called to the attention of SULLIVAN COUNTY DEMOCRAT within one week after error appears for any adjustment in the bill.

9. The Advertiser agrees that if his advertising is less in volume than the agreed minimum (number 3b), his rate will be in accordance with the rate schedule in effect at the date of contract signature.

10. SULLIVAN COUNTY DEMOCRAT agrees that if the Advertiser shall use an amount of advertising of sufficient volume to earn a lower rate, in accordance with the rate schedule in effect at date of contract signature, that the next lower rate will apply to all advertising used and that an amount will be credited to the account of the Advertiser to adjust space used to the lower rate.

11. SULLIVAN COUNTY DEMOCRAT reserves the right to increase the contract rate if basic costs increase, with a 30 day notice. The Advertiser has the option of (1) continuing at new rate, (2) adjust the column inch commitment, or (3) void this contract without penalty with a written notice prior to the rate increase.

12. The advertiser further agrees that this written contract constitute the whole contract as written and no oral agreements in relation to this contract shall be recognized.

Advertiser's Firm Name _____

Address _____

_____

Phone _____

Signed _____

(Signature of Authorized Officer)

Accepted by: _____ SULLIVAN COUNTY DEMOCRAT

Dated: _____

Fig. 11–6. A weekly newspaper display advertising contract. *(Courtesy Sullivan County Democrat)*

which are especially suitable to handcrafted products. Called *The Classified Mart, The Business Place, The Bargain Section,* or a variety of similar names, advertising costs in these section are often less expensive than in display sections. Ad rates for classified sections are usually computed by the word.

Magazines can also offer *ad bingos,* or *reader service* response capabilities. Here, numbers are printed in the ads, and a postcard is inserted in the back of the magazine with all of the reader service numbers. The reader interested in a particular product ad circles that number on the card, fills out name, address, and sometimes other demographic information, then mails the card. The magazine, or a private service, computerizes the responses and notifies the advertisers of these leads. In some cases, the service will send interested parties a brochure on your products which you supply. This service can be included in the cost of advertising the magazine. There is a longer timeframe on this type of service—often the first reports of reader interest will not reach you for four weeks or more after the magazine has come out.

Telemarketing as a Direct Response Method

Telemarketing use the telephone in an organized fashion to sell products or services directly to the consumer. The process makes effective use of consumer credit cards and toll-free phone numbers and can provide rapid sales response.

Telemarketing firms can handle the entire process for you, utilizing teams of callers or automated devices. You can also adapt the process for your own use. To assure a successful telemarketing operation, there are a number of prerequisites to consider.

A good *list of names* to solicit, and *accurate telephone numbers* are the primary tools. While all names and addresses in a zip code block can usually be located and will receive mail in a direct mail response program, comprehensive lists of telephone numbers are not as easy to obtain. Many individuals prefer unlisted phone numbers, and although these numbers can be obtained, it takes more effort. Telephone random dialing systems used in conjunction with a telemarketing program, for example, will usually pick up unlisted numbers in an area being worked.

Well-trained personnel, capable of speaking and responding to the potential consumer effectively on the phone, and a *script* or *spiel* are other important requirements for telemarketing. The caller must be able to give friendly and flexible responses in addition to the prepared sales script. The best-trained person will be ineffective without a well-researched *script*. The telemarketer has a very limited time to explain the reason for the telephone call, and to convince the person on the other end of the line about his or her sincerity and the consumer's need for your product.

There are several other pointers in developing a successful script. Testing can play an important role—it can provide you with positive and negative responses from potential customers. There are also professionals who specialize in the development of such scripts. Some telemarketers claim that within a very few seconds of talking with a consumer, they can accurately forecast whether or not the individual will make a purchase.

Computer-generated telemarketing systems can respond with almost human characteristics. These systems, designed to sell almost any product, individually and automatically dial all telephone numbers within a selected exchange. When someone answers, the human-voiced computer speaks and asks questions in a pre-set pattern. The system uses a script designed for the individual product, but has the capability of deviating from the script when certain questions are posed by the consumer. In most cases, the ultimate goal of this system is to generate sales leads. It does this by requesting that the person called gives a name and phone number to receive further information or a gift. A (non-computer) salesperson then follows up and tries to close the sale.

Certain products may lend themselves to immediate sale through telemarketing. In this case, the computerized telemarketing system requests that the buyer provides name, address, and a credit card number. The telemarketing units are checked regularly, and the product ordered is sent to the requesting consumer.

The downside of telemarketing is its high cost, the potential of strict government restrictions, and negative consumer reactions. In addition to telephone service expenses, costs include maintaining a staff of skilled sales persons throughout the day and into night-time hours. There may also be the need for operator availability 24 hours per day if you are marketing to a wide response area. Perhaps the most important problem facing the telemarketing industry is governmental regulations resulting from abuses by unscrupulous telemarket operators, and many complaints by people annoyed by the intrusion of the system.

If you feel that your craft product lends itself to telemarketing, you can try it on a limited basis. Start by locating a suitable list of names to call. These might be people who have seen your products at shows and whose names you have collected, or names purchased from a list company in your section of the country. The list might be limited to people who have demonstrated an interest in craft products or products similar to yours, and who are known purchasers at a selected dollar level. The list can be secured with telephone numbers alongside each name.

Next, develop a script for your product. Remember to have answers available to questions you feel people might ask. You may want to offer a product guarantee. If you accept credit card charges, use this for product payment. If not, be prepared to accept checks. Be aware that it is difficult, without recourse to costly legal action, to collect bad checks. This is especially true of out-of-state checks.

Select a noninvasive timeframe to make your telemarketing calls. Very early morning hours are taboo, as are mealtime hours. Use your judgment on hours to call—choose times you would feel comfortable receiving such calls, and remember to allow for different time zones if your calls are national or international.

Direct Response Ad Cost

There are a number of ways to determine your *effective ad costs* in direct response advertising. Costs relate directly to the number of orders or inquiries received through the advertising medium. If you are checking television or radio advertising costs, on the other hand, your *calculations are based on CPM (the cost per thousand) listeners.* This, incidentally, is why ratings are so important in the TV and radio industries. When ratings go up, so do advertising rates. If you are using telemarketing to sell your product, the costs are based on the number of calls made to the selected audience and the number of responses. You would have to make a judgment on whether cost calculations should be based on direct sales or sales leads.

The more closely and correctly you define your potential buyer (narrow your target market), the more cost-effective your direct response advertising costs become. What this means is that the more people who are likely to respond to your message, the lower your total costs. To define your buyers requires a thoughtful analysis of demographics of the magazines, newspapers, or other media to match them to your target audience. The closer you come to the target, the more effective your ads are likely to be, e.g., the more people will buy.

Analyzing Direct Response Results

What type of results should you expect from your direct response advertising?

Experts in the field forecast results in a variety of ways. You will find that they always leave a wide gap between the high and low expectations.

It bears repeating: direct response is not an exact science. The average consumer has the ability to throw off almost any research, and an uncanny talent for continually changing positions, desires, needs, thought patterns, and purchasing habits. Absolutes one day can change completely the next day. With these warnings in mind, consider the following examples.

Some direct mail people feel that they have been successful if they generate between 5 and 55 orders per 1000 direct response letters mailed. Others feel a campaign has been successful if it achieves a 2% response. As you can readily recognize, the range between projected low and high response figures is great.

Magazine adherents say they are comfortable when their return on a full-page ad shows fractional response, such as a ¼% to several responses per 1000 of the magazine's total circulation. If the ad is smaller, the anticipated response is less.

The key in all direct response advertising is to: (1) target your advertising to the correct population and, (2) market a product with a high enough profit margin so that even a modest direct response is profitable.

Chapter Highlights

- Direct response advertising allows you to communicate with potential buyers one-on-one.
- The direct response process offers many communications options

including direct mail, publication advertising, postcard ads, free-standing inserts in newspapers and magazines, card packs, catalog sales, and telemarketing.

- Some of the factors affecting the increase in the effectiveness of direct response advertising are the increase in toll-free telephone numbers, widespread computer use, increased numbers of working family members, more disposable income, heavy traffic on highways and in shopping centers, and fear of crime.
- Handcrafted products are especially adaptable to direct response selling methods.
- One-step response occurs when a buyer orders the product directly from the ad and the product is delivered. There are no intervening steps like requests for information, sales calls, or followups.
- The two-step response by a consumer requires two separate actions. The first is a request for information; the second a product purchase.
- Test your campaign by sampling to determine the effectiveness of your mailing package (Fig. 11–7).
- The two main components of a direct mail campaign are the mailing list and the mailing package.
- Your direct response package can be mailed using first-class or bulk-rate postage.
- A card-pack mailing allows you to put information about your product together with others and to reach potential purchasers at a lower cost than individual mailings.
- Syndicate or catalog direct response marketing places information and photographs of your product in a sales packet or booklet with other products.
- A free-standing insert is a section inserted into a magazine or newspaper. It can be used for a direct response ad about your product.
- An advertorial is an advertising piece that looks like an editorial piece of the paper or magazine in which it appears.
- You can purchase split-runs of newspapers or magazines. This permits segmentation of the market you are trying to reach.
- Telemarketing requires an accurate list of names and telephone numbers to solicit.

- Well-trained personnel are vital to a successful telemarketing operation.
- After names, telephone numbers, and trained personnel are in place, an effective telemarketing program requires a good script or "spiel" to tell the story and sell your product.
- Direct response costs are often calculated by the cost per thousand readers or viewers, or by the cost per response or order received.

- Test the price, the format or layout of your mailing package, and any offer made in the package.
- If, for example, you have selected telemarketing rather than direct mail as a method to sell your craft product, not only can you test the price structure, but you can also experiment with a number of different telephone "spiels" to see which is the most effective.
- Each direct response method that you have selected to market your craft product has an area that lends itself to testing.
- Only test one item in your mailing package or direct response program at a time in order to determine which item may be a factor in the success or failure of the technique. If you do more than one, the results of the test can be confusing.
- Log the responses received from the test mailing or other direct response technique. Your expectations of the results will govern whether you move forward with your campaign or make adjustments in the current method.
- If the response differences between packages or programs tested are small, you may consider that they are normal statistical variations.
- Once your test mailing establishes that your mailing package is satisfactory, or the direct response technique selected is working, do not make any changes, or you are liable to alter the results.

Fig. 11–7. Some suggestions for testing your product direct response mailing packet.

The Times Herald
RECORD

40 Mulberry St., Middletown, N.Y. 10940
(914) 343-2181

LOCAL DISPLAY ADVERTISING CONTRACT

Effective Date _____

WE BOTH AGREE

That in consideration of the terms of this mutual agreement the undersigned will furnish advertising copy to The Times Herald-RECORD for a period of 13/26/52 weeks from the above date, the text of which shall be satisfactory to The Times Herald-RECORD. A contract of 52 weeks will continue automatically for successive periods unless either party notifies the other in writing of intention to terminate at least thirty (30) days before the beginning of any continuation term.

This advertising is to occupy a minimum space of_____ inches per year with a minimum of_____ i n c h e s each and every week/ month.

This advertising shall be billed at_____ per column inch, daily and_____ per column inch Sunday, providing the terms of this agreement are not violated.

If the advertiser should use less than the required number of inches weekly, monthly, or yearly as agreed, the contract becomes void, and the earned rate will be charged in accordance with the rate in effect.

Failure to meet payment terms will be considered a breach of this contract and billing at the earned rate as set forth on the rate card may be imposed. If it shall be necessary to employ an attorney to collect advertising charges due hereunder, the advertiser agrees to pay court costs, the disbursements incurred by such attorneys and his fees for service in connection with such collection and it is further agreed that reasonable attorney's fees herein shall be 30% of the advertising charges sought to be collected.

Sample

A REFUND TO YOU

If the quantity of advertising purchased by advertiser qualifies advertiser for a lower rate, the Times Herald-RECORD shall give appropriate credit in accordance with the rate card upon the anniversary date hereof.

This agreement shall not be invalidated by reasons of insertions of advertising copy in wrong locations or by failure to publish such copy. Publisher shall not be held responsible for any failure to publish and any errors will be limited to the cost of the advertising space actually occupied by the error.

The rate card and the terms and conditions thereon attached hereto which is part of this contract, is subject to change at anytime, including but not limited to replacement of bulk or monthly minimum annual rates with rates based entirely on monthly lineage, effective thirty (30) days after written notice by The Times Herald-RECORD with respect to advertising copy published after the effective date of change. However, the advertiser has the right to cancel this contract as of the effective date of any rate change by notice in writing to The Times Herald-RECORD not later than fifteen (15) days before the effective date of any rate change. The Contract may not be assigned by the advertiser without the written consent of The Times Herald-RECORD.

FIRM NAME_____

FIRM ADDRESS_____

_____PHONE_____

SIGNED_____

SALESPERSON_____

ACCEPTED FOR THE
TIMES HERALD-RECORD_____

ACCOUNT NO._____

CREDIT APPLICATION

☐ **attached**

☐ **already on file**

Fig. 11–8. A daily newspaper display advertising contract. *(Courtesy Times Herald Record)*

12. ROP Depth Requirements

Five-column ROP advertisements are not permitted.

Six-column ROP advertisements must be a minimum of 7½ inches in depth. All other advertisements must be a minimum of one inch deep for every column wide.

All advertisements over 13 inches in depth will be charged for the full column depth (15 inches).

13. Contract and Copy Regulations   Refer to Advertising Policies (# 4).

14. Deadlines

For SUNDAY publication	4:30 p.m. Wednesday
For MONDAY publication	4:30 p.m. Thursday
For BUSINESS MONDAY publication	4:30 p.m. Wednesday
For TUESDAY publication	4:30 p.m. Friday
For WEDNESDAY publication	11:30 a.m. Saturday
For THURSDAY publication	4:30 p.m. Monday
For FRIDAY publication	4:30 p.m. Tuesday
For GO magazine publication	4:30 p.m. Tuesday
For NEIGHBORS publication	4:30 p.m. Friday
For SATURDAY publication	11:30 a.m. Wednesday
For SUNDAY MAGAZINE publication	4:30 p.m. Tuesday
For TV & VIDEO GUIDE publication	4:30 p.m. 10 days prior

Advance deadlines for holidays, color ads, and double-trucks.

15. Mechanical Requirements

The Times Herald-RECORD is a 6 column tabloid size newspaper printed by the offset process. Mats for advertising purposes are not acceptable. Offset reproduction proofs are preferred and will assure advertisers better quality in reproduction.

Screens may be 65, 85, or 100 line only.

Advertisements over 13 inches in depth will be charged as full column depth (15 inches). Double trucks will be charged as 13 columns. Advertisers should allow an additional day for copy preparation.

Page Size: Tabloid - 10¼" x 15

	Picas	Inches
Single Column	9½	1⁹⁄₁₆
2 Column	20	3¼
3 Column	30½	5
4 Column	41	6¾
6 Column	62	10¼
Double Truck	130½	21¾

TV & VIDEO GUIDE MECHANICAL REQUIREMENTS

TV & VIDEO GUIDE is published every Sunday and is a quarterfold, 5 column by 10 inch size.

	Picas	Inches
Single Column	7½	1¼
2 Column	16	2⅝
3 Column	24½	4
4 Column	33	5½
5 Column	41½	6⅞

Fig. 11–9. Mechanical advertising requirements for a daily newspaper. (Courtesy Times Herald Record)

CHAPTER 12

Television and Radio Exposure for Your Craft

Television and radio have a great deal in common as communication vehicles, It is important, however, to know their similarities as well as their differences if you are to use each to secure exposure for your product. While radio is strictly an audio medium, i.e., radio broadcasting produces sound waves only, television adds a visual perspective to its audio impact. Both radio and TV not only serve as sources of entertainment, but also as important informational and advertising vehicles. Each has the capacity to get people to respond. In the field of marketing, this means that television and radio can be used to expand the market for your craft product.

Using TV to Market Your Craft

Manufacturers and purveyors of products and services spend billions of dollars annually to market their wares on TV. It is essentially a mass market medium that should be considered if you have, or can envision, large-scale production, or if by establishing an important image you can position your product in a higher price range. Television permits potential consumers to inspect a product in full color while listening to commentary about it in the comfort of their own living room. In today's marketplace, television viewing has become a habit. It cuts across all socio-economic lines, encompassing nearly every age group, sex, and income level. When potential buyers see you and your creations on television, it adds to your credibility as a craftperson and enhances the value of your crafts.

While the cost of using television to promote a craft product may seem prohibitive, this chapter will deal with a number of affordable ways to secure TV exposure for your crafts and for yourself. It will explain how to harness the power of relatively inexpensive publicity and creative approaches to the media as well as the use of paid advertising.

It is helpful in any event to understand the medium if you are considering it either for paid advertising or free exposure.

Years ago, there were only a small number of television channels and program outlets available for television exposure. Today, with the increase of local stations, cable channels, and syndicated programs, many opportunities exist for free television coverage as well as limited-cost advertising. Even small business entrepreneurs, such as craftpeople, can now find television advertising, particularly on local or cable channels, effective. In addition, the growth in the number of stations offers opportunities to appear as guests on talk shows, news programs, and special productions.

All television stations are not the same. Some reach large metropolitan markets and some reach neighborhoods or localities. Generally, the larger the market, the more expensive advertising will be and the more difficult it will be to schedule personal appearances or arrange for product mention.

The largest groupings of stations, each responding to a central administration, are called *networks*. Some major networks are NBC (National Broadcasting System), ABC (American Broadcasting System), and CBS (Columbia Broadcasting System). Advertising rates on these networks are usually prohibitive for a small business, often running in the tens of thousands, and in some instances, hundreds of thousands of dollars per advertising spot. The size of the audiences help justify network charges for commercials. The major networks each have several hundred local station affiliates to whom they broadcast some or many programs.

Local TV stations broadcast to a limited area market. Many are

network affiliates, but as television has grown as an advertising medium, nonaffiliated local stations have been springing up throughout
the country. The ad rates for these nonaffiliated stations are usually
considerably less than either network or local affiliate stations. They
may not only be affordable, but often more productive for craftspeople
who seek recognition in specific local markets.

Cable TV stations may broadcast locally, regionally, or nationally.
Examples of nationally-broadcast cable networks include CNN (Cable
News Network), Nickelodeon, and A & E (Arts and Entertainment).

Lower cost advertising space on cable stations competes with both
local stations and TV networks. Some local cable stations offer advertisers the opportunity to place ads on the nationally-broadcast shows they
carry. In addition, because many local cable stations or companies have
well-defined area parameters, they offer an opportunity to deliver a
message to a specific audience.

In considering paid television advertising, it is important to review
the demographic profile of the network, channel, or cable to identify
how many of its viewers match the profile of your potential purchaser.
Fig. 12–1 shows a typical information sheet from a TV station for advertisers giving the demographic coverage of the station. Fig. 12–2 shows
a typical order form or contract from the same station, and Fig. 12–3 is
a program schedule.

Using Radio to Market Your Craft

Like television, radio is a source of entertainment. Like TV, too, it
has promotional and advertising potential for companies large and
small. Radio is considered a strong personal medium, i.e., it develops a
one-on-one relationship between the individual broadcasting and the
individual listener.

A highly mobile medium, radio can be tuned in almost anywhere,
including the millions of vehicles on the road throughout the country.
Industry sources indicate that there are approximately 13,000 individual radio stations in the country, and approximately eighteen radio networks like Mutual, ABC, NBC, CBS, Unistart, and SMN. These are
central radio organizations which provide groups of individual stations
and local affiliates with programming. Network systems are expected to
grow as satellite transmission options increase. Radio is available in AM

MARKET COVERAGE

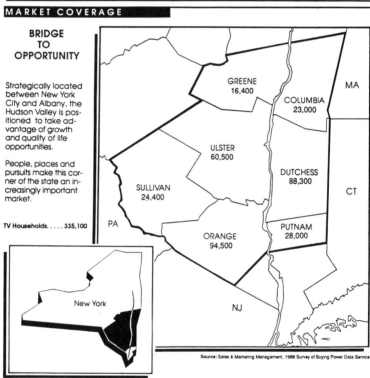

BRIDGE TO OPPORTUNITY

Strategically located between New York City and Albany, the Hudson Valley is positioned to take advantage of growth and quality of life opportunities.

People, places and pursuits make this corner of the state an increasingly important market.

TV Households. 335,100

Source: Sales & Marketing Management, 1988 Survey of Buying Power Data Service

721 Broadway • P.O. Box 1609 • Kingston, New York 12401 • Phone 914/339-6200 • Fax 914/339-6264

Fig. 12–1. Television station's demographic information for advertisers. Map shows areas of coverage and the number of households reached by this TV station. *(Courtesy WTZA-TV, Channel 62)*

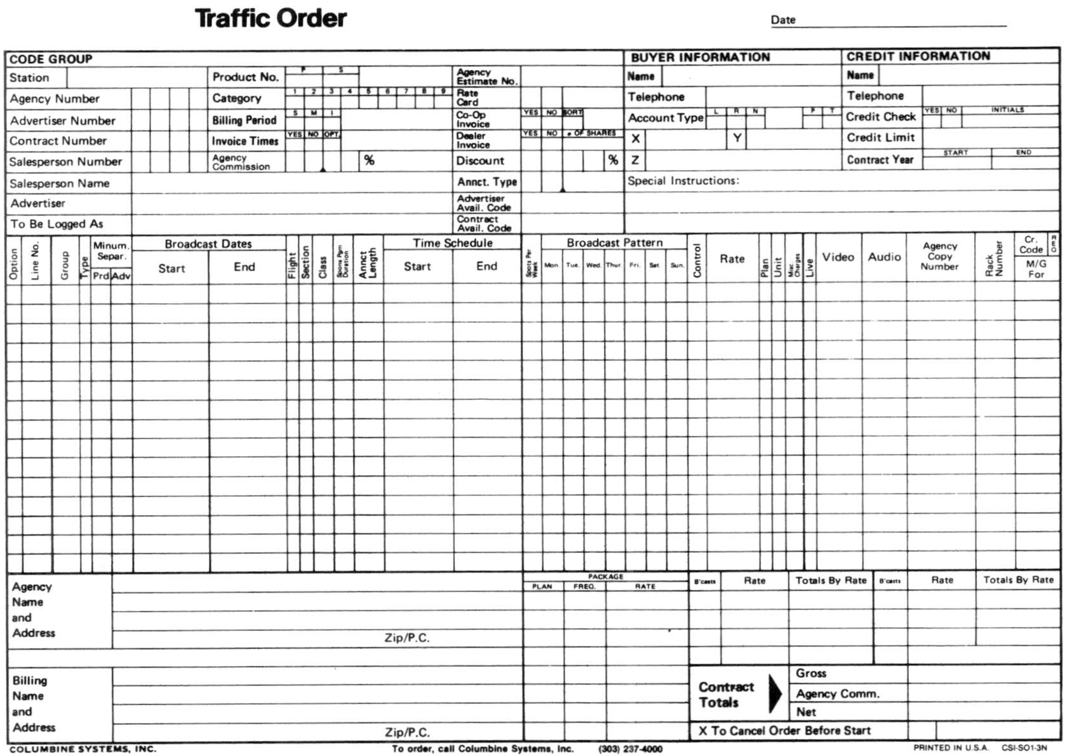

Fig. 12–2. Television station's Traffic Order or contract form. *(Courtesy WTZA-TV, Channel 62)*

WTZA-TV
Programming Schedule

WTZA-TV Associates
P.O. Box 1609
721 Broadway
Kingston, New York 12401
914-339-6200
Fax 914-339-6264

Effective Fall, 1991 (As of 10/09)

Time	Monday-Friday	Saturday	Sunday	Time
6:00 AM	Cardinal O'Connor's Daily Mass			6:00 AM
6:30	Ag Day 10/21		Christian Lifestyles	6:30
7:00	CNN Headline News 10/21	U.S. Farm Report	CNN Headline News	7:00
7:30	This Morning's Business 10/21	CNN Headline News	Various	7:30
8:00	CNN Headline News 10/21	Wall Street Journal Report	Little Mermaid	8:00
8:30	. CNN Headline News	On The River (R)		8:30
9:00	Donahue	Various	Captain Planet (R)	9:00
9:30		Various	Scholastic Match-Up (R)	9:30
10:00	* Sally Jessy Raphael	Various	Various	10:00
10:30		Coach's Show	Various	10:30
11:00	* Jenny Jones	WWF Wrestling	Various	11:00
11:30			Various	11:30
12:00 N	* $100,000 Pyramid	Big East Football	Various	12:00 N
12:30 PM	WTZA Afternoon Movie		Various	12:30 PM
1:00			WTZA Cinema Sunday I	1:00
1:30				1:30
2:00				2:00
2:30	The Disney Afternoon			2:30
3:00	DuckTales / Chip 'N' Dale	Death Valley Days		3:00
3:30	Tale Spin / Darkwing Duck	Have Gun Will Travel		3:30
4:00		Captain Planet	Specials/ WW Of Disney	4:00
4:30	* Teenage Mutant Ninja Turtles	Superboy		4:30
5:00	* The Cosby Show	Super Force		5:00
5:30	WTZA News 5:30pm Edition	Tarzan		5:30
6:00	A Current Affair 10/21	Scratch	On the River	6:00
6:30	WTZA News 6:30pm Edition	Scholastic Match-Up	Broadcast New York	6:30
7:00	Inside Edition 10/21	WKRP In Cincinnati II	Specials	7:00
7:30	WTZA News 7:30pm Edition	Siskel & Ebert		7:30
8:00	WTZA 8 O'Clock Movie	WTZA 8 O'Clock Movie	WTZA 8 O'Clock Movie	8:00
8:30				8:30
9:00				9:00
9:30				9:30
10:00	WTZA News 10:00PM Edition	WTZA Late Movie	A Current Affair Extra	10:00
10:30	CNN Headline News			10:30
11:00	WKRP In Cincinnati		Scratch (R)	11:00
11:30	Gunsmoke M-Th	WTZA Late Movie	Various	11:30
12:00 M		Gunsmoke	CNN Headline News	12:00 M
12:30 AM	WTZA News (R) M-Th			12:30 AM
1:00 AM	Video Power M-Th 10/21	CNN Headline News		1:00 AM
1:30 AM		WTZANews		1:30 AM

* WTZA News Brief   Schedule subject to change.

Fig. 12–3. Television programming schedule. Advertisers can select the time frame in which they want their ads to appear. *(Courtesy WTZA-TV, Channel 62)*

(amplitude modulation) and FM (frequency modulation) with FM dominating the field because of its reception potential.

Statistics indicate that while about one-third of all radios are used outside the home, the average home has six to eight radios, and adult listenership averages twenty-four hours a week.

The large number of radio stations throughout the country provides opportunities to test market your products. Most radio stations feature special formats (country/western, talk, easy rock, religious, etc.) These formats permit you to segment and target specific audiences for your craft product.

Experience has shown that radio requires a high number of advertising spots to impact a market. Consider that the attention level of the average radio listener is relatively low since most people tune in while they are doing something else and that, like TV viewers, radio listeners are exposed to hundreds of advertising messages daily. Effective radio advertising, therefore, requires commercials with strong impact and a heavy repetition schedule.

Figs. 12–4, 12–5, and 12–6 show typical information for advertisers on radio—demographic profile, contract, and rate sheet.

TV and Radio Exposure Methods

As we mentioned previously, there are a number of ways to secure television and radio exposure for your craft product. In addition to *buying advertising time*, you can, at minimal cost, use television and radio *talk and giveaway shows* for product exposure; you can devise ways to get your product or your business on the *news;* use *barter* or the *per-inquiry system* to generate sales, or seek ways to present yourself and/or your product in connection with *specific program formats.* Each approach has particular advantages, uses, and cost-benefit ratios.

If you have the time and/or the money, most advertising and promotional methods can be used concurrently. If you are on a tight budget, analysis of the profit potential of each method is important. Advertising, for example, frequently involves production costs as well as time/space charges. It does, however, let you say what you want to say about your product. Being a talk show guest, on the other hand, while it might be less costly, can often subject you and your work to questions and subjective or gratuitous comments to suit program formats or the host's personality.

PRIMARY COVERAGE AREA

SULLIVAN COUNTY

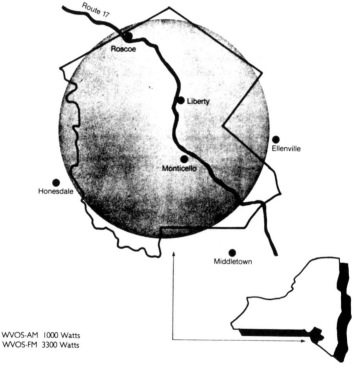

WVOS-AM 1000 Watts
WVOS-FM 3300 Watts

Fig. 12–4. Radio station demographic map indicating the station's area of coverage. *(Courtesy Radio WVOS)*

CONTRACT/ORDER FORM

WVOS
1240 AM
95.9 FM

The Wireless Works, Inc. ▪ P.O. Box 150, Liberty, NY 12754
Office: (914) 292-5533 ▪ News: (914) 292-2094

CUSTOMER NAME: _____   DATE _____

ACCOUNT NUMBER: _____   LOG DESCRIPTION _____

CO-OP: _____

START DATE: _____   END DATE: _____

AFFIDAVIT: YES/NO   SCRIPT AFFIDAVIT: YES/NO

DEDUCT 15% COMMISSION: YES/NO

SPOT LENGTH: _____   TOTAL SPOTS _____

UNIT COST: $ _____   TOTAL COST: _____

	MON	TUES	WED	THU	FRI	SAT	SUN
ROS (5AM - MID)							
DAYTIME: (6AM - 7PM)							
AM DRIVE (6AM - 10AM)							
MIDDAY: (10AM-3PM)							
PM DRIVE (3PM-7PM)							
EVENING: (7PM-MID)							
SPONSORSHIP or EXACT TIME							

NOTES: _____

All announcements are subject to station approval and government regulations. Should less than the number of units ordered be used, the rate earned for the actual time used shall apply. The station's rate card, to which reference is made, shall be a part of this contract. A finance charge of 1.5% per month (18% annual) will be charged on the unpaid balance of past due accounts.

The Wireless Works, Inc. shall have no liability for commercial time which is ordered but not aired except to run make good commercial time at a client's request at a time mutually agreeable with the client and The Wireless Works, Inc.

BY: _____   BY: _____
        (for advertiser)   (for station)

Fig. 12–5. A radio station contract between the station and the purchaser of advertising time or spots. *(Courtesy Radio WVOS)*

WVOS
1240 AM
95.9 FM

Mountain Broadcasting Corp. / P.O. Box 150, Liberty, NY 12754
Office: (914) 292-5533 / News: (914) 292-2094

LOCAL RATES - NET
Effective May 1, 1990

ANNUAL CONTRACT RATES

LEVEL:		1	2	3	4	5	6	7	8
TAP	30 sec	5.55	5.85	6.15	6.60	7.35	7.60	8.30	9.05
	60 sec	7.75	8.15	8.60	9.25	10.30	10.70	11.60	12.70
DAYPART	30 sec	6.55	6.90	7.25	7.75	8.65	8.90	9.75	10.65
	60 sec	9.15	9.65	10.15	10.90	12.05	12.50	13.60	14.90
EXACT	30 sec	9.15	9.65	10.15	10.90	12.05	12.50	13.60	14.90
	60 sec	12.85	13.55	14.20	15.10	16.90	17.50	19.10	20.90
NEWSCASTS	60 sec	14.80	15.60	16.40	17.15	18.55	18.90	20.25	22.90
ANNUAL VOLUME MIN. FOR RATE		23,000	18,000		0,000	6,500	4,800	3,400	1,950

Sample

SHORT TERM RATES

		Per Week: 15 times Per Month: 30 times Per Quarter: 78 times	25 times 60 times 130 times	40 times 100 times 182 times
TAP	30 sec	12.30	11.60	10.85
	60 sec	17.30	16.25	15.20
DAYPART	30 sec	14.50	13.60	12.75
	60 sec	20.30	19.10	17.85

SATURATION PACKAGES

15 Per Day	30's: 10.10	60's: 14.15
25 Per Day	30's: 9.35	60's: 13.10

Ten percent discount on orders placed for 52 weeks without change.
Add-ons to a consistent schedule without a break at the earned rate.
Weather, Remotes, and other special programs quoted on request.
Unfulfilled contracts are subject to short rate to the rate earned.

Fig. 12–6. Radio station advertising rates for 30-second and 60-second spots. *(Courtesy Radio WVOS)*

TV Advertising

Television ads are sold on a *supply and demand basis.* During a period when the demand for space is not great, the cost can be a fraction of exactly the same space when demand is at its height. A series of one-minute TV spots, for example, during a low-demand time might cost $2,500 while the exact same space might run $10,000 or more when demand is high. National elections or the World Series are examples of peak advertising demand times, while the post-Christmas season is usually a low-demand advertising time period.

The price of ad spots is also determined by a number of other factors. The rating that a particular show generates affects the cost of a TV spot as does the time in which the commercial appears. Prime time carries a higher advertising price tag than one o'clock in the morning. If, however, you are marketing a product for insomniacs, the 1:00 AM spot may achieve more for you than the prime-time spot.

Advertising space is also frequently sold in packages containing time spots throughout a particular day, or a series of different timeframes and dates. These packages are sold by the station and also through packagers or agents.

While some television channels and radio stations will produce ads for you at low or no charge, many advertisers prefer to use agencies to produce and place creative commercials. Advertising agencies receive a commission, generally 15%, from the media. They also charge the advertiser a fixed retainer fee, cost-plus production fees, or combination of both.

Modern camcorders and recording devices also make it possible for you to produce your own video and audiotapes. If you are seeking to include sophisticated techniques, you can rent editing time and production advice at the studio. If you do your own commercials, be sure to time them accurately and produce them in formats compatible with the station's equipment. Radio spots are generally sold in thirty- and sixty-second segments; television in ten-, fifteen-, thirty-, and sixty-second spots.

If you are not using an agency, you begin the process by designing and producing an advertising spot, and then pay the TV station for airtime to play and replay the spot at selected times. Your promotional budget will determine how many plays, or times your commercial will be seen and heard. You will have two budgetary charges to consider: the production cost, and the airtime cost.

When you decide to use television advertising as a medium for selling your craft product, make sure that you start with a plan. These are some of the steps that you might want to consider:

- *Develop the budget.* Carefully research the costs. Secure all cost data in writing so that your projections are accurate and you are in a position to control possible cost overruns. Be prepared to stick to your budget.
- *Decide who your audiences are and their geographic locations.* If you are aware of the target consumers' income levels and any other personalized information that might influence product sales, include this data in your resource bank.
- *Decide if you are going to use an advertising agency to produce and place your commercial.* It is beneficial to meet with several agencies before making up your mind about which one, if any, best suits your needs. The process will give you an insight into what has to be done, what the agencies will do, and for what price.
- *Secure demographic and psychographic market studies* from the channels you are considering for advertising and determine which channel offers the best match for your product.
- *Make sure that your ads are developed for your target market* and are technically correct for the channel or channels you select. Commercials must fit the time specifications. If you fall short by a few seconds, you will lose valuable airtime. If you run over, your ad may not be accepted or it may be cut short on airing. Your master tape must also meet the specifications of the station. Most important, your commercial must depict your product, stimulate people to want it, and tell them where or how to buy it.
- *Select and purchase your television spot time.* The television day is divided into seven timeframes. If you know your audience, you may be able to select the best time designation(s) for your craft product promotion. Television time frame designations include:
    Mornings (7 AM to 9 AM), Monday through Friday
    Daytime (9 AM to 4:30 PM), Monday through Friday
    Early Fringe (4:30 PM to 7:30 PM), Monday through Friday
    Prime Time Access (7:30 PM to 8:30 PM), Sunday through Saturday
    Prime Time (8 PM to 11 PM), Monday through Saturday
    Prime Time (7 PM to 11 PM), Sunday only
    Late News (11 PM to 11:30 PM), Monday through Friday
    Late Fringe (11:30 PM to 1 AM), Monday through Friday

- Television stations issue *rate cards* in which they detail the charges for advertising space. This cost information is generally offered to the potential purchaser in timeframe designations (e.g., Early Fringe or Prime Time) and number of spots (e.g., 25 spots or 100 spots). Discounts are usually available when purchasing a number of spots by contract or special package. You should be aware that you can frequently *negotiate TV spot rates* and packages with the station's advertising people. The rate charges are most often dependent on the station's open airtime.

- After your TV ads have aired, *review your sales results* closely. If you are using more than one TV station, note which produces the most sales or inquiries. If you are using more than one ad and/or more than one time slot, determine which ad and which slot draw the best results. Keep a record of response times so that you can record the speed with which results or sales flow into your office from various advertising efforts. The use of the toll-free phone numbers and the acceptance of credit card purchases (both of which make it more convenient for the customer but more costly for you) can provide you with an almost instantaneous knowledge of the pull of each commercial.

TV Ad Production—Whether your TV commercial is commercially prepared, or you plan on handling the project yourself, there are basic preparation steps and some basic principles to understand. If your commercial is being developed by an ad agency, a copy team and creative artist are usually involved in the production.

A TV commercial consists of two parts, a visual or motive portion, and an audio section of spoken word, music, or other sounds. Both segments are integrated onto the film or video strip.

In preparing a commercial, always keep in mind two factors. First, because TV commercials function within strict time limitations, every second of the production must be accurately timed and pull its weight. Second, since television commercials, once viewed, are usually not retained in hard copy or videotape, they must make a memorable impact when they are seen.

Although the audio section of the commercial should be relevant to the video portion, the visual should be capable of speaking for itself. Product benefits and intangible inherent rewards can be highlighted with voice-overs or with clearly legible print-overs.

- Always make sure that all elements of the commercial—action, video, and audio—complement each other. The objective is for the viewing consumer to understand and react to the message of the commercial.
- Limit the number of messages in the commercial so that the viewer is not confused or overburdened. If you are selling style, your video should express style; if you offer originality or unique works, these qualities should permeate your commercial.
- The rationale of television advertising is that it is more effective to display a story than to tell it. Remember that you are paying for the visual message—otherwise you could be on radio—and make sure that your visual carries its weight.
- The ad copy should enhance the visual, strengthen motivation and/or provide further information.

A TV commercial begins with a *script*. This is the spoken or voice-over portion of the ad. It should be creative, simple, brief, informative. The words should be easy for the reader to speak and pronounce, and simple for the listener to recall.

The *visual segment* of an ad can be developed either along with the verbal portion, or after it has been written. Usually the visual section is laid out in *storyboard* format. The storyboard is a series of rough sketches which highlight the key or lead scenes to be filmed.

A storyboard consists of two frames per scene with the top frame depicting the visual impact of the ad. This frame, in rough form, represents the video screen. The lower frame describes the video and audio portions of the segment in words, and is a synopsis of the script. Storyboards, representing the transition from rough creative work to finished ad, average six to twelve or more frames. It is at this point in the creative process that one can most easily make changes or additions. If an agency is producing the commercial, customer approval of the concepts and focus is usually required at this point.

After the creative work, in storyboard or other form, is approved, the ad enters its production stage. The first phase of production is the *shooting*. This is the filming or videotaping of the scenes that will form the commercial. Quite often the shooting requires a number of repetitious *takes* or *repeats.*

Cinematographers or video photographers use a variety of techniques to enhance the quality or style of the video ad. You may recognize some of the techniques, such as fade-outs, dissolves, fade-ins, zooms, etc., from work with your home camcorder. The photographer will shoot a great deal more film than can be used so that there is opportunity for selecting various views or lighting effects, for example.

When the shooting is done, the film or video is turned over to an editor who places the scenes in proper sequence, selects the best takes, adds titles and special effects, combines sound, and any other musical requirements. It is at this point in the process that certain corrections or changes can still be made in the ad spot. Once the editing has been completed, the finished ad spot is reviewed and, if satisfactory, duplicated for use on TV stations.

What Works in a TV Craft Commercial?—Of course, different products require different treatments, but some basic themes can get creative juices started. These include the selection of rare materials or those with unusual qualities—delicacy, strength, purity, intrinsic design, or artistic merit; the craftsperson at work in any phase of the production process; the product or products themselves in utilitarian, decorative, or creative settings; the display of ribbons, awards, other honors accorded the product or its maker; and satisfied purchasers or recipients using the product.

Radio Advertising

Radio advertising is purchased very much the same as TV advertising time. Radio spots are sold for placement in specific daily time periods, and in specific quantities based on budgetary constraints. Radio spots are sold on a supply and demand basis with advertising costs often based on the popularity of the individual shows. Time periods before, during, and after local news programs, for example, are usually in great demand, and thus cost more. Spots can also be purchased in packages.

The steps suggested for television advertising are in the main applicable to radio advertising as well.

- Design a budget and work within it.
- Decide who and where your audience is.
- Secure radio station rate cards and demographic information.
- Select a station and format that reaches your target audience.
- Plan, develop and produce your radio spots.

- Choose your radio timeframes and purchase your radio spots.
- After your radio spots have run, review the product sales for results.

Radio Ad Production—The production of the radio advertising spot requires the same attention as a television ad, and, except for television's visual segment, has many of the same components. To its advantage, the creative and production costs of a radio ad spot are far less than a TV ad.

A budget for producing the radio spot and purchasing airtime must be developed. A script for the radio spot must be written, and sound effects and music to complement the ad must be selected. A person or people must be chosen and rehearsed to read the commercial. A studio capable of taping the music and the voice portions of the ad spot separately must be located. When the two sounds are satisfactorily completed, they must be mixed onto a master tape. Duplicates of the completed master advertising tape have to be produced so that they can be sent to the selected radio station advertising departments.

If you are using an agency, all of this is handled by agency staff. If you are not using an agency, in many areas you can discuss production of the commercial by the station staff. Some smaller stations offer this service without charge, and some will give or sell you tape duplicates that can be used on other stations as well.

Talk Show Appearances

You can secure valuable exposure for your craft product by personal appearances on *talk show* or *special interest programs* on both radio and television. You can familiarize yourself with this process by watching and listening to talk-show hosts interviewing entertainers, authors, artists, designers, inventors, entrepreneurs, or others. Network shows generally have wide listening and viewing audiences. Local and cable station talk shows generally have coteries of devoted followers as well as those who might be attracted by specific guests or topics.

In addition to talk shows, there are many special interest shows or show segments. News programs frequently feature special events, new products, exhibitions, etc. Cooking programs may use decorative tableware or accessories; home decorating programs seek out products to complement particular themes, or people who can give expert advice.

Holiday feature producers are always on the lookout for something new or different. Producers have the responsibility of finding guests who can fit into their formats. For shows that run daily or weekly, the task of finding appropriate guests is an enormous chore, and if you can meet the criteria and are willing to invest the time and effort, producers will welcome you. In most instances, however, unless you are already a celebrity who is being sought by the producer, the costs for travel and lodging will be yours.

Appearances on these shows add to the credibility of your product and build your reputation as a craftsperson. While they do not always generate significant immediate sales results, serendipitous contacts often grow out of such appearances. Manufacturers, educators, decorators, buyers, investors, and others who are among the viewers may see more in your product than even you can envision and open doors to new markets or greater opportunities. Frequently, a guest appearance on one show creates invitations to other shows or requests for interviews by editorial and feature writers.

Despite the lure of the these shows, and making allowance for serendipity, it makes sense to be selective in those you approach for a guest appearance. Seek out those whose audience is likely to include your potential buyer, those who can influence potential buyers, or those who can enhance your reputation as an authority or expert in a specific field.

In order to get invited for guest appearances, you must have a product of special interest; an area of special expertise, talent or knowledge; a story that catches the attention of the talk-show host or the program's producer; an ability to communicate; a sense of self confidence; and a personality that projects well on TV or radio. If you know your product well and have developed some interesting related sidelights about the product and yourself, you should have no difficulty handling an appearance on the talk-show circuit.

You should be aware, incidentally, that many radio show interviews do not require your presence at the station, but are taped over the telephone. This makes it more convenient and less costly to be heard on radio shows across the country than on television shows which may require extensive, expensive travel.

It is worth watching talk shows for extended periods to determine their audience orientations, the type of guests, topics, products, or services that are featured, and the role of guests. It is also worthwhile to find out which shows are filmed or broadcast live and which are taped for later presentation. The latter offer a chance to correct "bloopers" just as radio taping does.

If you believe that a particular show or shows can benefit from your appearance and vice versa, the first step is a query letter or phone call to the show producer. You can obtain the name and address of the producer by contacting the station. A letter querying interest should be followed within a week or two by a phone call. An initial phone call should be followed promptly by a letter.

Your letter or call should be carefully developed to introduce yourself, your product, and the way you believe the show can benefit from your appearance. If you call, indicate that you are also sending a letter and a photograph, sample, or videotape of your product or products. In your conversation or correspondence, point out several interesting pegs that might grab the attention of the producer, host, and audience. These pegs could include timely association with special events or commemorations, holidays, or happenings in the news. If you create products for babies, offer to appear during National Baby Week. If you work in fashion, suggest an appearance following announcement of the latest fashion showings or the announcement of the world's best or worst dressed. If you can relate your work in some credible way to a popular book, play, or musical, or to a timely political event that can give the producer another view on a "hot" topic, by all means do so. Be prepared to discuss your own background and your ability to present yourself on the air. If you have a press kit or biographical information sheet that provides information about yourself and your product, include it with your letter.

When you are invited to appear on a talk show, live or taped, obtain all of the necessary information about the show. Learn exactly where and when you have to appear so that you are on time. Find out who your contact person at the TV or radio studio is to be. Make sure that you know what to bring with you, whether any special makeup is required, or special attire expected or preferred. If you believe it adds to the show and you will be demonstrating production as well as finished products, ask if work clothes might be appropriate.

If you would like any specific questions asked by the host, and he or she agrees to this process, find out how and when these questions should be presented. Also, find out whether you can name your product, discuss its price, and where it can be ordered, or, if not, how the station will respond to inquiries. Make sure that the producer and the host have enough information about you to introduce you accurately, and that they know how to pronounce your name.

If you have not received any special instructions for attire, your appearance should be treated as a business occasion and you should dress accordingly. Even if you have submitted in advance a list of questions and information for your introduction, be sure to bring copies with you. If you can afford to do so, samples of your work are very much appreciated by producers, hosts, and crew members. If your products are costly, homebaked goodies, cookies, or candies also warm the atmosphere.

Arrange to have the show videotaped for future reference. If you can, bring a blank videotape to the studio, and ask the producer to make a copy of the show or the segment of the program in which you appear.

Finally, after you have completed your appearance, remember to send a thank-you note to the host, the producer, and anyone else you worked with at the studio. Add them to your holiday card list, and periodically contact them with ideas for other appearances. Producers frequently move from show to show, so it is worthwhile to maintain contact with them.

The TV Giveaway Show

There are many prize giveaway shows in both the television and the radio marketplaces. These shows may offer exposure opportunities for your craft products. Consider *placing your craft products on one or more giveaway shows as prize or consolation items.* If, for example, you produce a craft product geared specifically to children, you might offer one or several items to a giveaway program with a children's audience. If your product has appeal for a general audience, you might target adult quiz shows that give product prizes.

You can offer your product directly to the show producer, or you can use a firm that specializes in the placement of products as prizes on giveaway shows. Be prepared to pay a fee for this service. If you are dealing in a relatively small television or radio market area, you can handle the contact process personally. Begin by making sure that you have selected the correct type of show, and that your product matches the show's conceptual design.

Radio giveaway programs, for example, might offer prizes for the fourth, tenth or twelfth person calling the studio with a specific message. Or, the station might offer awards for the first person giving the correct answers to a series of questions posed by a radio personality. Giveaway shows like Name That Tune, Wheel of Fortune, and Jeopardy are TV possibilities for prize awards.

If you want to handle prize placement yourself, prepare a letter to the show producer describing your product, and indicating your willingness to provide a certain number of your products as giveaways in return for credit on the show. Include a photo of the product along with its retail value. About a week after your letter, call the producer to find out if your offer has been received, if it has been considered, and whether or not it has been accepted. If you receive a positive response, determine how the product will be delivered to the station, the required timeframes and who will be handling the details at the studio or station. If your offer is rejected, try to discover why. It may be that the producer only deals with packagers or it may be that he or she does not see the match of your product with the show. Ask for a frank opinion on the merits of the product and for suggestions of other shows you should approach.

If the market for your product is currently local, do not go too far afield in your initial search for giveaway shows. Determine the effectiveness of the process first. If the results are satisfactory and your product sales increase, you can then attempt to move into other show giveaway areas.

Bartering for Advertising Space

You can *barter for* or *purchase bartered TV or radio advertising space.* Listed in many telephone books, nationwide, are companies known as barter houses who have available blocks of bartered advertising space. This space may have been traded for other products or services, or purchased by the barter house. You can often buy this advertising space at a discount. Barter packages usually apply to specific calendar periods and to specific schedule times. If your needs can be answered by these periods and schedules, you may find a bargain opportunity. Conversely, if these are periods and times which do not fit your target audience, you can be wasting your money.

In addition to selling bartered TV advertising space, there are firms who allow you to barter or trade your services or products for selective TV or radio advertising space. They usually charge a fee for this service and, additionally, barter for full-priced rather than discounted advertising space, just as the other company trading with you will expect to pay full price for your bartered craft products.

There are times that radio or TV stations require prizes for their giveaway programs, and may be willing to barter with you directly. You can find out by sending a brief letter describing your craft product, accompanied by a product photograph, plus an explanation of what you are seeking from the station in the way of traded advertising space. Send the letter to the station manager or target the specific show producer.

Per-Inquiry Advertising

Some television and radio stations may not be able to fill selective advertising time slots continuously. To try to make a profit from these slots, certain stations will work with an advertiser on a *per-inquiry basis*.

The per-inquiry system works in this fashion. The television or radio station indicates the availability of a certain number of advertising spots in selected timeframes. These stations are prepared to use this time for per-inquiry advertising, and provide the ad space at no charge. As a per-inquiry advertiser, you will usually be asked to provide a prepared audio or video advertising spot. In addition to the product sales material in the script, the ad spot will contain a phone number or address designated by the station. All responses received to the ads will be directed to this special address or number at the station. As a per-inquiry advertiser, you will be required to pay the station a predetermined sum for each inquiry received or each product sold through the station's advertising. The exact details are arranged between station and advertiser.

To find out if a television or radio station participates in, or will consider, per-inquiry arrangements, you have to check with the station advertising department. A letter describing your product, and a request to participate in such a per-inquiry program, should be sent to the stations with whom you are interested in working.

Fund-Raising Auctions and Charity Programs

Public broadcasting radio and television stations and charitable organizations regularly conduct *fund-raising appeals* and *auctions* on the air. In the former case, donors are offered gifts of varying value in return for their contributions at various levels. In the latter case, donated articles are auctioned to the highest bidders. In both cases, donations of your products are examples of the positive gains of giveaways—both in increased exposure for your products and helping worthy causes. Audiences for public broadcasting are invariably more open to originality and creativity than the general public. Exposure in this milieu, provided that your name and address are correctly stated, can be especially beneficial, and dollar for dollar worth more than paid advertising.

Chapter Highlights

- Radio and television are both sources of entertainment and advertising vehicles.
- In today's marketplace, television has become a daily viewing habit, and cuts across all socioeconomic lines.
- Some television stations reach into large metropolitan markets and others into small local markets. Generally, the larger the market, the more expensive the advertising and vice versa.
- Local TV stations are those that broadcast to a specific local market.
- Syndicated television stations broadcast their signals to more than one market.
- Radio is a highly mobile medium that can be tuned in almost anywhere. It is available in AM and FM, with FM stations dominating the field.
- Radio requires a high frequency of advertising spots to impact a market.
- Television advertising spots are sold to the advertiser on a supply and demand basis.
- When preparing to use television or radio advertising to sell your craft product, always develop a budget to monitor costs.
- Advertising time designations for TV ads include morning, daytime, early fringe, prime time access, prime time, late news, and late fringe.
- Radio advertising spots are purchased using similar time designations.
- The talk show route for either television or radio is a good method to gain exposure for your craft product.
- The most effective method to use to place yourself on talk shows is

to select the programs, and write directly to show producer or host requesting placement.

- Craft products can be used as prizes or gifts on television and radio giveaway shows. This can be an effective method for obtaining exposure for your craft item.
- The barter system permits you to trade your products for advertising space on radio and television.
- Instead of paying directly for advertising space, per-inquiry advertising on radio or television provides you with the opportunity to place ads and pay for only responses.
- A TV ad consists of two parts: a visual or motive portion and an audio section.
- A radio advertising spot is less expensive to produce than a television advertisement.

CHAPTER 13

The Craft Marketing Plan

Your Marketing Plan—A Strategy Map

While every facet of business operation contributes to the bottom line, it is the entire process of getting a product or service to a buyer that generates the income. This entire process, from the product itself to closing the sale, is *marketing*. An organized, disciplined, and creative approach to marketing opens the door to new business opportunities and enhances the business you already have.

The objective of this book is to help you develop that organized, disciplined, and creative approach. One of the best ways to insure that this is accomplished is to show you how to use the tools that have proven themselves over and over again in the business world. One of these tools is the *marketing plan*.

In contrast to the business plan, which is primarily designed for lenders or investors, and to give you an overall grasp of your operation, the marketing plan is developed to organize and project your efforts from product to profit.

An effective craft marketing plan is designed to help you make sound judgments on the development of your product, the people you are designing it for, and the process of getting them to buy it. In most instances, a marketing plan will project plans for a season, a quarter or a full year. In some instances, however, long-range marketing plans—for 3, 4, or 5 years—will be helpful. The latter might be the case if you are planning a heavy investment that requires a lengthy payback period. If your plan covers an extended period of time, you should recognize and allow for potential business climate changes.

The marketing plan is like the roadmap that you mark up for your vacation trip. Only the adventurous would consider taking an extensive, expensive journey without pre-planning. There are too many hazards that can waste your time, get you lost and cause you all manner of difficulties.

In order to avoid these pitfalls, the wise approach is to preplan. You start out by asking yourself where you are going, what routes you will travel, and how long the trip will take. You will consider time, routes, stopovers, costs involved, and alternative possibilities in case of emergencies.

Your craft marketing plan is a business roadmap. It lets you establish priorities, direction, and schedules. It gives you the option of developing strategies to maintain and build business. Your marketing budget delineates how operating and promotional funds will be used. Your projection of programs and schedules will provide an objective way to measure performance at specific points in time.

The marketing plan, therefore, spells out the goals you hope your product or products will achieve for your business, details the programs and projects you will use to accomplish these goals, and sets a practical timeframe in which to make things happen. It is designed to direct you to achieve a set of marketing objectives.

Elements of the Marketing Plan

While your business plan gives you and your banking and investment sources "need-to-know" financial information about your company, your craft marketing plan can help you launch a campaign to generate the income necessary to make your business successful. If you believe that your marketing plan presents a strong case for success, you may want to include it as an addendum to your business plan. The important point to recognize about a marketing plan is that it can provide not only the guidance and organization you will need, but also the impetus to move forward. Your marketing plan can be brief or lengthy, simple or complex, as long as it leads to systematic thinking about your product and business, and effective coordination of employees, partners, or representatives, if you have them. A good marketing plan should also prepare you for any sudden changes in the business environment.

A plan is a form of organized thought broken down into a number of segments. These segments might include, but are not limited to, the following general categories.

The Executive Summary

As discussed in the section on business plans, an *executive summary* or *overview* is written after the plan is completed. It then can be placed either at the beginning or the end of your marketing plan. It should highlight all the salient points of the plan in capsule form, and be easy to read and follow. The summary lets you quickly review your work, make sure that it covers all the bases, and is logical, credible, and workable. It allows others who may be reviewing your plan to have the basic information necessary to evaluate it.

Your summary will express what your marketing program has been, where it is at this time, and what is proposed for the future. It will give an overview of the opportunities and pitfalls that face your craft production enterprise, and the realistic business goals you have set. It will cover the short and long-term strategies you envision to make your marketing plan functional, and the tactics you propose to meet contingencies. It will summarize your schedules and areas of responsibility for project fulfillment. It will highlight budgetary allocations and evaluation checkpoints for staying on target.

The Mission Statement

You must always understand exactly what business you are in and why. Sometimes, in the heat of creativity, it is easy to forget. It is also important for others who read the plan to have a clear understanding of the business mission.

The *mission statement,* or *statement of intent,* helps keep your purpose in focus. You can stay more easily on track if you know where you want to go. The mission statement should also highlight for yourself and for current or eventual employees what you consider to be the most important business objectives. For example, if customer service is more important than maximizing profit, say so.

In its most elementary form, the mission statement for a craft production and sales business might simply state: *"This business has been developed to create the XYZ craft product and to sell this product at a profit. It is established that the market for this product will be single adults, male and female, between the ages of 25 and 45 years of age. The sales goal for the first year will be 1100 craft pieces with a 12% increase projected for the following two years."*

A Situational Analysis

It is also important to define the present business environment of your market, and the place your product or products have in that market. You should also pinpoint the relationship of your craft business to others in the field. An effective situational analysis will provide comparisons, reviews, and studies to demonstrate trends and determine directions.

A situational analysis might also include relevant research on the economic, social, cultural, and political attitudes, or trends that might impact on your business.

Two examples serve to highlight the nature of this impact. They demonstrate why it is important for you to be knowledgeable about trends, far and wide.

In the first instance, a store in the United States carrying a line of handcrafted Gorbachev dolls regularly saw modest sales of two or three dolls weekly. During the three days of the attempt to overthrow the Soviet leader, the sales of these dolls spurted to outstrip the supply. Individuals may have seen the purchase of the dolls as an opportunity to pick up a collector's item or a chance to purchase a product at a low cost that would rise rapidly in value.

In a similar marketing example during the same time period, stores selling Lithuanian handcrafted products saw their sales drop abysmally during the Soviet government take-over. This time the reason had to do with the entire customer base. The takeover activity was so intense that potential purchasers remained home glued to their television sets and did not go out to shop.

Such events may have caught even seasoned forecasters off base, but other more easily predicted events and trends should enter your thinking. What, for example, will be the effect of the European Common Market? Of developing countries receiving favored nation status? Of tariff trends? Of Middle East tensions and the cost of energy?

Marketing Goals and Objectives

While your mission is an overall statement of purpose, your marketing goals and objectives should be specific, and should define the expected results of your marketing efforts in numbers, percentages, and dollars.

A word of caution is in order. Inflated goals and projections may make you feel good, but only until you recognize that they cannot be achieved. Don't be tempted to kid yourself. It is healthy to be optimistic, but optimism should be tempered with realism.

Previous business experience establishes a base on which to project goals with some degree of assurance. If you are starting off with a brand new product and must forecast a goal, the task is not as simple. In this case you must rely on judgment and research to achieve a reasonably good perspective of the entire market or industry.

Market Information and Research

Research into available information cannot only help you set realistic goals, it can also help you develop the programs to implement these goals. Research will give you the norms as well as current condition of the craft industry, it should give you insights on your competition as well as potential opportunities and threats, and it should highlight what the market is looking at and for. Research can help you forecast your potential in the market segments best suited for your craft product line. Today, more than ever, markets are breaking down into segments, each with clearly discernable purchasing habits.

The information is out there and a great deal of it is easily available. Craft industry trade journals and magazines as well as those devoted to marketing in general are good sources and should be regular must reading. The government has considerable data available. Many public libraries offer government publications, and catalogs listing such publications and are available from the Government Printing Office.

Informal research is also a valuable tool. Discussions with colleagues, competitors, suppliers, bankers, and other knowledgeable people can provide a great deal of marketing intelligence.

Marketing Strategies

Intelligence agencies, worldwide, collect data from a wide range of sources. Once collected and sifted through, a great deal of this information finds its way to analysts who are responsible for developing strategies based on the data.

After you have done your research and interpreted the data, you, too, develop a strategy based on it. The *strategy* becomes the linchpin of your plan. It will determine the segments of the market or markets you will target, and the approach or approaches you will use for each segment.

This is the point in which the elements in the marketing mix—product, price, promotion, place, packaging, purpose, projecting and positioning—play a prominent role. These have been discussed at some length in preceding chapters. The strategic moves you plan should be viewed from each of these perspectives.

As part of your strategic thinking, look at your product from your consumer's viewpoint and not your own. Think about whether the craft product line you are producing and trying to sell is what the market really wants. Are there any modifications or changes in your product that will make it more marketable? Are there any ways in which your product can be adapted to new markets or different segments of existing markets?

Evaluate the pricing. As you work through your strategic program, try to develop a pricing framework that you feel your market will respond to. On one hand, make sure that you have left sufficient leeway to make a reasonable profit. At the same time, do not outprice yourself in the marketplace. Strike a happy medium. You may also want to consider list prices, discounts, allowances, credit terms, special coupons, and other pricing situations.

You will discover that there are literally hundreds of ways to promote your craft product. Your strategic planning will have to winnow out and select the most effective methods within your budget. Advertising in large daily newspapers or taking television spots on major networks to promote a craft article can be tremendously expensive and may, in certain instances, prove to be a waste. Small weekly newspapers and cable television targeted to a specific audience may fit within your budget and be more effective. Your research should provide you with guidance in this area. If, for example, your craft product is targeted strictly to a college market, college newspaper or college radio station advertising may deliver your message at a far lower cost than major media.

There are many ways to move your craft product into the hands of the consumer. Personal selling, direct mail, sales promotion, publicity, and advertising are just some of the standard methods. What direction will you take to inform and motivate potential customers to buy your craft products?

Your strategic planning may point to craft fairs as the most economical place to reach your market. There are craft fairs and there are craft fairs! Some shows cater to the general public while others offer craft producers an opportunity to showcase and sell their wares to wholesalers as well. If you are prepared for the wholesale market, the latter type of craft show would be a wise, strategic selection.

Many people react to packaging, in fact, they may purchase based on what they see and can handle. In your strategic thinking, you may want to consider special packaging for your craft product. An interesting box, bag, or a creative type of packaging may induce the consumer to purchase your craft article faster than an off-the shelf, unpackaged item.

If the craft article you produce must compete with others that are similar, your strategy should include plans for positioning the product in the marketplace. You may want to look at the differences you can define or create between these products. These differences should be highlighted in your promotional material, your displays, and other communication activities. Minor changes in the production of your craft article may place you in a more positive position. Such factors as quality, options, style size, and guarantees can help differentiate your product and position it advantageously in the marketplace.

Programs and Schedules

It is not enough just to design a program for your marketing plan. A *schedule* or *timetable* must be developed to remind you when things must be started, worked through, and completed. This schedule will provide a checklist to assure that each section of the promotional program goes off on time and that nothing is left out.

If you are the only person working on the craft marketing program in your business, the responsibility for starting and completing the work is yours alone. If, however, other people are involved, a definite line of responsibility for the schedule should be developed.

Budget

Almost everything you plan to do will have dollar signs attached. The objective of a *budget* is to project what the costs will be and to establish whether there are sufficient funds to handle them. A budget helps control costs and can limit overruns. It is important to include all of the costs involved with the marketing of your craft product. Your costs will include such items as operational overhead, material costs, labor charges, promotional expenses.

A budget can be viewed as a projected profit and loss statement. On the income side of the budget worksheet, the sales of your craft products are projected. On the expense side of the budget worksheet, the costs of the raw materials for your craft articles, production, marketing, administration, and other expenses are projected. Once you decide on the budget for your product line, it should serve as the basis for your entire marketing operation. Periodically, your actual income and expenses should be compared to those you have budgeted. An actual budget evaluation can tell you whether you are going overboard on expenses, or whether your promotional program has increased your income beyond expectations.

Contingency Planning

Your craft marketing plan should always include a plan and a budget to meet unforeseen contingencies or other than projected circumstances. Preplanning saves stress, strain, and money. Preplanning, or *contingency planning* is the response to the words "What if?"

What if your craft item is designed specifically to be marketed to young adults and your market area changes so that it is dominated by senior citizens? Your contingency plan might suggest that you move your sales effort to another area in which there are more young adults. Your contingency plan can call for the redesign of your craft product to appeal to grandparents, or you might change your packaging to appeal to seniors.

It is important that you maintain a close watch over changing markets. You must be ready to make a determination whether the change is a brief aberration or a permanent change. To make contingency plan changes when they are not really necessary can harm a current market.

Evaluation

When you think that everything has been included in your plan, your job still is not finished. It is important to evaluate the plans as you have developed them, and to set objective standards for evaluating the results when they are experienced.

The basic questions to ask in evaluating your marketing program are: "Did the program work? If not, why not?"

Chapter Highlights

- The entire process, from production to closing the sale, is encompassed within a marketing framework.
- In order for marketing to be really effective, it is important to adopt an organized, disciplined, creative approach.
- The marketing plan is designed to project your efforts from product to profit.
- Your craft marketing plan is actually a business roadmap which establishes priorities, direction, and schedules.
- Your craft marketing plan also spells out the goals for your product, details the programs that will be used to arrive at these goals, and develops a timeframe in which things should happen.
- An effective marketing plan includes, but is not limited to, the following broad categories: An *executive summary* which is an overview of the plan you have devised. A *mission statement* delineating exactly what business you are in and why. A *situational analysis* which helps define the current business environment vis-à-vis your craft product and others in the field. A listing of *goals and objectives* which defines anticipated results of your projected marketing program, and *market and research information* that can help you in your quest to reach realistic goals. Your plan should also discuss

market strategy which is the linchpin of your plan and detail *programs and schedules* to set timeframes for action. A *budget* must also be included in your marketing plan so that you know ahead of time exactly what you expect the operational costs to be. Every good program should also have a *contingency plan* built in to meet unforseen problems.

Your Craft Marketing Plan Worksheet

Use this worksheet to lay out your craft product marketing plan. Eliminate any area of the plan that you do not wish to develop. Go into as much detail as you desire. If you require additional space, add as many pages as you need.

COMPANY OR CRAFT PRODUCT NAME: _____

DATE OF PLAN: _____

EXECUTIVE SUMMARY: _____

_____

_____

_____

_____

MISSION STATEMENT: _____

_____

_____

_____

_____

_____

SITUATIONAL ANALYSIS: _____

_____

_____

MARKETING GOAL/OBJECTIVES: _____

_____

_____

_____

_____

MARKETING RESEARCH: _____

_____

_____

_____

_____

MARKETING STRATEGIES: _____

_____

_____

_____

_____

PROGRAMS & SCHEDULES: _____

_____

_____

_____

MARKETING BUDGET : _____

_____

_____

_____

_____

EVALUATION: _____

_____

_____

_____

_____

CONTINGENCY PLANNING: _____

_____

_____

_____

CHAPTER 14

Keeping Business Records

An Introduction to Business Records

No matter how small your business is, you must keep accurate records to show how money comes in and goes out. It is important that you know where you stand financially so that you can make business decisions based on facts. It is also necessary that you have proper information for banks and suppliers whom you may ask for loans and credit. You are also required to keep accurate records for federal, state, and sometimes local tax purposes, and for payroll, if you have employees.

The effort of keeping business records is not as complicated as it may first appear. In fact, is very logical.

The business records you will keep will come under the general heading of *bookkeeping* or *accounting records.* Even if you employ a full or part-time bookkeeper and retain an accountant, it is vital that you understand every phase of the recordkeeping function. The information in this chapter will not only give you the understanding you need if anyone else is to do the actual work, but it will also give you the technical know-how to do the work yourself if necessary.

No matter who does the work, the end result is the preparation of two financial statements. The first of these is sometimes referred to as the *P & L Statement* or the *Statement of Income and Expenses.* The second is the *Statement of Assets and Liabilities,* which is sometimes called the *Balance Sheet.* Each of these statements is prepared at least once a year; although some businesses need them once a month (monthly), once every three months (quarterly), or once every six months (semi-annually).

Computerized Recordkeeping

Today, with the use of a relatively low-cost computer and business software, the entire bookkeeping process has been simplified and demystified. Almost every business process that you require or want can be handled rapidly with your computer. You can keep complete records, get extensive reports, and prepare all types of transactions, including issuing your checks. The information can be provided on the screen of the computer, or printed out for permanent reference. In many instances, software, the programs used to run a computer, can be purchased specifically for your needs. At other times, available software for general business purposes will adequately suit your needs. The information in the following pages has been prepared so that you will have a broad understanding of the business record process. It has both computer and noncomputer applications.

The P&L Statement

The Statement of Profit and Loss is designed to tell you how much of a profit or loss resulted from your business activities during a particular period of time. The essential elements of a Profit and Loss statement are really very simple.

If you take all of your *business income* and compare it to all of your *business expenses* for a specified time period, you can tell if you have made a profit or loss. The expenses, of course, are the monies you pay out to run the business. The income is the money you take in. If your expenses are larger than your income, you have lost money. To find out how much, you would subtract the total of your income from the total of your expenses. If the expenses are less than the income, you have made a profit. In order to find out how much, you would subtract the total expenses from the total income.

So that you have an idea of how easy it is to really prepare a profit and loss statement, let's use an example.

On January 1, you officially started your craft business. In the month of January, you spent $150.00 for salaries, $100.00 for supplies, $50.00 for rent, $50.00 for auto expenses, $50.00 for interest on loans, $15.00 for your telephone bill, and $85.00 for advertising your craft product. All together, these expenses added up to $500.00. During the month of January, your customers paid you $1000.00 for products that they purchased from you. Your profit and loss statement for January would look like Fig. 14–1.

Cash or Accrual Basis

There are two methods used to report income and expenses. One is the *cash basis,* and the other is the *accrual basis.* Your accountant or tax advisor will recommend the basis which is best for you. Most small businesses use the cash basis—that is, they report only actual cash in and cash out of their businesses for each period. Incidentally, in ac-

---

ANYTOWN CRAFT PRODUCT COMPANY
PROFIT AND LOSS STATEMENT

For period beginning January 1, 19--, and ending January 31, 19--

Income:

Products Sold To Customers		$1000.00
Total Income		$1000.00
Less Expenses:		
Salaries:	$150.00	
Supplies:	$100.00	
Rent:	$ 50.00	
Auto:	$ 50.00	
Interest:	$ 50.00	
Telephone:	$ 15.00	
Advertising:	$ 85.00	
Total Expenses		$ 500.00
Profit for the Month		$ 500.00

Fig. 14–1. Simple Profit and Loss Statement.

counting terms, cash includes checks and money orders. If you do not have an accountant or tax advisor, you will find the cash basis simpler to use than the accrual basis.

An accrual is really a means of assigning income and expenses to the period or product where they really belong. Using the cash basis does not report your business position precisely, as credit transactions, payables, and receivables do not show up exactly in cash basis reporting. The accrual basis, generally used by larger companies, takes into account the actual billings (or gross sales) regardless of whether they have been paid or not. It also reports all expenses incurred by the business, regardless of whether these have been paid or not. If you buy on credit or permit your customers to pay on credit, your actual costs and income are not fully reflected on a cash basis. The accrual basis reports the actual costs of supplies used during the period, even if more were purchased than used, and even if they were not paid for during the period. The accrual system also gets into prepaid expenses (expenses which are paid for before they are used such as insurance, or auto licenses). Another name for these prepaid expenses is deferred charges to expenses or simply deferred charges. All this means is that the charge is deferred or put off until it is used. Because the accrual system takes into account the *payables* (what a business owes) and the *receivables* (what is owed to the business), it also gets involved in estimating how many of the receivables will eventually be paid and in *setting up reserves* for possible losses.

We are discussing the accrual system, not because you will be using it in most instances, but because you should understand that the cash basis which you will generally be using will not be precisely accurate for a profit and loss statement. Over a period of time, however, the ups and downs caused by receivables and payables will even out. By comparing P & L Statements for successive periods, you will have a fairly good idea of how your business is doing. For tax purposes, you will have to choose one method and stick to it.

The Balance Sheet

We have been talking chiefly about statements of Income and Expenses or P & L Statements. These statements will tell you how much money you made or lost in a particular period of time. Suppose, however, you wanted to know exactly how much your business was worth at any particular time. The P & L Statement can not tell you this, but a *Balance Sheet* or a *Statement of Assets and Liabilities* can. An asset is anything of value that the business owns. There are several kinds of assets. *Current assets* are in the form of cash or something that reasonably can be expected to become cash in the near future. Usually the near future is considered to be a year or less. In addition to cash, accounts receivable are considered to be current assets if they are due and payable in a year or less. Notes receivable, that is notes which have been given to you as promises to pay, due and payable in a year or less are also considered to be current assets. Merchandise for sale is also a current asset and is listed on the balance sheet at your cost.

Fixed assets are those of a more permanent nature and those which will ordinarily not be turned into cash in the ordinary course of business; although they have a real value, and could be turned into cash if necessary. Furniture and fixtures, installation equipment and tools, vehicles, land and buildings, are generally listed among the fixed assets of a business.

We have said that an asset is anything of value that the business owes. On the other hand, *a liability* is any financial obligation of the business, or in other words, anything the business owes. There are *current liabilities*, which are those which are due and payable, some notes payable and certain taxes. There are *fixed liabilities,* which are due and payable over a comparatively longer period of time. If, for example, you purchase a truck to haul your craft products for $3,600.00, and finance it over three years, the truck will become a fixed asset of your business. The amount you will have to pay the bank within the first year of purchase will be a current liability. The balance due in the second and third years will be a fixed liability. If you have a mortgage on the property, the mortgage is a fixed liability.

If you remember that an asset is anything of value that your business owns, and a liability is anything the business owes, you will find it simple to prepare and understand a Balance Sheet. This sheet will provide you with net worth information at any given time. There is a very simple formula which the Balance Sheet uses:

Net Worth = Assets – Liabilities

In other words, if you subtract what you owe from what you own, you get the business's net worth.

Look at the following example. In order to go into business, you invest $2500.00 of your own money and you borrow $2500.00 from relatives. You deposit the money in your bank. From this money you purchase $200.00 in supplies and raw material, a truck worth $3,600.00 on which you make a down payment of $720, and sign a note for the balance with the bank. You buy a desk, filing cabinet, and adding machine for a total of $300. Now, you want to know what the net worth of your business is: Your Balance Sheet would look something like the example provided in Fig. 14–2.

ANYTOWN CRAFT PRODUCT COMPANY
BALANCE SHEET

As of January 1, 19--

CURRENT ASSETS:
Current on hand and in banks	$3,780.00	
Supplies or merchandise for sale	$ 200.00	
Total Current Assets		$3,980.00

FIXED ASSETS:
Furniture and Fixtures	$ 300.00	
Truck	$3,600.00	
Total Fixed Assets		$3,900.00
TOTAL ASSETS		$7,800.00

CURRENT LIABILITIES:
Notes to relatives payable in one year or less	$2,500.00	
Note to bank for truck, payable within one year	$ 960.00	
Total Current Liabilities		$3,460.00

FIXED LIABILITIES:
Note to bank for truck payable after one year	$1,920.00	
Total Fixed Liabilities		$1,920.00
TOTAL LIABILITIES		$5,380.00
	NET WORTH	$2,500.00

Fig. 14–2. Sample Balance Sheet.

Money Flow

We will talk more about all of the elements which are reported in the financial statements when the general ledger and the journals are discussed. These are specific books you will be keeping. In the meantime, we will follow in a logical sequence the flow of money for your business, and the procedures you will need to know to monitor this flow.

One of the basic principles of business recordkeeping is that the records must be clear enough, and recorded in such a way that it is possible to follow every transaction clearly and easily through the records.

The Checking Account

One very preliminary business procedure is the opening of a *checking account* into which all business funds are deposited and from which all business costs and expenses are paid. Your checking account then becomes a running history of the cash transactions of your business.

In most areas where there is more than one bank, it pays to shop around to learn what banks charge and what services they offer for checking accounts. Some banks charge a specified fee for each deposit and each check issued. Some banks charge a fee only if the balance in the account drops below a certain specified amount. Other banks do not charge for checking account service if a savings account with a specified minimum balance is maintained. Some banks charge for printing your checks and others offer these printed checks free. There can be differences in services and charges for business and personal checking accounts. All of these things should be taken into account.

More important, however, should be the bank's attitude toward business loans. Some banks are notoriously conservative in their loan policies, and others are known to be more understanding of the needs of new or small businesses. You can determine the general attitude of a bank by discussing it with your accountant or tax advisor, if you have one, or more directly, by talking to a bank official yourself. When you talk to a banker, remember that the bank needs customers—these are depositors and borrowers—and you are thinking of becoming a customer of the bank. Ask your banker to tell you why you should be doing business with his bank rather than the one down the block. In most cases, he will respect your business-like approach, and will remember you when you need to borrow funds.

When you open a bank account, you are assigned a special computer number for your account. This number appears on printed deposit slips and on your checks. When you put money—cash and checks—into your account, you must prepare a *deposit slip* for the bank. This deposit slip lists the amount of cash in the deposit, and then itemizes the individual checks which are also being deposited. It is a good idea to make out every deposit slip in duplicate, that is one copy for the bank and one for your files. The deposit slip you make out will include the name of your account, your account number, the date of the deposit, and the amounts being deposited in cash and checks. Your copies of the deposit slips will serve as control records of income as long as you deposit all of the money which comes into your business. You can also add any other relevant information to your copy of the deposit slip. For example, you might keep a record of who each check came from and for what.

When you want to take money out of a checking account, you issue and sign a check. When you open your checking account, the bank will supply you with several hundred checks. Each check you fill out is an order to the bank to pay a specified person or firm. A check contains a space for the date, the payee, the amount in both numbers and words, and your authorized signature. It says, "Pay to the order of _____,"
which is where you put the name of the person or firm to whom you are writing the check (the payee). The check continues with space for the amount of the check both in words and figures so that there can be no mistaking the amount you want to issue. If there is a difference between the amount you write in figures and the amount indicated in words, the amount in words is used by the bank. The check also contains a blank space for your signature, and is not valid until you sign it with the same signature which is on file at the bank.

The Checkbook—Every checkbook has a section in which you can keep a record of the running balance in your account as you make deposits and issue checks. The form of this section or check stub differs from bank to bank, but the principle is the same. You start out with a certain amount of money which you have deposited to your account. As you issue each check, the amount of money in your account is reduced by the amount of each check. As you add money to the account by making additional deposits, the amount of money in your account goes up by the amount added. The record of deposits and checks issued is called a *check register*. Everytime you make a deposit or issue a check, you must record it in the register if you are to have accurate knowledge of your bank balance.

It is a good idea to fill in the information on the check register before you write a check so that you do not forget to mark it down and adjust your balance. Forgetting to record checks issued can lead to being overdrawn at the bank and to unnecessary charges and embarrassment.

The check register should show the date and amount of each deposit, the balance after the deposit is made, the date and amount of each check, to whom the check was issued, for what it was issued, and the balance in the account after the check is issued. For example: The beginning balance in your account is $5,000.00. You issued during the month a check for $200.00 to the X Company for supplies, leaving a balance of $4,800.00. You paid the telephone company $15.00, leaving a balance of $4,785.00. You paid the Morning Newspaper $85.00 for advertising, leaving a balance of $4,700.00. You issued a check to the truck garage for $50.00 for gas, oil, and repairs, reducing your balance to $4,650.00. You paid your landlord $100.00 for rent, reducing your account balance to $4,550.00, and you paid the bank $50.00 for a payment on your loan. When you subtracted the $50.00 your checkbook balance showed $4,500.00.

The Bank Statement—At the end of specified periods of time, usually monthly, the bank sends you a statement showing its records of all the transactions made in your account. This report form is called a *bank statement*. The bank includes with your statement all of the checks you issued which have been turned in by people or firms to whom you issued them for payment by the bank from your account. It is important to check the bank statement within a short time after receiving it. Checking your bank statement and comparing it to your check register to make sure that the actual balances are the same is called *reconciling the statement*. A *Bank Reconciliation* should be done to make sure that neither the bank nor you have made a mistake in recording deposits or checks issued. Bank statements contain a form for reconciliation, or you can prepare a form like this:

The first reconciliation prepared for your account will show the Beginning Balance at 0 (zero). Each month after that, the Beginning Balance should be listed as the Checkbook Balance of the month before.

**ANYTOWN CRAFT PRODUCT COMPANY
BANK RECONCILIATION**

Month of January, 19--

Beginning Balance	$_____
Plus Total Deposits Made During Period	$_____
= Total Cash Available	$_____
Less Total of All Checks Issued During Period	$_____
= Checkbook Balance	$_____
Plus Outstanding Checks (Issued but which have not yet been paid by bank)	$_____
THIS SHOULD EQUAL BANK BALANCE ON YOUR STATEMENT	$_____

Fig. 14–3. Bank reconciliation form.

After you enter the Beginning Balance, compare your deposits listed in the check register with those listed on your Bank Statement. If they are the same, add up the deposits and list the total as Total Deposits Made During Period. The addition of your Beginning Balance to your Total Deposits gives you the Total Cash Available. Now, if you subtract the Total Checks Issued (and bank charges if they appear on your statement), you should get your Checkbook Balance. This figure should be the same as the balance shown in your checkbook register.

The Bank Statement you have received will include all of the checks the bank has charged to your account. There may be some checks which you have issued but which have not yet been turned in for payment by the bank by the people or firms to whom you issued them. These are called *Outstanding Checks.* To find out which they are, put the checks you have received with your Bank Statement in numerical order and compare them with your checkbook. Keep a list of all these checks *which have* not *yet been returned.* List these outstanding checks with their amounts on your bank reconciliation and add them to the amount listed as your Checkbook Balance. The total you now get should reconcile with (equal) the Bank Balance on the Bank Statement.

If your actual checkbook balance does not match the Checkbook

Balance in your reconciliation, chances are that you have made a mistake in addition or subtraction in your checkbook. Another possible reason might be that you have neglected to subtract a bank service charge from your balance. It is also possible, though it does not happen often, that the bank has not recorded a deposit that you have made, or has charged your account incorrectly for a check. Look at the lower right corner of a check that has cleared the bank and has been returned to you with your statement. You will note the computer print figure which the bank has deducted from your account for that check. This amount should be the same as the amount you originally wrote on the check. Occasionally when a number is illegible, the computer operator at the bank may read 7 as a 1 or a 9, or confuse another set of figures. If this should happen, the bank should be notified and an adjustment requested.

Another reason that your Bank Balance on the reconciliation does not match the balance shown by the bank statement is that you might have made an error in listing and totaling your outstanding checks. Occasionally checks may be outstanding from one month to another, and sometimes checks which you have sent out have been lost in the mail, or by the people to whom you sent them. When you list outstanding checks, therefore, you should carefully check the list of outstandings from the previous month and carry over those which are still outstanding.

Although it may sound complicated, the Bank Reconciliation is really a simple procedure when you take it step by step. It is terribly frustrating to follow through the whole procedure, and find that you are off by a few dollars or even a few cents. When you recheck, the error can usually be spotted. Oftentimes it is a matter of having reversed a number in copying it (a transaction), so that what should be $5.62 is copied as $6.52 or $5.26. A useful clue to finding a transposition is that the amount of money which you differ by will be divisible by 9. In the example of $6.52 instead of $5.62, the difference is $.90; $5.26 differs by $.36—both divisible by 9.

There are occasions when the reconciliation does not balance out after a few efforts to find the mistake. It is a good idea to put the work aside for awhile, and look at it again after you have had a chance to do something else. When you look at it fresh, the mistake often becomes obvious.

Petty Cash

We have pointed out that all monies received by the business should be deposited in the checking account and all monies paid out of the business should be paid out by check.

Most individuals and business today have a variety of credit cards with which they can pay bills, large and small. There are times, however, when it is necessary to pay just a few cents for something, or to give a delivery person a tip, or take a customer to lunch where credit cards may not be accepted. At times like this, a check is inconvenient. For such purposes, you should issue one check to yourself for *Petty Cash* in the amount of $50.00 or $100.00, or whatever amount you feel meets these small cash needs for a certain period of time. When you cash this check and use the monies to pay the minor cash expenses of your business, you should keep a record of each expenditure by writing it in a diary, small notebook, or in a petty cash slip in your office. It is important to keep all these records for tax purposes. Every legitimate business expense reduces the amount you pay for income tax. You should, therefore, keep a record of the date, to whom the cash was paid, and for what. If, for example, you spend $50 a week in cash, by the end of the year you have spent $2600. If you are able to substantiate $2600 in business expenses for tax purposes, you can save money.

Bookkeeping Records and Procedures

Every business procedure that you initiate can provide your craft business with better control. Federal, state, and local regulations require that certain business records must be maintained. The records that you keep will tell you where your income is coming from and what expenses are generated. The records will let you know what areas of your craft business require more attention, effort, promotion, and control. Most important, your business decisions are usually based on this collection of information.

The business information that you collect can be written up manually, or records can be maintained in part or wholly by computer. Over the years, computers and software have become less expensive and more user-friendly. This means that the equipment is easy to use for bookkeeping functions, inventory control, and for all types of business communications.

Included in this section will be information on the *General Ledger,*

Accounts Receivable, Accounts Payable, Inventory and the *other book-keeping records* available to you. Bookkeeping procedures and principles are standardized so that anyone who needs the information will be able to understand exactly what has happened.

The General Ledger

The *General Ledger* contains an account for every item that will eventually go on the Balance Sheet and the Statement of Profit and Loss. Petty Cash, which we have already discussed, is one of these accounts.

You will recall that each statement is based on a formula or an equation. To summarize these equations once again:

• Your Income Less Your Expenses Equals Your Profit.
• Your Assets Less Your Liabilities Equals Your Net Worth.

If you think about it for a moment, you will recognize that if you *change any part of each formula,* you will *change the end result.* Since every business transaction makes a change, and since it is hard to remember every single transaction over a period of time, it is necessary to keep accounts of each transaction. Even if you had a superhuman memory and could actually remember each transaction, you would need to keep records to provide proof of a transaction for legal and tax reasons.

These accounts are kept in a General Ledger or in a series of separate ledgers. Accounts must be kept for all current assets, all fixed assets, all deferred charges and all current and other liabilities. There is also a Net Worth Account which is sometimes called a Proprietorship Account or Equity Account. The ledger also carries the accounts for Income (sometimes called Sales or Revenue), and for all expenses.

There are several kinds of income and several kinds of expenses. The income from *sales of your craft products,* and the income from *sales of service* are usually recorded in separate accounts. Service in the craft business, for example, might be charges for the repair of customer's jewelry pieces if your craft happened to be jewelry. Income from *interest earned,* if you are selling your products on credit, is also a separate account. Expense accounts include those for *material, labor, and other job costs,* and for each of the *overhead expenses.* Overhead expenses are those which are necessary to maintain your business, such as rent, light, heat, advertising, office supplies, vehicle expense, etc.

Each account is on a separate page. The page itself is divided into two sides like a T. You purchase these pages in an office supply store, or from an office supply firm. The name of each account is at the top of the page. The left side of the page is used to enter the costs of assets and additions to assets. The right side of the page is used to enter deductions from assets. The liability accounts and the net worth accounts are handled in opposite fashion.

If we take a business situation similar to the one we have previously discussed, it would appear in the General Ledger similar to the example in Fig. 14–4.

Example—The transactions we are recording in the ledger sheets are a) the investment of $2500.00 of your cash; b) the addition of $2500.00 cash borrowed from relatives; c) the purchase of a truck for $3600.00 on which you paid $720.00 down and signed a bank loan for the $2800.00 balance; d) the purchase of office furniture for $300.00; e) and the purchase of merchandise for $200.00. The accounts would then appear:

ANYTOWN CRAFT PRODUCT COMPANY
GENERAL LEDGER

CASH

a) Jan. 1	$2500.00	c) Jan. 1	$ 720.00
b)	$2500.00	d)	$ 300.00
		e)	$ 200.00

MERCHANDISE

| e) Jan. 1 | $ 200.00 | |

TRUCK

| c) Jan. 1 | $3600.00 | |

FURNITURE and FIXTURES

| d) Jan. 1 | $ 300.00 | |

NET WORTH

| | | Jan. 1 | $2500.00 (a) |

LOANS and NOTES PAYABLE

| | | Jan. 1 | $2500.00 (b) |
| | | | $2800.00 (c) |

Fig. 14–4. General ledger transactions—asset and liability accounts.

If you were at this point to prepare a Balance Sheet, you would take the balance of each account, which is done by taking the difference between each side of the account. Then you would add up the assets (Cash, Merchandise, Truck, Furniture and Fixtures). From this total you would subtract the liabilities (Loans and Notes Payable). Using the formula, Assets − Liabilities = Net Worth, you would get Cash $3780.00 + Merchandise $200.00 + Truck $3600.00 + Furniture and Fixtures $300.00, for a total of $7880.00 in assets. From this you would subtract Loans and Notes Payable of $5380.00. This would give you the $2500.00 balance in your Net Worth Account. If you recall the Balance Sheet, Fig. 14–2, you will see that the Statement was prepared in just the manner described.

The accounts which have just been discussed and illustrated are asset and liability accounts and the Net Worth account. But income and expense accounts must also be entered in the General Ledger.

All income accounts are entered in the same way as the net worth account; that is, additions are added on the right side and deductions are entered on the left side. This is because income accounts represent an addition, even if only temporarily, to the net worth of your business. All expense accounts are entered in the opposite way because they represent decreases, even if only temporarily, to the net worth.

You sometime hear the words *debit* and *credit* used in reference to an account. The debit side of an account is the left side and items entered on that side are called debits. The credit side of an account is the right side, and items entered on the right side are called credits.

We have said that asset and expense accounts are increased by (debit) entries to the left side, and liability, net worth, and income accounts are increased by (credit) entries to the right side. The difference between the sides is called the *account balance.*

In order to keep the books in balance, a debit entry to one account always requires a credit entry to another account and vice versa. Sometimes, one entry may require several opposite entries to balance out. If you look back at our truck purchase in Fig. 14–4, you will note that the $3600.00 debit to the truck account was balanced by a $720.00 credit to the cash account and a $2880.00 credit to the Loan account. No two businesses will keep their ledgers in exactly the same order, or keep all of the same account headings.

The theory of the General Ledger has been explained so that you can understand how to set it up for your business or to follow what your accountant or bookkeeper is doing for you. There are several variations on the ledger procedure which will be discussed later in this section.

Other Bookkeeping Records

If you had nothing else to do but enter every transaction as it happened into an account, you might be able to get away with just keeping a General Ledger. But you are running your craft business and also working at it. So, in most instances, you do not have the time to make the entries immediately. On the other hand, if the entries are not made immediately, there is a danger of not making them all. For this reason, it is advisable to keep a *book of original entry*. The classic or traditional method of doing this is to use a General Journal in which a page would look like Fig. 14–5.

The *General Journal* contains a daily record of all transactions. Then, when there is time, the record is used to *post,* or enter, to the various accounts.

Another way that this can be handled is to maintain separate journals for each kind of business transaction. Thus, you might have a *Cash Receipts Book* in which you would enter each income item that came in daily with a notation of its source.

All payments, to whom they were made and for what, could be listed in your *Cash Payments Journal.* This can also be posted on a daily basis.

Your *Sales Journal* could contain a daily written record of every sale and to whom it was made. This journal could also contain information as to whether the sale was cash or credit and the credit terms.

GENERAL JOURNAL (ANYTOWN CRAFT PRODUCT COMPANY)			
DATE	**ACCOUNT & EXPLANATION**	**DEBIT**	**CREDIT**
a) Jan. 1	Cash	$2500.00	
	Net Worth—Opening Investment		$2500.00
b) Jan. 1	Loans Payable		$2500.00
	Cash—Loans from relatives	$2500.00	

Fig. 14–5. Sample General Journal page.

Your *Purchases Journal* could record every purchase made and its source and payment terms.

The Cash Receipts and Cash Payments Journal are sometimes combined into a single book called a *Cashbook.* The difference between the receipts and payments at any time should equal the cash on hand and in the bank.

If your craft business uses the cash basis for reporting, one of the most efficient bookkeeping systems is a large book containing anywhere from 10 to 24 columns on a page. This can combine the entire cashbook and the accounts book of the general ledger. A sheet in this book might look something like Fig. 14–6.

The columns would continue and cover Rent, Interest, Petty Cash, and other routine categories.

Fig. 14–7 shows the right and left sides of another type of standard journal.

To make the system even more efficient, there are several business supply firms which provide cashbook systems combined with checks and a check register. You can find these systems by checking with your accountant or banker or by inquiring directly at a business supply firm. The checkbook combination is considerably more expensive than the traditional checkbook and ledger, but it is much more convenient. It is also simpler to understand and use, and saves a great deal of time. In a small business, when time is a valuable commodity, it is sometimes worth the additional expense to save time.

In these systems the checks have built-in carbons so that as you write a check, a record is automatically kept of the check number, to whom it is issued, for what, and the amount. The record is kept on large multi-columned sheets. You label the columns as you would the combined cashbook and ledger previously discussed. If you write a check to Mr. Landlord, for example, in the amount of $100.00, you would then enter the $100.00 under the column headed Rent. At the end of each month, when you are doing your bank reconciliation, you would also total your columns across the page. As a control, your income from all sources would equal your total deposits. The total of all expenditure columns would equal the total of all checks issued.

A computer and appropriate software, can rapidly handle the business transactions discussed. Your accountant can probably provide you

COMBINATION CASHBOOK AND LEDGER ANYTOWN CRAFT PRODUCT COMPANY						
(1) Date	(2) Name	(3) Explana-tion	(4) Amount	(5) Bank Balance	(6) Deposits	(7) Income from Sales

Fig. 14–6. Sample Cashbook-Ledger combination.

COMBINATION CASHBOOK AND LEDGER ANYTOWN CRAFT PRODUCT COMPANY				
(7) Other Sources	(8) Auto Expenses	(9) Office Expenses	(10) Net Salaries	(11) Payroll Taxes

Left side of a journal page.

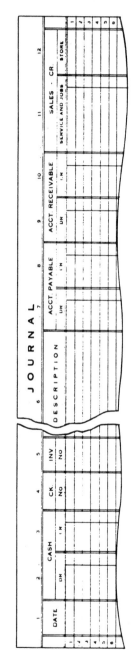

Right side of a journal page.

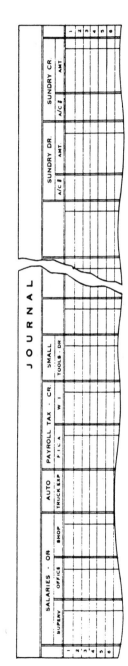

Fig. 14-7. Sample page headings of another type of journal.

with advice about developing an effective computer system for your business.

Accounts Receivable

A *receivable* is a bill that someone else owes you, and it is an asset of your business. No matter what system of bookkeeping you use, you must keep an accurate record for each of the firms from whom you buy and to whom you sell. To keep a complete record of sales, you would keep a daily sales journal in which you would enter each sale made, the name and address of the customer, the terms of the sale, and the amount. You would then take the sales journal entries and post (enter) them individually on each customer's page in the debit side of the Accounts Receivable Ledger. A simplified method is to keep all of your sales invoices (record of sales) in numerical order, and make the entries to the customer's account directly from the invoice. The invoices must, in any instance, then be carefully preserved as evidence of the sale.

When the customer pays the bill or pays on account, the payment is first recorded in your cash income record book. It is then posted to the credit side of the customer's account in the Accounts Receivable Ledger. At the end of each month, you would make your customer's statements from their account pages. The statement would indicate the amount they owed at the beginning of the month (the beginning balance) plus their purchases during the month, less the amounts they paid during the month. The difference would be the amount they currently owe you or the total balance due. This system can also be computerized easily. The total of all the account balances will give you the total of your accounts receivable—an asset on your Balance Sheet.

Accounts Payable

A *payable* is a bill that you owe. It is a liability of your business. The purchases you make from suppliers or vendors should be entered daily in a purchase journal. From there, they are posted (credited) to the vendor's account in your Accounts Payable Ledger. When you pay a bill, your payment is listed in your cashbook and posted (debited) to the vendor account. You can tell how much you owe any vendor or supplier at any time if you subtract the payments from the purchase amounts. This system can also be computerized. As with your receivables, the balances in each of the vendor accounts (what you still owe) should be totaled and posted to your Balance Sheet as a liability of the business.

Inventory

Your purchases will also form the basis of your inventory records. Inventory is the material, supplies, or craft merchandise you have available for sale. It is an asset of the business. Since it can easily be converted into money, and generally represents a sizable investment, inventory must be watched carefully. The recordkeeping is part of your control over inventory. Computer software programs are available, or can be developed for inventory control of your craft businesses.

When you buy an item for resale or manufacturing and receive a purchase invoice, in addition to entering it in your purchase journal and your payable to vendors account, you should record it as an addition to your inventory record. When items are sold or manufactured, the inventory record should be reduced accordingly. Periodically, an actual count should be made of everything you have remaining in inventory. This count should correspond to the records. If it falls below, you will know either that the recordkeeping has not been accurate, or that you have been victimized by theft. If you are manufacturing, be sure to keep accurate records of any materials destroyed or broken in the process and show this as a reduction of your inventory. This is usually kept as a separate account, called "Breakage or Loss."

Other Aspects of Record Keeping

There are other aspects of record keeping. Among them are payroll records, various tax records, sales and purchase discounts, or other more specialized records which your business may need. For more detailed information about these other recordkeeping formats, ask the advice of your tax advisor or accountant.

Chapter Highlights

• Keeping business records is not a complicated procedure. It is just an orderly record of what you do with your money and products.

- Although bookkeeping procedures may be handled manually, low-cost computers have simplified the entire proces.s
- The Profit and Loss Statement lets you know how much of a profit or loss resulted from your business during a given time period.
- If you take all of your business income and compare it to your business expenses over a certain period of time, you will know if you have made a profit or lost money.
- There are two business bases used to report income and expenses—the cash basis and the accrual basis.
- The Balance Sheet is a statement of your businesses assets and liabilities.
- An asset is anything of value that you or your business owns.
- A liability is any financial obligation of your business—anything the business owes.
- All business funds are deposited into your checking account. Business expenses are also paid from your checking account. Your checking account is a complete record of your business's cash.
- A bank statement is a record sent to you by your bank of all transactions made into and out of your checking account.
- Checking your bank statement and comparing it to your checks and book register is called reconciling your bank statement.
- The addition of your total deposits to your beginning bank balance give you the total cash available to you.
- Subtracting all of the checks the bank paid and any charges from this total shows you how much you have left in your account. Outstanding checks, those written but not yet paid by the bank, are added to your checkbook balance to equal the bank's record of your balance.
- Any mathematical errors need to be found and corrected—these mistakes will usually be in your register.
- Petty cash expenditures are used to pay small bills or expenses where a check or credit card might not be applicable. A record should always be maintained for money laid out for any petty cash expenditures. The permanent record of your petty cash account is kept in a General Ledger.
- The General Ledger or a suitable computerized format also contains an account for every item that will eventually go on the Balance Sheet and P & L Statement.
- There are several kinds of income and several kinds of expenses.

Information on both will fit into a specific area in your bookkeeping system.

- Expense accounts include those for materials, labor, job costs, and overhead expenses.
- Income accounts include monies in from the sales of your craft products and the sale of your services. In the instance of a craft business, for example, service funds can result from payment for repairs.
- The General Journal contains a daily record of all transactions.
- All payments, to whom they were made and for what, could be listed in a Cash Payments Journal.
- Your Purchases Journal could record every purchase made, its source, and payment terms.
- A payable is a bill that you owe. It is a liability of your business. The total of your payables entered on your Balance Sheet under liabilities.
- A receivable is a bill that someone else owes you, and is an asset. The total of receivables is entered on your Balance Sheet under assets.
- All purchases you make from suppliers or vendors should be entered daily in a purchase journal.
- Inventory is the material, supplies, or craft merchandise you have available for sale.
- There are numerous other records that a business must maintain. Among these are payroll records, tax records, sales and purchase discount records, etc. Your tax consultant or accountant can advise you on what records you will need to keep.

CHAPTER 15

The Craft Business Plan

The Business Side of Crafts

Whether you are working in wood, leather, fabric, metals, glass, ceramics, or any other material, plans are essential to produce your product. While experienced, creative, one-of-a-kind artists frequently develop a plan and a process almost subconsciously or simply let each piece of work flow out of their reservoir of talent, even they will sketch the original idea. They will experiment with colors and variations in the design, with textures and tools, and with various raw materials.

Forethought saves time, money, and aggravation. It is particularly important if you are going to produce articles in multiples or variations on a theme.

It makes sense when you start work on a craft project to develop the patterns and the plans you will follow. Once everything is planned, the next step is assembling the necessary tools and materials. When everything is in place, you can begin to turn out the product in an orderly process. Every activity requires a plan, preparation, and organization.

The business end of a craft enterprise similarly calls for planning, organizational discipline, and preparation. If you expect to seek funding from banks, friends, relatives, or other individuals to begin your business, for operational purposes, or for expansion, the lenders will want to know about your plans and the structure of your business. They will also want to know about you, about your track record, if any, about your business acumen, your ability to organize, to monitor expenses, and to foresee and deal with the problems your business might encounter. A well-prepared business plan will tell a lender a great deal about you and your likelihood of success.

Even if you do not have to borrow, a business plan is a valuable tool. If you are investing your own or your family's capital in your craft business, you should ask yourself the same questions a banker might. It makes a lot of sense to answer these questions before you proceed. The answers will give you a handle on the soundness of the financial structure you are building. Once you develop your business plan, you will have a clear and constant understanding of your operation so you can spend more time on its artistic end, creating new products and adding to your income sources.

A business plan for a craft operation consists of a number of components which will give you a clearcut picture of how your craft business will be conducted.

All the elements of a crafts business plan have been explained in the chapters of this book. This chapter, in effect, brings together all of the previous material into a usable model. Knowing the elements of your plan will help you focus on profit potential. Do your business plan after you have read about or skimmed the rest of this book.

The Business Plan

Your business plan begins with an outline. It should be neatly typed, double-spaced, and preferably on white paper. Leave margins at the top, bottom, and right and left sides of the paper. Follow the general format discussed below and the pertinent information about your craft business will fall into place.

A business plan for your craft operation should include an introduction, an analysis of the craft business environment and the competition, a description of your product or products, a projection of business growth, your marketing plan, statements of projected income and expenses, estimated profits or losses over a period of several years, statements of assets and liabilities (what you own and what you owe), other financial information and explanations pertaining to the operation, applicable research and development (R & D) factors, the people in the organization (including yourself), an organizational chart, a projected marketing program, and an evaluation of risks or feasibility.

There will be some overlap as each section approaches the subject from a different perspective.

The Introduction

The brief opening section of your business plan is the first time a reader will be exposed to your business. Remember as you write the introduction that although your business is very familiar to you, it may be startlingly new and different to someone who does not know much about artists and craftpeople and their business. The words you use and the information you supply should have the strength to convince a lender that your business is viable and has potential.

The first part of your business plan introduction should very briefly describe your craft business, your product or product line, your purpose for being in business and the objectives you hope to achieve. Do not ramble. Each description should be written in only a few sentences. It should be clear and concise, and formal in nature. The presentation should demonstrate that you are serious, sensible, and solid, as well as talented, creative, and skillful. Try to keep this part of the introduction to one page of double-spaced typed copy. If you can tell the story in less space, so much the better.

The second section of the introduction should tell how long you have been in operation and give the legal structure of your business— corporation, partnership, sole proprietorship—with appropriate dates if there have been changes. It might also briefly describe any business strategies that you have used since you started. This will indicate your flexibility, and your ability to evaluate and make beneficial changes.

You should also should describe in more detail the craft product or products you produce, or plan to produce.

And finally, your introduction should briefly identify your customer base or potential and discuss how your product can satisfy this market. You will add further information about this subject later in the business plan.

An Analysis of the Craft Business Environment

This analysis will tell the reader that you have investigated and understand your craft business marketplace. With this in mind, discuss your overall market potential and its size. Break down the markets into segments and explain why you have decided to target each segment.

There are certain factors that influence customers and their demands. You should discuss these factors as they relate to your craft products. You should be able to detail potential customer needs, how often they purchase craft products like yours, their average expenditure for these products, and how they react to your packaging, displays, and advertising, if any. A statement about your pricing can be included in this section along with any comments about customer reactions to price changes. If possible, include the income level of the customer population to whom you have sold or are targeting. If your records indicate any seasonal or cyclical influences such as the Christmas-Chanukah holidays, Mother's or Father's Day, June graduations, showers and weddings, etc., include this information in this section.

If there are any laws that you are aware of that may specifically affect the sale of your craft products, you should mention your conformance. In addition, you should include your recognition of and responsiveness to government standards and requirements. For example, if you are producing ceramics to serve or hold food, your products should be lead-free. If you are producing clothing, you should include washing or cleaning instructions.

It is also important to present a realistic evaluation of the competition you foresee. Most people are aware that the craft industry has competition on many levels: other craft people who produce similar products, overseas competitors, individuals who make inexpensive knock-offs, and more. With craft fairs, mall shows, boutiques, galleries, and catalogs increasing in visibility, lenders wonder about how much the market can support. You should analyze and discuss the nature and degree of the competition you foresee, whether it is direct or indirect, and how it affects your pricing as well as your other marketing plans.

Dealing with this subject gives you a chance to detail the qualities of your product and other positive factors which will enable it and you to succeed in the competitive world.

Your Craft Product

A description of the product or products is essential. Talk about the material from which it is crafted, the design and styling, approximate size or sizes, where and how it can be used, and anything else about it that might be important to a lender. If the product is copyrighted or trademarked, include this information. Emphasize the product's quality and distinguishing features. Mention if it has won awards or has been purchased by collectors, museums, or been accorded any other mark of recognition. Include details about cost and pricing, and method of distribution.

If you plan on coming out with new designs or products in the near future, this should be stated. You may want to detail your sources and access to supplies and raw materials, indicating their reliability, uniformity, or other factors which might affect your work and your business.

Good photographs of your craft products can accompany and enhance your business plan.

Planning for Business Growth

Some people are lucky and find their business mushrooming almost beyond their capacity to produce. Most craftpeople, however, require serious planning for business expansion. Planning includes investigation and evaluation of products, markets, staff, and other factors that can increase your business potential. A discussion of your investigation and evaluation should be included in this section of your business plan. Are you considering doing more shows, opening a shop, catalog sales or other forms of direct marketing, wholesaling, adding representatives, or simply adding to your product line?

It is equally important that you maintain your current market-share. This is the segment of the marketplace that you have won for yourself through product sales. This maintenance of current market-share requires certain strategies which you may have already developed and honed to a fine degree. Consider your current strategies and write them out in this section of the outline.

Economists and weather people usually forecast future activities based on current knowledge and experience. Forecasting is a valuable tool if it is based on experience—yours or other people's—and reasonable assumptions. Look three years or five years down the line and conservatively forecast what business you might expect to be doing. Consider both your present product line as well as any new products you anticipate. Translate your forecasts into dollar estimates. When we say that forecasting should be based on reliable assumptions, we mean that you must have some ideas about costs, conditions, etc. three or five years away. Consider the factors that might affect these projections. Keep abreast of the field. Think about both the worst-case and best-case scenarios. A conservative forecast is generally most credible.

Marketing for Business

Certain marketing basics should be included in your craft business plan. You should discuss the geographical areas in which you expect to sell your products. Describe any distribution plan you have established or expect to set up. Discuss any sales approach that you are using or plan to use to move your product. Are you selling to craft shops? Is your product in museum shops or boutiques? A craft cooperative? Regularly appearing in local or regional juried craft shows? Mall shows? Catalogs? Galleries?

Your current and projected advertising and public relations material should also be detailed. If sample copies of campaign literature are available, they can be included. If funds are needed for advertising, public relations, or promotion, the budget for these items should be estimated.

If you maintain a showroom for your craft products, or have designed special display booths for shows, include this information in the outline. Photographs can also be included.

Operating Your Craft Business

The financial health of a business operation is generally judged on the information in two statements. The first is a statement of earnings. This is also called a Statement of Profit or Loss or a Statement of Income and Expenses. Profits or earnings are the surplus of income over expenses. The second is a Balance Sheet, or a Statement of Assets and Liabilities. Assets are what you own, including receivables; liabilities or payables are what you owe.

A third statement, a Cash Flow Analysis, is sometimes also developed. This reports or projects how actual cash moves in and out of your business, and shows how your cash receipts and expenses are scheduled and affect your actual cash on hand at any point in time. It is applicable if you are selling on credit either to individuals or businesses. It also lets a lender know that you plan to have enough cash on hand at any point to meet unexpected situations.

If you are operating a business currently, you can develop these statements from information at hand. If you are planning a business, you can develop pro-forma statements based on your best estimates or projections.

The expenses of a business include the cost of materials, packaging, transportation, salaries, utilities, advertising, office supplies, professional costs such as legal and accounting, services such as cleaning, snow removal, tax preparation, and repairs, rentals or real estate taxes, mortgage payments and other expenses, interest, etc. In addition to these numbers or projections, discuss any property involved with your business. Describe such facilities as to size, location, and special features. If you own or lease production equipment, in addition to the the dollars involved, you should include its age, condition, and its anticipated lifespan.

If you maintain an inventory, calculate its value. Inventory is an asset. If your products have a lifespan, or breakage factor, include this information. Discuss inventory allowances if you make them for theft, discontinued lines, seconds or imperfects, samples, etc.

If you subcontract some of your production, include this information along with your costs for this service. You might mention the work history and reputation of the subcontractors if these factors add to the quality image of the product.

If you are like most craftpeople, you are sensitive to quality and quality control. This is probably because your craft products are in fact an extension of yourself. It is wise to include information about this production aspect in the business plan. A description of how quality control is established and maintained in the production of your crafts delivers an effective message.

Craft Business R & D

Most progressive businesses conduct research and development programs. Craftpeople by their very nature are great experimenters. You may take this aspect of your business for granted as you try working with new materials or with the same materials in different ways, or applying the same materials and techniques to different products. Investigating and experimenting with materials, techniques, and applications is the research of the craftperson. Development consists of designing and making the prototype, or sample product, and creating production plans based on the prototype or sample.

If your business functions in this manner, regularly producing new craft designs, patterns, objects, etc., include this information in your business plan. Spell out the details of costs, marketing, and the potential of new product lines.

The People in Your Craft Company

Business and financial people take great stock in the character, talent, and business acumen of individuals who manage businesses. This includes you. Lenders and investors look closely at backgrounds, track records, and reputations.

Starting with yourself, list every one of the top management or production people in your operation. Describe the individual, resume style, and detail his or her qualifications for the particular job. If possible include a photograph. Describe the person's functions and salary or projected compensation. If there are employment contracts or special agreements involved, describe them. For example, are there buyout clauses and patent rights or assignments, or restrictive covenants? This information may be particularly relevant if the individual is creating craft pieces intended for duplication.

An Organizational Chart

If your staff is large you can include an organizational chart in the report. The chart will graphically show the lines of authority and responsibility, the chain of command, who reports to whom in the various divisions or departments of the organization.

Capital Needed

This is the point at which you discuss your need for a loan, investment, or financial participation to start, maintain, or expand your venture.

If you are looking for a loan, you must show that you are able to pay it back. If you are looking for an investment, you must be able to show that the investor will make a profit on his or her investment over and above what it could earn in the bank. If you are looking for participation, you must be able to show that the return could be more than a salary.

This section should explain the financial statements, or projections discussed above including:

- The terms of existing debts.
- If your company is a corporation, the names of any stockholders and how they achieved their equity.
- Any capital contributions and/or investments in your company and from whom.
- The use you made of any prior capital invested in your company.

When you detail the potential return on the investment you are seeking, remember that this section will be closely scrutinized by the financial people. It should be as realistic as possible, conservative, and based on reasonable assumptions.

If, through trade magazines, you can obtain financial comparisons with companies similar to yours, this information can bolster your assumptions. Past experience is also an important factor.

You should also detail how you will spend the money you are seeking. For equipment? Materials? Labor? Buildings or vehicles? Advertising and promotion? It is important for a lender to know whether his or her funds are being used for capital improvements or operating expenses.

Your Business Risks

Unless you are a born pessimist, when you start up a business, you feel that nothing will go wrong. You expect to make a profit, perhaps not from the moment the doors are open but soon.

The fact of the matter is that there are a great many businesses out there that do not make it. Any good business plan, therefore, deals with an analysis of possible risks.

There are two types of risk analysis—qualitative and quantitative.

The *qualitative* risk analysis asks what can go wrong and what the possibilities are of its actually happening? The analysis is predicated on similar types of business operations and any known possibilities. Industry trade journals and government data and fact books are usually used to obtain this information.

The *quantitative* risk analysis looks at such standardized factors as breakeven points and payback periods. How long will it take, given a realistic scenario, to get to the breakeven point, considering the rate of payback on your investment and/or borrowings? This is the crux of what some lenders call a feasibility study. It is the test of whether or not an investment in your business is sound. This may be another area in which you might want to consult with your accountant.

Optional Additions

Additional supporting material can make your business plan even more acceptable to people in the financial world. This material might include testimonials from satisfied customers, credit references from vendors and financial institutions, and copies of articles about you and your products. You could also include copies of leases, franchise agreements, property, health, life and liability insurance coverage, incorporation papers, and legal information that impacts on your business.

The Executive Summary

When you have completed your business plan, it is a good idea to develop an executive summary. The summary should be a brief capsule of the entire plan to give a reader with limited time a rapid overview of the complete report. The summary can be placed either at the end of the report or at the beginning.

Either a table of contents or an index is also important if your plan is more than a few pages long.

Your business plan will serve you well long after you have secured the capital you need for your business. It will serve as a guide to follow and a standard by which to measure your success. If you have the self-discipline to update your business plan periodically, it will force you to think clearly about what you have achieved and where and how you can make your business grow.

Chapter Highlights

- Planning ahead when preparing to sell your craft product can save you time, money, and aggravation.
- If patterns, plans, tools, and everything else required are in place, you can begin to turn out your craft product in an orderly fashion. The business end of the craft profession requires the same attention.
- Once your business plan is developed, you will have a clear and constant understanding of your operation.

- The components of your business plan are an introduction; an analysis of the business environment; product description; information about profit, loss, assets, and liabilities; research and development data; an organizational chart and description of the business leadership; a marketing program; and an evaluation of risks and feasibility.
- The business plan introduction is a description of your craft business.
- The environmental analysis portion of your business plan concerns market potential and general economic factors concerning your business.
- One of the important portions of your business plan is a complete description of the craft product you are producing.
- Everyone plans for business growth. This segment of your business plan explains how you envision growth for your product and business.
- A section of your business plan is reserved for a marketing plan. This piece describes in detail how you expect to place your product in the marketplace and sell it to the consumer.
- The financial information about your business operation is covered in your business plan. It is detailed and covers every dollar aspect of the operation.
- In order to stay ahead of the competition, progressive businesses conduct research and development programs. A section of your business plan should be devoted to this business aspect.
- It is important to describe in your business plan the talents of the people who make decisions in your organization. Space should be provided for this important information.
- If your organization is small, there is no need for an organization chart; however, if your company is large, such a chart should be part of your business plan.
- Some businesses require capitalization. Many business plans are developed specifically to seek capital. In this section of the plan, you will detail your monetary requirements.
- The subject of business risks is discussed in this portion of the business plan. There are two types of risks: qualitative and quantitative.
- Additional options and supporting material about your business can be included near the end of your business plan presentation.
- All of the information discussed in your business plan can be put together in abbreviated form in the plan's executive summary.

YOUR CRAFT BUSINESS PLAN

Use this worksheet to lay out your craft business plan. Eliminate any areas of the plan that you do not which to develop. Go into as much detail as you desire. If you require additional space add as many pages as you need.

COMPANY OR CRAFT PRODUCT NAME: _____

DATE OF PLAN: _____

INTRODUCTION: _____

_____

_____

_____

_____

BUSINESS ENVIRONMENT ANALYSIS: _____

_____

_____

_____

_____

PRODUCT DESCRIPTION: _____

_____

_____

_____

_____

BUSINESS GROWTH PROJECTIONS: _____

_____

_____

_____

_____

MARKETING PLAN: _____

_____

_____

_____

_____

PROFIT AND LOSS PROJECTIONS: _____

_____

_____

_____

_____

RESEARCH AND DEVELOPMENT: _____

_____

_____

_____

_____

COMPANY LEADERSHIP INFORMATION: _____

_____

_____

_____

ORGANIZATION CHART: _____

_____

_____

_____

BUSINESS RISK EVALUATION: _____

_____

_____

_____

OPTIONAL ADDITIONS: _____

_____

_____

EXECUTIVE SUMMARY: _____

_____

_____

_____

_____

Marketing Glossary

Ad Spot—15-, 30-, or 60-second audio messages aired by a radio station, or audiovisual messages aired by a television station promoting a particular product or service.

Advertising Agency—A professional communications company that assists businesses with designing their ads and placing the ads in selected media.

Barter—The business of trading a service or product for another individual's service or product. Money is usually not used in a barter transaction.

Brochure—A written and pictorial promotional tool providing descriptive information about a product for the consuming public.

Budget—A written outline of projected income and expenses over a selected time period.

Buyer Behavior—A process whereby a consumer reacts favorably or unfavorably to a particular product for a series of different reasons. As a result, the consumer makes a decision either to purchase or reject a product.

Column Inch—A measurement used by newspapers to sell advertising space. The ad space is generally sold in column inch increments, which is a depth of one inch on the newspaper page. The width of a newspaper column inch may vary from newspaper to newspaper.

Competition—An individual, group, or organization sets up a business selling the same or similar products as yours, and thus has the potential of rivaling yours. As competitors, they attempt to convince consumers to purchase their products rather than yours.

Consignment—A process whereby a craft producer places products in a retail outlet for sale to consumers. The products are placed in the shop or outlet on a "loan basis," and are only paid for by store management after a sale has been completed. The shop receives either a set fee or a percentage of the product's selling price.

Consumer Goods—Products that are destined ultimately to be used by members of the purchasing public.

Contract or Piecework—This is a process whereby an individual outside your company contracts to make or assemble products for you at an agreed-upon price per unit. Your company may benefit by avoiding employment taxes and fringe benefits.

Cost of Product—Each product costs a specific amount to produce. In addition to such items as raw materials, product costs include labor, freight, shipping, handling, packaging, labeling, operating expenses, insurance, taxes, professional fees, general office, travel and sales expenses.

Demographic Research—A research process for determining who consumers are by their age, geographic area, income, education, sex, etc.

Depreciation—Articles with specific lifespans such as vehicles, buildings, tools, etc. are "written off" or depreciated as they age over the life of the individual asset. Each item has a time span in which it is deemed to be commercially useful. An accounting mechanism called depreciation is used to set aside funds with which to purchase new equipment after the lifespan of the article has been reached.

Developmental Stage—The stage in a product's life cycle where an item is being created, designed and prepared for the marketplace.

Discretionary Income—The money people have left from their incomes after purchasing all of their life necessities such as food, clothing, and shelter, and after the necessary government taxes have been paid.

Direct Mail—A promotional technique used to sell a product to the consumer using the mail or other mass communications system as the vehicle.

Fixed Costs—These are costs that remain approximately the same no matter how many units or items you produce, such as rent or mortgage payments.

Getting Press—Receiving attention for a product in the form of publicity and editorial coverage from the media.

Growth Stage—The stage in the life cycle of a product where the item is accepted by the marketplace and it experiences sales growth.

Image—A visual or word picture of a product developed by the marketer which is designed specifically to interest consumers in the product.

Innovation—The creative development of a new product, or the redesign of a current product to meet the demands of the marketplace.

Introductory Stage—The stage in a product's life cycle where a newly-created item is being introduced to the marketplace.

Juried Show—A show in which craft products are first judged before being allowed to exhibit at a show. The items are reviewed by an individual or team of experts and must meet certain established criteria.

Life Cycles—The different business time periods through which a product passes from its beginning or startup to its decline as a result of a lack of consumer interest.

Markdown—The difference in cost to the consumer between the original price for a product and the reduced price for which it is finally sold.

Markup—Each product costs a certain amount to create and market. The selling price of the product is increased a certain percentage over costs to create profit for the producer. This percentage is called markup.

Market—The demand developed by a wide variety of purchasing consumers for a product; or, the group of consumers you feel will buy your product.

Marketing—An activity of business by which consumers are informed about the results of a craftsperson's efforts, and have the opportunity to procure the products. The process of matching products with markets.

Market Research—The system by which a producer attempts to learn about the consumer market and market demands.

Maturity Stage—The stage in the life cycle of a product where the item begins to saturate the marketplace and demand for the product starts to slacken.

Media—The press—newspapers, magazines, journals, newsletters—and other public information sources—radio, television, cable TV.

Multiple Pricing—Packaging a number of the same or related products together and pricing them to sell as a single unit. This is a promotional sales technique.

Niche Market—A small, specialized section of the market in which to sell a specific product. Competition is usually sparse in niche markets especially if the producer is first in the niche with an idea that is significantly different.

PSA—Public Service Announcement. Space allotted by radio or television stations at no charge for nonprofit organization messages.

Package of Satisfaction—The feeling of physical and psychological satisfaction, and the positive image engendered when a consumer purchases a product.

Packaging—The container or housing in which a product is displayed in the marketplace, or the holder in which it is placed for storage or consumer shipment.

Place—The physical accessibility of a product or the method used to assure that a consumer may find a particular product in the marketplace.

Positioning—A collection of perceptions that the consumer has about a product. The group of perceptions that are developed by the product or by the marketer of the item, especially concerning product image as it relates to markets targeted.

Press Conference—An invitational gathering of members of the press designed to provide a forum for special information about a new company product or event.

Press Kit—A collection of publicity pieces, photographs and other information about a product or company that is distributed to the media. For convenience, the information is usually kept together in a folder or envelope.

Price—The cost a consumer pays or is willing to pay the seller of a product for an item that he or she wishes to purchase.

Price Lining—Selectively selling a product to a target market in a specific price range.

Pricing Formula—Total cost of goods sold *equals* cost of materials *plus* cost of all labor including personal and family labor *plus* all other expenses of the business.

Product—The creation of a useful or decorative item by a craftsperson. The resulting creation may be simple or complex, inexpensive or expensive.

Product Personalization—The individualization of products by initials, names, symbols, etc., to enhance the sales potential of the item.

Profit and Loss Statement—A summary of the results of doing business over a specific time period. This business statement will indicate the profits that have been made or the losses that have been incurred by the business.

Promotion—A combination of publicity, advertising, and other promotional efforts on behalf of a product designed to alert consumers to the existence and desirability of an item.

Psychographic Research—A system for learning how consumers react by determining how they think and how they behave.

Public Relations Agency—A professional communications company that assists businesses with placing their publicity and promotions in selected media.

Publicity—The audio, visual, and written expressions about a product that are developed by a marketer to interest and sell the product in the consumer marketplace.

Sales Tax—Almost every state has regulations governing the tax that product producers must charge and add to the price consumers pay for an item. Each state sales tax or revenue department provides the applications and forms necessary for producers to collect sales tax in a given state or locality.

Segmentation of a Market—The division of a consumer market into specific groupings. Once divided, the marketer may target each segment in a special way to reach the purchasing consumers.

Show Booth—An assigned exhibit space at a show in which craft and other products are shown and made available for sale to the viewing consumer. The booth or exhibit area may simply be a space, a table, or an ornate, specially-designed booth.

Telemarketing—The use of the telephone as a promotional vehicle to sell products to the consumer public.

Test Marketing—Setting up a system to test a new product or promotion before attempting to sell it to the entire consumer market.

Variable Expenses—These are expenses that are directly related to creation of a product: the more product you make, the higher these costs. They are often computed on a per unit basis. These expenses include such items as cost of materials, labor and shipping costs.

Venue—An exhibition area, hall, fairgrounds, convention center, show place, etc., in which events are conducted.

Wholesaling—Selling a line of products to a buyer rather than to the ultimate consumer. The buyer or wholesaler may then sell the line of products to the consumer. Products sold this way command a lower price but larger quantities.

Resources

The resource information that follows covers many areas of interest to the the craftsperson. The focus is on product marketing, but related subject areas are also included. Because of the magnitude of each subject area, only a representation of available sources is provided in these pages. Additional information is available by checking such sources as craft directories, telephone books, chambers of commerce and business directories, national, state, and regional art councils, and trade journals.

Craft Show Promotion Companies

The list that follows is representative of craft show promotion companies that may be useful to your marketing efforts. It is not a complete listing, but is designed to suggest to you the marketing possibilities and the assistance available. There are many show promotion firms, small and large, throughout the United States and Canada.

It is suggested that you contact the individual promoters for their annual show schedules.

A few words of caution: Before signing a booth space contract with any promotion company, it is suggested that you read the promoter's contract carefully. Understand your obligations to the promoter and the show venue. Be prepared to observe regulations such as the booth set-up rules, show hours, food restrictions, etc. Look carefully for any special charges that may be levied for electricity, signs, labor, etc.

ACC Craft Fair
P.O. Box 10
New Paltz, NY 12561

Artisan Promotions, Inc.
83 Mount Vernon Street
Boston, MA 02108

Artrider Productions, Inc.
4 Camelot Road
Woodstock, NY 12488

Cavalcade of Crafts
25 Landfield Avenue
Monticello, NY 12701

Contemporary Crafts Market
777 Kapiolani Boulevard - Suite #2830
Honolulu, Hawaii 96813

DMC Expositions, Inc.
P.O. Box 581406
Dallas, TX 75258

Jinx Harris Shows, Inc.
3 Harwich Court
Merrimack, NH 03054

Harvest Festival
111 Liberty Street
Petaluma, CA 94952

Sylvia Henry Exhibits
404 Jefferson street
Massapequa, NY 11758

Heritage Markets
Box 389
Carlisle, PA 17013

George Little Management Inc.
2 Park Avenue - Suite #1100
New York, NY 10016

MII Productions, Inc.
P.O. Box 938
Vernon, CT 06066

Market Square
P.O. Box 220
Newville, PA 17241

Ron Meyers Productions, Inc.
P.O. Box 7021
Gulfport, MS 39506

Offinger Management Company
Gift Retailers Manufacturers & Reps Assoc.
1100-H Brandywine Boulevard
P.O. Box 2188
Zanesville, OH 43701

Palm Beach Promotions, Inc.
6070 North Federal Highway
Boca Raton, FL 33487

Raab Enterprises, Inc.
P.O. Box 33428
North Royalton, OH 44133

Bill Riggins Promotions, Inc.
610 East War Memorial Drive
Peoria, IL 61614

4/3/95

Wendy Rosen Shows, Inc.
Buyers Market of American Crafts
3000 Chestnut Avenue - Suite 300
Baltimore, MD 21211

410-889-2933

Rose Squared Productions
12 Galaxy Court
Belle Mead, NJ 08502

United Craft Enterprises
Box 326
Masonville, NY 13804

Woodwill Corporation
P.O. Box 186
Hauppauge, NY 11788

Arts Councils

While craft producers may work alone developing and turning out their creations, there are many arts and crafts councils available which provide opportunities for craftspeople to meet and compare notes with others. These councils also offer support in a variety of different areas including technical assistance, information about craft shows, listing of craft courses, and other material of a nature helpful to the marketing effort. Craftspeople may call on the services and advice of national arts councils and organizations with strong ties to the craft industry.

Regionally-based arts and crafts councils can be located by contacting area chambers of commerce, business organizations, and directories.

National Councils

American Artists' and Craftsmen's Guild
P.O. Box 193
Westmont, IL 60559

American Arts and Crafts Alliance
145 West 86 Street
New York, NY 10024

American Craft Council
72 Spring Street
New York, NY 11012

American Crafts Retailers Association
P.O. Box 653
Cockeysville, MD 21030

Crafts Center, The
2016 O Street NW
Washington, DC 20036

National Association for the Cottage Industry
P.O. Box 14850
Chicago, IL 60614

National Endowment for the Arts
Nancy Hanks Center
1100 Pennsylvania Avenue NW
Washington, DC 20506

State Councils

Alabama State Council on the Arts
1 Dexter Avenue
Montgomery, AL 36130

Alaska State Council on the Arts
619 Warehouse Avenue - Suite 220
Anchorage, AK 99501

Arizona Commission on the Arts
417 West Roosevelt
Phoenix, AZ 85003

Arkansas Arts Council
Heritage Center - Suite 200
225 East Markam Street
Little Rock, AR 72201

California Arts Council
601 North 7th Street - Suite 100
Sacramento, CA 95814

Colorado Council on the Arts and Humanities
770 Pennsylvania Avenue
Denver, CO 80203

Commonwealth of Pennsylvania Council on the Arts
216 Finance Building
Harrisburg, PA 17210

Delaware State Arts Council
State Office Building
820 North French Street
Wilmington, DE 19801

**District of Columbia Commission on the Arts
and Humanities**

111 East E Street NW - Suite B500
Washington, DC 20004

Florida Arts Council
Department of State—Cultural Affairs Division
The Capitol
Tallahassee, FL 32399

Georgia Council for the Arts
2082 East Exchange Place - Suite 100
Tucker, GA 30084

Hawaii State Foundation on Culture and the Arts
335 Merchant Street - Room 202
Honolulu, HI 96813

Idaho State Commission on the Arts
304 West State Street
Boise, ID 83720

Illinois Arts Council
100 West Randolph - Suite 10–500
Chicago, IL 60601

Indiana Arts Commission
47 South Pennsylvania Street
Indianapolis, IN 46204

Iowa State Arts Council
State Capitol Complex
Des Moines, IA 50319

Kansas Arts Commission
700 Jackson - Suite 1004
Topeka, KS 66603

Kentucky Arts Council
Berry Hill
Frankfort, KY 40601

Louisiana State Division of the Arts
P.O. Box 44247
Baton Rouge, LA 70804

Maine Arts Commission
State House Station 25
Augusta, ME 04333

Maryland State Arts Council
15 West Mulberry Street
Baltimore, MD 21201

Michigan Council for the Arts
1200 6th Avenue - Suite 1180
Detroit, MI 48226

Minnesota State Arts Board
432 Summit Avenue
St. Paul, MN 55102

Mississippi Arts Commission
239 North Lamar Street
Jackson, MS 39201

Missouri Arts Council
Wainwright Office Complex
111 North 7th Street - Suite 105
St. Louis, MO 63101

Montana Arts Council
48 North Last Chance Gulch
Helena, MT 59620

Nebraska Arts Council
1313 Farnam-on-the-Mall
Omaha, NE 68102

Nevada State Council on the Arts
329 Flint Street
Reno, NV 89501

New Hampshire State Council on the Arts
Phenix Hall
40 North Main Street
Concord, NH 03301

New Jersey State Council on the Arts
4 North Broad Street
Trenton, NJ 08625

New Mexico Arts Division
224 East Palace Avenue
Santa Fe, NM 87501

New York State Council on the Arts
915 Broadway
New York, NY 10010

North Carolina Arts Council
Department of Cultural Resources
Raleigh, NC 27611

North Dakota Council on the Arts
Black Building - Suite 606
Fargo, ND 58102

Ohio Arts Council
727 East Main Street
Columbus, OH 43205

Oregon Arts Commission
835 Summer Street NE
Salem, OR 97301

Rhode Island State Council on the Arts
95 Cedar Street - Suite 103
Providence, RI 02903

South Carolina Arts Commission
1800 Gervais Street
Columbia, SC 29201

South Dakota Arts Council
108 West 11th Street
Sioux Falls, SD 57102

State Arts Council of Oklahoma
Jim Thorpe Building
Room 640
Oklahoma City, OK 73105

Tennessee Arts Commission
320 6th Avenue North - Suite 100
Nashville, TN 37219

Texas Commission on the Arts
P.O. Box 13406
Capitol Station
Austin, TX 78711

Utah Arts Council
617 East South Temple
Salt Lake City, UT 84102

Vermont Council on the Arts
136 State Street
Montpelier, VT 05602

Virginia Commission for the Arts
101 North 14th Street
Richmond, VA 23219

Washington State Arts Commission
Mail Stop GH-11
Olympia, WA 98504

West Virginia Department of Culture and History
The Cultural Center
Capitol Complex
Charleston, WV 25305

Wisconsin Arts Board
131 West Wilson Street - Suite 301
Madison, WI 53702

Wyoming Council on the Arts
2320 Capitol Avenue
Cheyenne, WY 82002

Cooperatives/Specialty Stores/Galleries

There are craft cooperatives, specialty stores, and galleries in towns and cities throughout the United States and Canada. These are shops where groups of talented craftspeople can display and market their individual craft products. These outlets, operated cooperatively by a craft group, or run by a business entrepreneur, can provide a convenient marketing outlet for the craftsperson. The following is a representative list of craft outlets that may be useful to your marketing efforts. Check the business section of your telephone book, the regional chamber of commerce, and area business directories for the names and locations of additional retail marketing outlets.

Craft Village Cooperative
2301 Kuhio Avenue
Honolulu, HI 96815
Cooperative craft gallery in mall setting—only products made in Hawaii exhibited and sold.

Delavan Center, Inc.
501–509 West Fayette Street
Syracuse, NY 13204
Gallery and craftsperson workshop.

Elder Craftsmen, Inc.
135 East 65 Street
New York, NY 10021
Sells crafts of people over age 55.

Florida Craftsmen, Inc.
235 Third Street South
St. Petersburg, FL 33701
Showcases and sells crafts.

Forty-One Madison
New York Merchandise Mart
2 Park Avenue - Suite 1100
New York, NY 10016
Craft/gift showcase site.

Adrien Linford
1320 Madison Avenue
New York, NY 10021
Near 93rd street.
Craft showcase and sales gallery.

Oregon School of Arts and Crafts
8245 SW Barnes Road
Portland, OR 97225
Sales gallery sells work by craftpeople from across United States.

Peters Valley Craftsmen, Inc.
Route 615
Layton, NJ 07851

The Studio Gallery
133 South Salina Street
Syracuse, NY 13202
Selects and sells unique craft items.

Valley Artisans Market
25 East Main Street
Cambridge, NY 12816

Craft Centers/Schools

The craft centers and schools listed below are representational of the type of schools available to you if you wish to hone your skills further. These centers offer a range of courses in many different craft categories. Check the craft magazines and trade journals for a complete craft school listing. Write directly to the schools to obtain their updated course catalogs.

American Woodcarving School
RD#2 Box 213
Belvidere, NJ 07823
Woodcarving.

Anderson Ranch Arts Center
P.O. Box 5598
Snowmass Village, CO 81615
Ceramics, woodworking crafts, etc.

Arrowmont School
P.O. Box 567
Gatlinburg, TN 37738
Ceramics, woodworking crafts, etc.

Augusta Heritage Center
100 Sycamore Street
Elkins, WV 26241
A full range of craft classes offered.

Basketry School
Route 3 - Box 325
Chloe, WV 25235
Basketry craft classes.

Baulines Craft Guild
Schoonmaker Point
Sausalito, CA 94965
Woodworking, ceramics, glass design, etc.

Bishop Certified Stencil Seminars
P.O. Box 3349
Kinston, NC 28502
Craft of stenciling.

Brookfield Craft Center, Inc.
P.O. Box 122
Brookfield, CT 06804
Classes in metalwork, weaving, ceramics, basketry, dollmaking, etc.

John C. Campbell Folk School
Route #1 - Box 14A
Brasstown, NC 28902
A full range of craft classes offered.

Chautauqua Institute
Box 1098
Chautauqua, NY 14722
Ceramic crafts.

Cooper-Hewitt Museum
2 East 91 Street
New York, NY 10128
Exhibition-related craft programs.

Colton Glass Center
Camp Colton
Colton, OR 97017
Glass crafts.

Coupeville Arts Center
P.O. Box 171
Coupeville, WA 98239
Classes offered in fiber, needlework, photography, etc.

Craft Center
Cedar Lakes Conference Center
Ripley, WV 25271
Classes in stained glass, weaving, woodworking, etc.

Dunconor Workshops
Box 149
Taos, NM 87571
Classes in jewelry crafting techniques.

Enamelist Society
P.O. Box 310

Newport, KY 41072
Classes in enameling.

Kay Fisher
The College of Miniature Knowledge
8800 Cook-Riolo Road
Roseville, CA 95678
Classes in the craft of making miniatures.

Gemological Institute of America
P.O. Box 2110
1660 Stewart Street
Santa Monica, CA 90406
Jewelry-oriented craft classes.

Guilford Handicrafts Center, Inc.
411 Church Street - P.O. Box 589
Guilford, CT 06437
Classes in pottery, jewelry, metalsmithing, etc.

Haliburton School of Fine Arts
P.O. Box 339
Haliburton, Ontario KOM 1SO, Canada
Classes in carving, basketry, glass, etc.

Haystack Mountain School of Crafts
Box 87
Deer Isle, ME 04627
Classes in ceramics, glass blowing, metal, etc.

Hill Country Arts Foundation
P.O. Box 176
Ingram, TX 78025
Classes in sculpting, ceramics, weaving, etc.

I.M.C. Needlecrafts, Inc.
55 Railroad Avenue
Garnerville, NY 10923
Source of craft how-to booklets.

Oregon School of Arts and Crafts
825 SW Barnes Road

Portland, OR 97225
Classes in ceramics, fibers, metal, wood, etc.

Penland School
Penland, NC 28765
Classes in ceramics, metals, glass, fibers, etc.

Pennsylvania Guild of Craftsmen
P.O. Box 820
Richboro, PA 18954
Classes in stained glass, ceramics, etc.

Peters Valley Craftsmen, Inc.
Crafts Education Center
Route 615
Layton, NJ 07851
Classes in blacksmithing, ceramics, wood, textiles, fine metals, etc.

The River Farm
Route #1 - Box 401
Timberville, VA 22853
Fiber crafts classes.

Sawmill Center for the Arts
P.O. Box 180
Cooksburg, PA 16217
Classes in woodcarving, basketry, etc.

Southwest Craft Center
300 Augusta
San Antonio, TX 78205
Classes on ceramics, jewelry, etc.

Thousand Island Craft School
324 John street
Clayton, NY 13624
Classes in weaving, carving, etc.

Vermont State Craft Center
Frog Hollow
Middlebury, VT 05753
Specializing in functional pottery.

Westchester Art Workshop
Westchester County Center
White Plains, NY 10606
Classes in fiber arts, jewelry, ceramics, sculpture, etc.

Trade Journals/Craft-Oriented Magazines

While there are magazines available that can be particularly useful in the marketing of your craft products, there are also journals which can impact on other areas of your business. It is suggested that you review copies of as many craft and craft-related magazines as possible in your local library. You can then subscribe to those magazines which you feel will be the most useful to your marketing efforts. In researching information about marketing your craft products, seek out marketing magazines, incentive journals, sales magazines, direct marketing newspapers, etc.

American Artist
1 Astor Place
New York, NY 10036

American Craft Magazine
72 Spring Street
New York, NY 10022

Art in America
980 Madison Avenue
New York, NY 10021

Artisan Crafts
Box 179
Reed Springs, MO 65237

Arts Magazine
23 East 26 Street
New York, NY 10010

The Crafts Fair Guide
P.O. Box 5062
Mill Valley, CA 94942

Craft Horizons
72 Spring Street
New York, NY 10022

Craftmakers/Wholesale Crafts
Box 481
Everett, MA 02149

Craft/Midwest
Box 42
Northbrook, IL 60065

The Crafts Report
700 Orange Street
P.O. Box 1992
Wilmington, DE 19899

Craft Show Digest
P.O. Box 3275
Falls Church, VA 22043

The Craftsman's Gallery
Box 655
Rockville, MD 20849

Creative Crafters Journal
P.O. Box 210
Honaker, VA 24260

Entrepreneur Magazine
P.O. Box 13787
Irvine, CA 92713

Galleries
P.O. Box 3705
Washington, DC 20007

Gift Reporter
1785 The Exchange
Atlanta, GA 30339

Interior Decorator's Handbook
370 Lexington Avenue
New York, NY 10064

Niche
The Magazine for Progressive Retailers
P.O. Drawer 1217
Hunt Valley, MD 21030

The Professional Crafter
P.O. Box 692
Mariposa, CA 95338

Profitable Craft Merchandising
News Plaza - P.O. Box 1790
Peoria, IL 61656

SAC
P.O. Box 159
Bogalusa, LA 70429

Show and Sell
P.O. Box 212
Santa Claus, IN 47579

Sunshine Artists
Sun Country Enterprises
501–503 N. Virginia Avenue
Winter Park, FL 32789

Craft Fair Guides & Listing Sources

The following list is representative of the craft fair guides available. The guides can be extremely useful to your marketing efforts. The list may suggest to you other sources of useful information on the subject. There are craft fair and event guides published in most local regions, and by area craft guilds and art councils. Newspapers and regional magazines publish lists of forthcoming events in their areas of coverage. The listings generally provide information on the place, date, and hours of craft shows well in advance of the scheduled programs.

American Craft Enterprises, Inc.
P.O. Box 10
New Paltz, NY 12516
Craft show calendar.

Art and Craft Catalyst
P.O. Box 433
Whitley, IN 4678
Art and craft calendar.

The Craft Connection Newspaper
P.O. Box 1280
Pine Grove, CA 95665
Craft calendar and information newspaper.

The Crafts Fair Guide
P.O. Box 5508
Mill Valley, CA 94942
Arts and craft show calendar.

The Crafts Report
700 Orange Street
Wilmington, DE 19801

Fairs and Festivals in the Northeast
Arts Extension Service - Division of Continuing Education
University of Massachusetts
Amherst, MA 01003
Fairs and festival calendar.

National Calendar of Open Competitive Art Exhibitions
5433 New Haven Avenue
Fort Wayne, IN 46803
Show Calendar.

SAC
The National News and Listings of Arts and Craft Shows
P.O. Box 159
Bogalusa, LA 70429

Sunshine Artists
Sun Country Enterprises
501–503 N. Virginia Avenue
Winter Park, FL 32789
Craft show calendar.

Arts and Crafts Resources

A craft operation, just like other businesses, requires different types of resource information. At one point, you may require additional information about marketing, or you may need some special data about a specific type of promotion. You may want some facts about the state sales tax, packaging, or business operation. The following is a representative list of some of the resource information available. It may suggest to you other sources of useful data. Your library is an excellent source of additional information as are craft and marketing journals.

Artist/Craftsperson Address Search Service
American Craft Council
72 Spring Street
New York, NY 10012
Mechanism for locating names of individal artists/craftspeople.

Craft Registry Database
American Craft Council
72 Spring Street
New York, NY 10012
Names and addresses of craftspeople by medium, location, scale or type of object.

Craft Supply Directory
225 Gordons Corner Plaza
Box 420
Manalapan, NJ 07726
A directory of craft supplies and equipment.

U.S. Small Business Administration
Office of Business Development
1441 L Street, N.W.
Washington, DC 20416
Videotapes, publications on marketing, financial management, management and planning, etc.

Check with your individual state **Small Business Administration** office for publications about marketing, business management, finances, etc. These offices are usually located and can be addressed at the individual state capitols. Check local telephone books and business directories for office addresses.

Marketing-Oriented Craft Industry Suppliers

Craftspeople require a great variety of supplies to produce their products. This raw material information is usually available in the manufacturers' catalogs which cater to each specific craft.

The listing which follows concerns itself primarily with marketing-oriented craft supplies. These are products whose prime purpose is the promotion and sale of your products.

Acrylic Designs, Inc.
100 River Street
Springfield, VT 05156
Custom signs.

Action Bag Company
501 North Edgewood Avenue
Woodale, IL 60191
Packaging for craft products.

Adcraft Manufacturing Company
2810 South 18 Avenue
Broadview, IL 60153
Promotional badges.

American Badge Company
15537 South 70 Court
Orlando Park, IL 60462
Promotional badges.

American Business Information
5711 South 86 Circle
P.O. Box 27347
Omaha, NE 68127
Mailing lists.

American Business Lists
5711 South 86 Circle
P.O. Box 27347
Omaha, NE 68127
Mailing lists.

American Color Printing
1731 NW 97 Avenue
Plantation, FL 33322
Printed catalog sheets.

American List Counsel, Inc.
88 Orchard Road - CN 5219
Princeton, NJ 08543
Mailing lists.

Apco Apeda Photo Company
525 West 52 Street
New York, NY 10019
Photo processing - B&W and color.

Beekman Plastics, Inc.
7424 Santa Monica Boulevard
Los Angeles, CA 90046
Brochure display racks.

Berlekamp Plastics, Inc.
2587 East Country Road 99
Fremont, OH 43420
Custom signs.

Berry and Homer, Inc.
2035 Richmond Street
Philadelphia, PA 19125
Photo processing - B&W and color.

Best Mailing Lists, Inc.
38 West 32 Street
New York, NY 10001
Mailing lists.

Ed Burnett Consultants, Inc.
99 West Sheffield Avenue
Englewood, NJ 07631
Mailing lists.

Chandler Designs, Inc.
383 Middlesex Avenue
Wilmington, MA 01887
Shrink packages for craft products.

Coleman Outdoor Products, Inc.
250 North Street - Francis
Wichita, KS 67212
Tents and canopies.

Color Optic Displays, Inc.
5670 Corporate Way
West Palm Beach, FL 33407
Literature displays.

Corr-Pac International
19 Kimberly Road
East Brunswick, NJ 08816
Packaging boxes.

Creative Energies
Route 4 - Box 733
Silver Springs, FL 32688
Indoor-oudoor craft booth canopies.

Darkroom Products, Ltd.
2949 11 Street
Rockford, IL 61109
Photo processing - B&W and color.

Diamond Brand Canvas Products
Highway 25
Naples, NC 28760
Tents and canopies.

Direct Press Modern Litho
3860 Akwood Road
Huntington Station, NY 11746
Printing supplies.

Hugo Dunhill Mailing Lists, Inc.
630 Third Avenue
New York, NY 10017
Mailing lists.

Finn Graphics
220 Stille Drive
Cincinnati, OH 45233
Custom signs.

Flourish Company
5763 Wheeler Road
Fayetteville, AR 72703
Indoor-outdoor craft booth canopies.

Freund Can Company
191 West 84th street
Chicago, IL 60620
Boxes and plastic containers for packaging.

Graphic Display Systems
1243 Lafayette Street
Lebanon, PA 17042
Portable exhibit booth display units.

Heritage Display Group
550 Vandalia Street
St. Paul, MN 55114
Modular exhibit booth displays.

Howard Displays, Inc.
2361 South State Street
Chicago, IL 60616
Custom signs.

International E-Z Up, Inc.
5525 East Gibraltar
Ontario, CA 91764
Indoor-outdoor craft booth canopies.

Itex
P.O. Box 2309
Portland, OR 97208
A barter company.

KD Kanopy
5758 Lamar Street
Arvada, CO 80002
Indoor-outdoor craft booth canopies.

Lapel Pin, Inc.
6381 Hollywood Boulevard - Suite 505
Hollywood, CA 90028
Promotional badges.

Lillian Vernon
510 South Fulton Avenue
Mount Vernon, NY 10550
Direct mail catalogers.

Midwest Photo Company
P.O. Box 686
Omaha, NE 68101
Photo processing- B&W and color.

Mobile Light Exhibits
617 East 28 Street
Charlotte, NC 28205
Lighting/exhibit booths.

National Bag Company
2233 Old Mill Road
Hudson, OH 44236
Plastic product packaging.

National Banner Company
11938 Harry Hines Boulevard
Dallas, TX 75234
Display banners.

Nationwide Shopper Service
144 South First Street
Burbank, CA 91502
Direct mail catalogers.

Nomadic Instand
P.O. Box 9113, Cathedral Station
Boston, MA 02118
Exhibit booth display units.

Normadic Structures, Inc.
7400 Fullerton Road
Springfield, VA 22153
Exhibit booth display units.

On Display
P.O. Box 42006
3400 Formex Road

Richmond, VA 23224
Exhibit booth display units.

On Tyme Products
6340 West Oakton
Morton Grove, IL 60053
Printing supplies.

Pacesetter Displays, Inc.
119 Seaboard Lane
Franklin, TN 37064
Exhibit booth display units.

Perry Printing Corporation
5100 West Brown Deer Road
Milwaukee, WI 53223
Printing supplies.

Postalia, Inc.
1423 Centre Circle Drive
Downers Grove, IL 60515
Small business postage meters.

Premiums Plus, Inc.
191 Post Road West
Westport, CT 06880
Direct mail catalogers.

Professional Displays, Inc.
746 Arrow Grand Circle
Covina, CA 91722
Exhibit booth display units.

Promo Cards
8829 Kennedy Boulevard
North Bergen, NJ 07047
Business cards.

Recognition Services
5415 N. College Avenue
Indianapolis, IN 46220
Promotional badges.

Edith Roman Associates, Inc.
876 Avenue of the Americas
New York, NY 10001
Mailing lists.

S D Modular Displays
1919 NW 19 Street
Ft. Lauderdale, FL 33311
Exhibit booth display units.

Scope Packaging, Inc.
240 West Fletcher
Orange, CA 92665
Packaging boxes.

Siegel Display Products
P.O. Box 96
Minneapolis, MN 55440
Product display racks.

Skyline Displays Northeast, Inc.
75 Glen Road
Sandy Hook, CT 06482
Exhibit booth display units.

Springfield Corrugated Box, Inc.
Westover Industrial Park
Building 7111
Chicopee, MA 01022
Packaging boxes for craft products.

Sunshell Designs, Inc.
201–1815 Pine Street
Vancouver, BC V6J 3C8, Canada
Tents and canopies.

Superb Case
415 Valley Street
Providence, RI 02908
Business cards.

Taymar Industries, Inc.
P.O. Box 12369

Palm Desert, CA 92255
Brochure and promotional holders.

U.S. Buyers Network
1320 Route 23
Wayne, NJ 07470
Direct mail catalogers.

Vista Color Lab, Inc.
2048 Fulton Road
Cleveland, OH 44113
Film/slide processing.

World Shelters, Inc.
7400 Fullerton Road - Suite 134
Springfield, VA 22153
Indoor-outdoor craft booth canopies.

Index

**Over a Century of Excellence
for the Professional
and
Vocational Trades and the Crafts**

Order now from your local bookstore
or use the convenient order form
at the back of this book.

AUDEL

These fully illustrated, up-to-date guides and manuals mean a better job done for mechanics, engineers, electricians, plumbers, carpenters, and all skilled workers.

CONTENTS

ELECTRICAL

House Wiring (Seventh Edition)
ROLAND E. PALMQUIST;
revised by PAUL ROSENBERG
5 1/2 × 8 1/4 Hardcover 248 pp.   150 Illus.
ISBN: 0-02-594692-7 $22.95
Rules and regulations of the current 1990 National Electrical Code for residential wiring fully explained and illustrated.

Practical Electricity
(Fifth Edition)
ROBERT G. MIDDLETON;
revised by L. DONALD MEYERS
5 1/2 × 8 1/4 Hardcover 512 pp.   335 Illus.
ISBN: 0-02-584561-6 $19.95
The fundamentals of electricity for electrical workers, apprentices, and others requiring concise information about electric principles and their practical applications.

Guide to the 1993 National Electrical Code
ROLAND E. PALMQUIST;
revised by PAUL ROSENBERG
5 1/2 × 8 1/4 Paperback 608 pp.
100 line drawings
ISBN: 0-02-077761-2 $25.00
The guide to the most recent revision of the electrical codes—how to read them, under-

stand them, and use them. Here is the most authoritative reference available, making clear the changes in the code and explaining these changes in a way that is easy to understand.

Installation Requirements of the 1993 National Electrical Code
PAUL ROSENBERG
5 1/2 × 8 1/4 Paperback 261 pp.
100 line drawings
ISBN: 0-02-077760-4 $22.00
A handy guide for electricians, contractors, and architects who need a reference on location. Arranging all the pertinent requirements (and only the pertinent requirements) of the 1993 NEC, it has an easy-to-follow format. Concise and updated, it's a perfect working companion for Apprentices, Journeymen, or for Master electricians.

Mathematics for Electricians and Electronics Technicians
REX MILLER
5 1/2 × 8 1/4 Hardcover 312 pp.   115 Illus.
ISBN: 0-8161-1700-4 $14.95
Mathematical concepts, formulas, and problem-solving techniques utilized on-the-job by electricians and those in electronics and related fields.

Fractional-Horsepower Electric Motors

REX MILLER and
MARK RICHARD MILLER

5 1/2 × 8 1/4 Har...
ISBN: 0-672-...

The in... ...tenance, re-
pa... ...e small-to-moder-
ate ...tors that power home
appl... ...d industrial equipment.

Electric Motors (Fifth Edition)

EDWIN P. ANDERSON
and REX MILLER

5 1/2 × 8 1/4 Hardcover   696 pp.
Photos/line art
ISBN: 0-02-501920-1 $35.00

Complete reference guide for electricians, industrial maintenance personnel, and install-
ers. Contains both theoretical and practical
descriptions.

Home Appliance Servicing
(Fourth Edition)

EDWIN P. ANDERSON;
revised by REX MILLER

5 1/2 × 8 1/4 Hardcover   640 pp.   345 Illus.
ISBN: 0-672-23379-7 $22.50

The essentials of testing, maintaining, and
repairing all types of home appliances.

Television Service Manual
(Fifth Edition)

ROBERT G. MIDDLETON;
revised by JOSEPH G. BARRILE

5 1/2 × 8 1/4 Hardcover   512 pp.   395 Illus.
ISBN: 0-672-23395-9 $16.95

A guide to all aspects of television transmission and reception, including the operating
principles of black and white and color re-
ceivers. Step-by-step maintenance and repair procedures.

Electrical Course for Apprentices and Journeymen
(Third Edition)

ROLAND E. PALMQUIST

5 1/2 × 8 1/4 Hardcover   478 pp.   290 Illus.
ISBN: 0-02-594550-5 $19.95

This practical course in electricity for those
in formal training programs or learning on
their own provides a thorough understanding
of operational theory and its applications on
the job.

Questions and Answers for Electricians Examinations
(1993 NEC Rulings Included)

revised by PAUL ROSENBERG

5 1/2 × 8 1/4 Paperback   270 pp.
100 line drawings
ISBN: 0-02-077762-0 $20.00

An Audel classic, considered the most thorough work on the subject in coverage and
content. This fully revised edition is based on
the 1993 National Electrical Code®, and is
written for anyone preparing for the various electricians' examinations—Apprentice,
Journeyman, or Master. It provides the license applicant with an understanding of
theory as well as of all definitions, specifications, and regulations included in the new
NEC.

MACHINE SHOP AND MECHANICAL TRADES

Machinists Library
(Fourth Edition, 3 Vols.)

REX MILLER

5 1/2 × 8 1/4 Hardcover 1,352 pp. 1120 Illus.
ISBN: 0-672-23380-0 $52.95

An indispensable three-volume reference set
for machinists, tool and die makers, machine
operators, metal workers, and those with
home workshops. The principles and methods of the entire field are covered in an up-
to-date text, photographs, diagrams, and tables.

Volume I: Basic Machine Shop

REX MILLER

5 1/2 × 8 1/4 Hardcover   392 pp.   375 Illus.
ISBN: 0-672-23381-9 $17.95

Volume II: Machine Shop

REX MILLER

5 1/2 × 8 1/4 Hardcover   528 pp.   445 Illus.
ISBN: 0-672-23382-7 $19.95

Volume III: Toolmakers Handy Book

REX MILLER

5 1/2 × 8 1/4 Hardcover   432 pp.   300 Illus.
ISBN: 0-672-23383-5 $14.95

Mathematics for Mechanical Technicians and Technologists

JOHN D. BIES

5 1/2 × 8 1/4 Hardcover 342 pp. 190 Illus.
ISBN: 0-02-510620-1 $17.95

The mathematical concepts, formulas, and problem-solving techniques utilized on the job by engineers, technicians, and other workers in industrial and mechanical technology and related fields.

Millwrights and Mechanics Guide (Fourth Edition)

CARL A. NELSON

5 1/2 × 8 1/4 Hardcover 1,040 pp. 880 Illus.
ISBN: 0-02-588591-x $29.95

The most comprehensive and authoritative guide available for millwrights, mechanics, maintenance workers, riggers, shop workers, foremen, inspectors, and superintendents on plant installation, operation, and maintenance.

Welders Guide (Third Edition)

JAMES E. BRUMBAUGH

5 1/2 × 8 1/4 Hardcover 960 pp. 615 Illus.
ISBN: 0-672-23374-6 $23.95

The theory, operation, and maintenance of all welding machines. Covers gas welding equipment, supplies, and process; arc welding equipment, supplies, and process; TIG and MIG welding; and much more.

Welders/Fitters Guide

HARRY L. STEWART

8 1/2 × 11 Paperback 160 pp. 195 Illus.
ISBN: 0-672-23325-8 $7.95

Step-by-step instruction for those training to become welders/fitters who have some knowledge of welding and the ability to read blueprints.

Sheet Metal Work

JOHN D. BIES

5 1/2 × 8 1/4 Hardcover 456 pp. 215 Illus.
ISBN: 0-8161-1706-3 $19.95

An on-the-job guide for workers in the manufacturing and construction industries and for those with home workshops. All facets of sheet metal work detailed and illustrated by drawings, photographs, and tables.

Power Plant Engineers Guide (Third Edition)

FRANK D. GRAHAM;
revised by CHARLIE BUFFINGTON

5 1/2 × 8 1/4 Hardcover 960 pp. 530 Illus.
ISBN: 0-672-23329-0 $27.50

This all-inclusive, one-volume guide is perfect for engineers, firemen, water tenders, oilers, operators of steam and diesel-power engines, and those applying for engineer's and firemen's licenses.

Mechanical Trades Pocket Manual (Third Edition)

CARL A. NELSON

4 × 6 Paperback 364 pp. 255 Illus.
ISBN: 0-02-588665-7 $14.95

A handbook for workers in the industrial and mechanical trades on methods, tools, equipment, and procedures. Pocket-sized for easy reference and fully illustrated.

PLUMBING

Plumbers and Pipe Fitters Library (Fourth Edition, 3 Vols.)

CHARLES N. McCONNELL

5 1/2 × 8 1/4 Hardcover 952 pp. 560 Illus.
ISBN: 0-02-582914-9 $68.45

This comprehensive three-volume set contains the most up-to-date information available for master plumbers, journeymen, apprentices, engineers, and those in the building trades. A detailed text and clear diagrams, photographs, and charts and tables treat all aspects of the plumbing, heating, and air conditioning trades.

Volume I: Materials, Tools, Roughing-In

CHARLES N. McCONNELL;
revised by TOM PHILBIN

5 1/2 × 8 1/4 Hardcover 304 pp. 240 Illus.
ISBN: 0-02-582911-4 $20.95

Volume II: Welding, Heating, Air Conditioning

CHARLES N. McCONNELL;
revised by TOM PHILBIN

5 1/2 × 8 1/4 Hardcover 384 pp. 220 Illus.
ISBN: 0-02-582912-2 $22.95

Volume III: Water Supply, Drainage, Calculations

CHARLES N. McCONNELL;
revised by TOM PHILBIN

5 1/2 × 8 1/4 Hardcover 264 pp. 100 Illus.
ISBN: 0-02-582913-0 $20.95

The Home Plumbing Handbook
(Fourth Edition)

CHARLES N. McCONNELL

8 1/2 × 11   Paperback   224 pp.   210 Illus.
ISBN: 0-02-079651-X $17.00

This handy, thorough volume, a longtime standard in the field with the professional, has been updated to appeal to the do-it-yourself plumber. Aided by the book's many illustrations and manufacturers' instructions, the home plumber is guided through most basic plumbing procedures. All techniques and products conform to the latest changes in codes and regulations.

The Plumbers Handbook
(Eighth Edition)

JOSEPH P. ALMOND, SR.;
revised by REX MILLER

4 × 6   Paperback   368 pp.   170 Illus.
ISBN: 0-02-501570-2 $19.95

Comprehensive and handy guide for plumbers and pipefitters—fits in the toolbox or pocket. For apprentices, journeymen, or experts.

Questions and Answers for Plumbers' Examinations
(Third Edition)

JULES ORAVETZ;
revised by REX MILLER

5 1/2 × 8 1/4   Paperback   288 pp.   145 Illus.
ISBN: 0-02-593510-0 $14.95

Complete guide to preparation for the plumbers' exams given by local licensing authorities. Includes requirements of the National Bureau of Standards.

HVAC

Air Conditioning: Home and Commercial (Fourth Edition)

EDWIN P. ANDERSON;
revised by REX MILLER

5 1/2 × 8 1/4   Hardcover   528 pp.   180 Illus.
ISBN: 0-02-584885-2 $29.95

A guide to the construction, installation, operation, maintenance, and repair of home, commercial, and industrial air conditioning systems.

Heating, Ventilating, and Air Conditioning Library
(Second Edition, 3 Vols.)

JAMES E. BRUMBAUGH

5 1/2 × 8 1/4 Hardcover 1,840 pp. 1,275 Illus.
ISBN: 0-672-23388-6 $53.85

An authoritative three-volume reference library for those who install, operate, maintain, and repair HVAC equipment commercially, industrially, or at home.

Volume I: Heating Fundamentals, Furnaces, Boilers, Boiler Conversions

JAMES E. BRUMBAUGH

5 1/2 × 8 1/4   Hardcover   656 pp.   405 Illus.
ISBN: 0-672-23389-4 $17.95

Volume II: Oil, Gas and Coal Burners, Controls, Ducts, Piping, Valves

JAMES E. BRUMBAUGH

5 1/2 × 8 1/4   Hardcover   592 pp.   455 Illus.
ISBN: 0-672-23390-8 $17.95

Volume III: Radiant Heating, Water Heaters, Ventilation, Air Conditioning, Heat Pumps, Air Cleaners

JAMES E. BRUMBAUGH

5 1/2 × 8 1/4   Hardcover   592 pp.   415 Illus.
ISBN: 0-672-23391-6 $17.95

Oil Burners (Fifth Edition)

EDWIN M. FIELD

5 1/2 × 8 1/4   Hardcover   360 pp.   170 Illus.
ISBN: 0-02-537745-0 $29.95

An up-to-date sourcebook on the construction, installation, operation, testing, servicing, and repair of all types of oil burners, both industrial and domestic.

Refrigeration: Home and Commercial (Fourth Edition)

EDWIN P. ANDERSON;
revised by REX MILLER

5 1/2 × 8 1/4   Hardcover   768 pp.   285 Illus.
ISBN: 0-02-584875-5 $34.95

A reference for technicians, plant engineers, and the homeowner on the installation, operation, servicing, and repair of everything from single refrigeration units to commercial and industrial systems.

PNEUMATICS AND HYDRAULICS

Hydraulics for Off-the-Road Equipment (Second Edition)
HARRY L. STEWART;
revised by TOM PHILBIN

5 1/2 × 8 1/4 Hardcover 256 pp. 175 Illus.
ISBN: 0-8161-1701-2 $13.95

This complete reference manual on heavy equipment covers hydraulic pumps, accumulators, and motors; force components; hydraulic control components; filters and filtration, lines and fittings, and fluids; hydrostatic transmissions; maintenance; and troubleshooting.

Pneumatics and Hydraulics (Fourth Edition)
HARRY L. STEWART;
revised by TOM STEWART

5 1/2 × 8 1/4 Hardcover 512 pp. 315 Illus.
ISBN: 0-672-23412-2 $19.95

The principles and applications of fluid power. Covers pressure, work, and power; general features of machines; hydraulic and pneumatic symbols; pressure boosters; air compressors and accessories; and much more.

Pumps (Fifth Edition)
HARRY L. STEWART;
revised by REX MILLER

5 1/2 × 8 1/4 Hardcover 552 pp. 360 Illus.
ISBN: 0-02-614725-4 $35.00

The practical guide to operating principles of pumps, controls, and hydraulics. Covers installation and day-to-day service.

CARPENTRY AND CONSTRUCTION

Carpenters and Builders Library (Sixth Edition, 4 Vols.)
JOHN E. BALL;
revised by JOHN LEEKE

5 1/2 × 8 1/4 Hardcover 1,300 pp. 988 Illus.
ISBN: 0-02-506455-4 $89.95

This comprehensive four-volume library has set the professional standard for decades for carpenters, joiners, and woodworkers.

Volume 1: Tools, Steel Square, Joinery
JOHN E. BALL;
revised by JOHN LEEKE

5 1/2 × 8 1/4 Hardcover 377 pp. 340 Illus.
ISBN: 0-02-506451-7 $21.95

Volume 2: Builders Math, Plans, Specifications
JOHN E. BALL;
revised by JOHN LEEKE

5 1/2 × 8 1/4 Hardcover 319 pp. 200 Illus.
ISBN: 0-02-506452-5 $21.95

Volume 3: Layouts, Foundation, Framing
JOHN E. BALL;
revised by JOHN LEEKE

5 1/2 × 8 1/4 Hardcover 269 pp. 204 Illus.
ISBN: 0-02-506453-3 $21.95

Volume 4: Millwork, Power Tools, Painting
JOHN E. BALL;
revised by JOHN LEEKE

5 1/2 × 8 1/4 Hardcover 335 pp. 244 Illus.
ISBN: 0-02-506454-1 $21.95

Complete Building Construction (Second Edition)
JOHN PHELPS;
revised by TOM PHILBIN

5 1/2 × 8 1/4 Hardcover 744 pp. 645 Illus.
ISBN: 0-672-23377-0 $22.50

Constructing a frame or brick building from the footings to the ridge. Whether the building project is a tool shed, garage, or a complete home, this single fully illustrated volume provides all the necessary information.

Complete Roofing Handbook (Second Edition)
JAMES E. BRUMBAUGH
revised by JOHN LEEKE

5 1/2 × 8 1/4 Hardcover 536 pp. 510 Illus.
ISBN: 0-02-517851-2 $30.00

Covers types of roofs; roofing and reroofing; roof and attic insulation and ventilation; skylights and roof openings; dormer construction; roof flashing details; and much more. Contains new information on code requirements, underlaying, and attic ventilation.

Complete Siding Handbook (Second Edition)
JAMES E. BRUMBAUGH
revised by JOHN LEEKE

5 1/2 × 8 1/4 Hardcover 440 pp. 320 Illus.
ISBN: 0-02-517881-8 $30.00

This companion volume to the *Complete Roofing Handbook* has been updated to reflect current emphasis on compliance with building codes. Contains new sections on spunbound olefin, building papers, and insulation materials other than fiberglass.

Masons and Builders Library
(Second Edition, 2 Vols.)
LOUIS M. DEZETTEL;
revised by TOM PHILBIN
5 1/2 × 8 1/4 Hardcover 688 pp. 500 Illus.
ISBN: 0-672-23401-7 $27.95
This two-volume set provides practical instruction in bricklaying and masonry. Covers brick; mortar; tools; bonding; corners, openings, and arches; chimneys and fireplaces; structural clay tile and glass block; brick walls; and much more.

Volume 1: Concrete, Block, Tile, Terrazzo
LOUIS M. DEZETTEL;
revised by TOM PHILBIN
5 1/2 × 8 1/4 Hardcover 304 pp. 190 Illus.
ISBN: 0-672-23402-5 $14.95

Volume 2: Bricklaying, Plastering, Rock Masonry, Clay Tile
LOUIS M. DEZETTEL;
revised by TOM PHILBIN
5 1/2 × 8 1/4 Hardcover 384 pp. 310 Illus.
ISBN: 0-672-23403-3 $14.95

WOODWORKING

Wood Furniture: Finishing, Refinishing, Repairing
(Third Edition)
JAMES E. BRUMBAUGH
revised by JOHN LEEKE
5 1/2 × 8 1/4 Hardcover 384 pp. 190 Illus.
ISBN: 0-02-517871-7 $25.00
A fully illustrated guide to repairing furniture and finishing and refinishing wood surfaces. Covers tools and supplies; types of wood; veneering; inlaying; repairing, restoring and stripping; wood preparation; and much more. Contains a new color insert on stains.

Woodworking and Cabinetmaking
F. RICHARD BOLLER
5 1/2 × 8 1/4 Hardcover 360 pp. 455 Illus.
ISBN: 0-02-512800-0 $18.95
Essential information on all aspects of working with wood. Step-by-step procedures for woodworking projects are accompanied by detailed drawings and photographs.

MAINTENANCE AND REPAIR

Building Maintenance
(Second Edition)
JULES ORAVETZ
5 1/2 × 8 1/4 Paperback 384 pp. 210 Illus.
ISBN: 0-672-23278-2 $11.95
Professional maintenance procedures used in office, educational, and commercial buildings. Covers painting and decorating; plumbing and pipe fitting; concrete and masonry; and much more.

Gardening, Landscaping and Grounds Maintenance
(Third Edition)
JULES ORAVETZ
5 1/2 × 8 1/4 Hardcover 424 pp. 340 Illus.
ISBN: 0-672-23417-3 $15.95
Maintaining lawns and gardens as well as industrial, municipal, and estate grounds.

Home Maintenance and Repair: Walls, Ceilings and Floors
GARY D. BRANSON
8 1/2 × 11 Paperback 80 pp. 80 Illus.
ISBN: 0-672-23281-2 $6.95
The do-it-yourselfer's guide to interior remodeling with professional results.

Painting and Decorating
REX MILLER and GLEN E. BAKER
5 1/2 × 8 1/4 Hardcover 464 pp. 325 Illus.
ISBN: 0-672-23405-x $18.95
A practical guide for painters, decorators, and homeowners to the most up-to-date materials and techniques in the field.

Tree Care (Second Edition)
JOHN M. HALLER
8 1/2 × 11 Paperback 224 pp. 305 Illus.
ISBN: 0-02-062870-6 $16.95
The standard in the field. A comprehensive guide for growers, nursery owners, foresters, landscapers, and homeowners to planting, nurturing, and protecting trees.

Upholstering
(Third Edition)
JAMES E. BRUMBAUGH

5 1/2 × 8 1/4 Hardcover 416 pp. 318 Illus.
ISBN: 0-02-517862-8 $25.00

The esentials of upholstering are fully explained and illustrated for the professional, the apprentice, and the hobbyist. Features a new color insert illustrating fabrics, a new chapter on embroidery, and an expanded cleaning section.

AUTOMOTIVE AND ENGINES

Diesel Engine Manual
(Fourth Edition)
PERRY O. BLACK;
revised by WILLIAM E. SCAHILL

5 1/2 × 8 1/4 Hardcover 512 pp. 255 Illus.
ISBN: 0-672-23371-1 $15.95

The principles, design, operation, and maintenance of today's diesel engines. All aspects of typical two- and four-cycle engines are thoroughly explained and illustrated by photographs, line drawings, and charts and tables.

Gas Engine Manual
(Third Edition)
EDWIN P. ANDERSON;
revised by CHARLES G. FACKLAM

5 1/2 × 8 1/4 Hardcover 424 pp. 225 Illus.
ISBN: 0-8161-1707-1 $12.95

How to operate, maintain, and repair gas engines of all types and sizes. All engine parts and step-by-step procedures are illustrated by photographs, diagrams, and troubleshooting charts.

Small Gasoline Engines
REX MILLER and
MARK RICHARD MILLER

5 1/2 × 8 1/4 Hardcover 640
ISBN: 0-672-23414-9 $1

Practical inform
maintain___ _____ __-cycle
en___ ___ _____ ____ers, edgers,
___ _____ _____owers, emergency
e_____ _____rs, outboard motors, and
ot___ _____ment with engines of up to ten
hor___power.

NEW EDITION FOR 1993

Truck Guide Library (3 Vols.)
JAMES E. BRUMBAUGH

5 1/2 × 8 1/4 Hardcover 2,144 pp. 1,715 Illus.
ISBN: 0-672-23392-4 $50.95

This three-volume set provides the most comprehensive, profusely illustrated collection of information available on truck operation and maintenance.

Volume 1: Engines
JAMES E. BRUMBAUGH

5 1/2 × 8 1/4 Hardcover 416 pp. 290 Illus.
ISBN: 0-672-23356-8 $16.95

Volume 2: Engine Auxiliary Systems
JAMES E. BRUMBAUGH

5 1/2 × 8 1/4 Hardcover 704 pp. 520 Illus.
ISBN: 0-672-23357-6 $16.95

Volume 3: Transmissions, Steering, and Brakes
JAMES E. BRUMBAUGH

5 1/2 × 8 1/4 Hardcover 1,024 pp. 905 Illus.
ISBN: 0-672-23406-8 $16.95

DRAFTING

Industrial Drafting
JOHN D. BIES

5 1/2 × 8 1/4 Hardcover 544 pp. Illus.
ISBN: 0-02-510610-4 $24.95

Professional-level introductory guide for practicing drafters, engineers, managers, and technical workers in all industries who use or prepare working drawings.

Answers on Blueprint Reading
(Fourth Edition)
ROLAND PALMQUIST;
revised by THOMAS J. MORRISEY

5 1/2 × 8 1/4 Hardcover 320 pp. 275 Illus.
ISBN: 0-8161-1704-7 $12.95

Understanding blueprints of machines and tools, electrical systems, and architecture. Question and answer format.

HOBBIES

Complete Course in Stained Glass
PEPE MENDEZ

8 1/2 × 11 Paperback 80 pp. 50 Illus.
ISBN: 0-672-23287-1 $8.95

The tools, materials, and techniques of the art of working with stained glass.

Just select your books, fill out the card, and mail today.

Money-Back Guarantee